Private Chronicles

ROBERT A. FOTHERGILL

✦✦

Private Chronicles

A STUDY OF
ENGLISH DIARIES

LONDON
Oxford University Press
NEW YORK   TORONTO
1974

Oxford University Press, Ely House, London W.1

GLASGOW NEW YORK TORONTO MELBOURNE WELLINGTON
CAPE TOWN IBADAN NAIROBI DAR ES SALAAM LUSAKA ADDIS ABABA
DELHI BOMBAY CALCUTTA MADRAS KARACHI LAHORE DACCA
KUALA LUMPUR SINGAPORE HONG KONG TOKYO

ISBN 0 19 212194 4

© Oxford University Press 1974

942
F82p
94675
Sept 1975

PRINTED AND BOUND IN ENGLAND BY
HAZELL WATSON AND VINEY LTD
AYLESBURY, BUCKS

To the memory of my mother,
who read this book in manuscript

Contents

✢✢

List of Plates

✠✠✠

The publishers wish to thank the following who have given permission for the illustrations to be reproduced: Courtauld Institute Galleries: p. 87; B. Cozens-Hardy: p. 54 right; Victor Gollancz Ltd: p. 182; Houghton Library, Harvard University: p. 119; H.M. The Queen: p. 86; Kilvert Society: p. 118; Mrs Penelope Lloyd: p. 151; National Galleries of Scotland: p. 23; National Portrait Gallery: pp. 22, 54 left, 55; Peter Owen: p. 183; Radio Times Hulton Picture Library: p. 150.

Preface

✚✚✚✚✚✚✚✚✚✚✚✚✚✚✚✚✚✚ ✚✚✚✚✚✚✚✚✚✚✚✚✚✚✚✚✚✚✚✚✚✚✚✚✚✚✚✚✚✚

TEMPTING though it is to preface this work with a disarming attempt to anticipate the reader's perception of its shortcomings, the book had better begin on page one and take its own chances. This page, meanwhile, is better employed as an occasion to express my gratitude for the sympathetic interest and assistance afforded me in the writing of the book and in its preparation for the press. Particularly I should like to thank: Atkinson College and Dean Harry Crowe, for granting me a year's leave of absence and generously providing for the costs of typing and duplication; Professor Bill Keith of the University of Toronto, for his continuing encouragement and critical interest; Janis Gilks, for preparing the typescript so painstakingly; Dr. Robertson Davies and Dr. George Whalley, for their advice and assistance; Elizabeth Waight, for putting aside her own work on Victorian diarists to give me a detailed critique of my text; Mr. Charles Prosser, Hon. Sec. of the Kilvert Society, and Mrs. Prosser, for their hospitality and help with the Kilvert photographs; Miss Audrey Bayley of Oxford University Press, for her most friendly and patient shepherding of the book to the press; and my wife, without whom the book would quite simply not have been written.

R. A. F.

Atkinson College
York University
Toronto
December 1973

Acknowledgements

✝✝

I am indebted to the following for permission to quote from the works mentioned.

Diary by E.B.B. (Elizabeth Barrett), edited by P. Kelley and R. Hudson: the University of Ohio Press and Mr. John Murray;

Boswell's London Journal and *Boswell on the Grand Tour: Germany and Switzerland,* edited by F. A. Pottle; *Boswell on the Grand Tour: Italy, Corsica and France* and *Boswell in Search of a Wife,* edited by F. Brady and F. A. Pottle; *Boswell: the Ominous Years,* edited by C. Ryskamp and F. A. Pottle; *Boswell in Extremes,* edited by C. McC. Weis and F. A. Pottle: the editors, Yale University, William Heinemann Ltd, and the McGraw Hill Company;

Byron: a Self-Portrait, edited by P. Quennell: John Murray Ltd.;

The Diary of Benjamin Robert Haydon, edited by W. B. Pope: copyright 1960, Harvard University Press and the President and Fellows of Harvard College;

The Diary of Ivy Jacquier: Victor Gollancz Ltd.;

The Diary of Alice James, edited by Leon Edel: Rupert Hart-Davis (Granada Publishing) and Dodd, Mead & Company;

The Diary of William Jones, edited by O. F. Christie: Coward, McCann & Geoghegan, Inc.;

Kilvert's Diary, edited by William Plomer, copyright 1944 by T. Perceval Smith, renewed 1972 by William Plomer: Jonathan Cape Ltd., Mr. F. R. Fletcher, and the Macmillan Publishing Company, Inc.;

The Journal of Katherine Mansfield, edited by John Middleton Murry: the Society of Authors as the literary representatives of the Estate of Katherine Mansfield, and Alfred A. Knopf, Inc.;

The Diaries of Anaïs Nin, Volumes I, II and III, edited by Gunther Stuhlmann, copyright 1966, 1967, 1969 by Anaïs Nin; Peter Owen Ltd., and Harcourt Brace Jovanovich, Inc.;

The Diary of Samuel Pepys, edited by R. Latham and W. Matthews: G. Bell & Sons, Ltd., and the Regents of the University of California;

The Diary of Dudley Ryder, edited by W. Matthews: Methuen & Company, Ltd.;

The Journal of Walter Scott, edited by J. G. Tait: Miss Margaret Tait.

1

✦✦✦

Introduction

THE case for undertaking a study of English diary-writing rests upon the extraordinary character and distinction of a handful of examples, some celebrated, others quite unrecognized. The reputations, as diarists, of Samuel Pepys, James Boswell, Fanny Burney, Dorothy Wordsworth, and Walter Scott are unassailably established. Benjamin Haydon, Francis Kilvert, and W. N. P. Barbellion (B. F. Cummings), while not exactly household names, are not unknown to fame; but not even this much can be said for people like Dudley Ryder, William Jones, and Ivy Jacquier. Yet their diaries, and those of some few others whose names will soon appear, comprise (it will be argued) the staple of English diary-writing. If the genre were to be robbed of these few remarkable books the heart would have been cut out of it. A study could still be written of the hundreds that would remain, but it would no longer be worth writing.

The following study does not claim to be an exercise in literary history. No attempt is made to lay out a comprehensive picture of English diary-writing, or to devote space on some principle of equity to every diarist of any note since Edward VI. Not only would such a book be a monster of indigestibility, but the limited function that it could serve has been very largely served already. The series of books published in the nineteen-twenties by Lord Arthur Ponsonby gave descriptive accounts of literally hundreds of English, Irish, and Scottish diaries, many of which existed only in manuscript and were known to very few people. Descended from a line of diarists himself, Lord Ponsonby unearthed an extraordinary collection of literary and antiquarian curiosities, along with three centuries of fine and varied diary-writing, and presented them to a fascinated public by means of lavish quotation and a description of the general character of each diary. The corpus thus established was greatly enlarged with the publication in 1950 of William Matthew's *Annotated Bibliography of British Diaries 1442–1942*, containing nearly twenty-three hundred items. And the list continues to lengthen as still more diaries are discovered and published.

This book undertakes to introduce some order into this welter of material. It seeks to establish conceptual perspectives that will cause English diary-writing to appear not as a heap but as an intricate and complex pattern. The attraction and the weakness of Lord Ponsonby's collections is that they consist in essence of anthologies of personalities, each one briefly overheard speaking in his or her own accents. His books grow by a process of simple accretion; they are incapable of developing. What he lacks is a way of perceiving the character and quality of a given diary not merely as a manifestation of the writer's personality, but as a function of its place in an evolutionary pattern. If the language can be found for treating diaries as books rather than as people, it will be possible to see diary-writing as a complex genre in which successive conventions of perception and expression impart a character to the most private and informal of writings. The patterns discernible are made the more interesting by the fact that until the late eighteenth century it was a genre virtually unconscious of its own existence.

The great mass of diary-writing is poor stuff, interesting only to the antiquarian or the social historian. Out of this monochrome wilderness emerge diaries, or passages therefrom, in which what may be called serial autobiography achieves a marvellous richness and vitality. The business of asserting a 'great tradition' of English diary-writing is inseparable from the effort to formulate the criteria that systematically express this 'greatness'. What takes place is a lengthy process of reciprocal adjustment between the works which insist on being prized, and the formulations which appear, after repeated examination, to be central. Thus the worth of a previously disdained or ignored work will reassert itself and force a modification of the criteria; or the growing stability of a critical formulation will expose the inferiority of a diary that has been claiming major importance. It should be pointed out that the criterion of historical importance operates rather peculiarly in this context. Obviously the usual sense of a work's having an influential impact on the development of the genre is out of place. Often remaining unpublished for centuries, most diaries had no impact whatsoever. At the same time, however, there is a perceptible evolution in the conventions of diary-writing, and the degree of prominence assigned to any given diary will depend to a considerable degree upon the date at which it was written. As in any genre, an average run-of-the-mill piece of writing might have been a noteworthy achievement fifty years earlier.

What considerations, then, governed the choice of a few score of diaries out of Matthews's twenty-three hundred? (The question of the further division into greater and less is left aside for the moment.) Possibly we should go a step further and ask for a working definition of the term 'diary' at this point. But this is one of those cases where definition will only obscure a relatively straightforward word. 'Diary' means what you think it means; moreover its usage appears to be indistinguishable from that of 'journal'. In this study the two terms will be used interchangeably, for variety's sake. The trouble with efforts at definition is that the Pepysian format—which I suspect is most people's unconscious norm—is continually sliding away on all sides into its many kindred forms. Surrounding the diary, at various points of the compass, lie meditations, letters, anecdote collections, occasional essays, rough-drafts, chronicle histories, commonplace books, and many more examples of more-or-less regular, more-or-less private writing. Haydon incorporates all of them at one time or another— and continues to call the book his diary. In general let it be agreed that a diary is what a person writes when he says, 'I am writing my diary'.

An important principle of selection is the concentration of this study upon what may be termed the 'personal' diary, that is to say the diary whose prime subject is the life of the writer, valued for its own sake. Thus it excludes, or places a low value upon, diaries which are chiefly devoted to matters involving the writer only indirectly, at a remove. Included in this class are diaries of public or political affairs—Lord Egmont and Charles Greville are prime examples—most travel diaries, at least of the sight-seeing variety, and diaries devoted to occupations, as for example expeditions, military campaigns or professional work. Writers' notebooks, for example those of Gerard Manley Hopkins and Henry James, are likewise excluded, as are diary records of special interests, such as sport, gardening, and theatre-going. It need hardly be said that many of the diarists included write at length of their travels, occupations, and interests, but only as these are elements in the texture of their lives.

With a few notable exceptions, all the diaries are English, written in England. In one sense the term 'British' might be more appropriate, since Scottish and Irish writers are included; however, the term 'English' is meant to convey that they all participate in the culture of England, although, like Boswell and Scott, they may live north of the border. The two most obvious exceptions are Alice James and Anaïs Nin. The former was living in England, and her diary is clearly a response to an experience of English life and society. The inclusion of the latter must be justified on different grounds. Of Danish-Franco-Spanish parentage, living in Paris and New York, writing in English, Anaïs Nin is an international writer. Her diary, which is still in the process of publication—indeed she is still writing it—has already become one of the classics of the genre which no study of the subject could afford (or would want) to omit.

The diaries listed in the bibliography are by no means the only ones to have been considered. Ponsonby and Matthews provided the main leads, though my estimate of a diarist's interest or importance has sometimes, upon inspection, differed from theirs. A few were discovered quite by chance. Ivy Jacquier, for example, I found in a secondhand bookstore; I have not come across a single reference to her anywhere. Now it is equally possible that by the same chance some important diaries have been entirely overlooked. Should this be the case, the study would of course be to some extent impoverished, but not, I believe, seriously impaired. The picture is more likely to be upset by the discovery and publication of hitherto lost or unknown diaries. Ryder, Boswell, Neville, and Elizabeth Barrett have all come to light since the publication of Ponsonby's surveys.

In preparing this study I have not attempted to study the original manuscripts. I have relied instead upon printed editions, and, as Ponsonby remarks, 'No editor can be trusted not to spoil a diary.'[1] Some editors should be exempted from this judgement, but in general it would not do to minimize the distance at which we stand from what the diarists actually wrote. Clearly this factor must impose limits upon what can be said with critical assurance. Moreover, even the most faithful editor, such as Pepys (at last), Boswell, Haydon, and Elizabeth Barrett have been blessed with, can transmit no more than what survives. The volume containing Boswell's 'Holland Journal' was lost within weeks of his finishing it; Madame D'Arblay vigorously pruned the diary she had kept when Fanny Burney; Haydon and Elizabeth Barrett ripped out their own pages by the dozen; Barbellion and Ivy

Jacquier edited their diaries for publication. As for the ravages of editors, committed in the names of brevity, purity, or thematic unity, some at least had the decency to indicate the extent of their depredations. After all of these factors have been assessed, it is probably true to say that among the first-rate English diarists, the only ones so far published whole and entire are Samuel Pepys and Walter Scott.

Alteration and excision by the author presents a different problem from that raised by an editor's tamperings. The question of textual integrity involved in the former case is a critical, not to say philosophical one, and will be considered at some length in Chapter 3. Editors, meanwhile, have brought an array of considerations to their labours. The most respectable motive behind the amputation of a diary is the desire to make it readable. Commonly this means the abridgement or distillation of an unwieldy original, through the elimination of whatever is considered stodgy, pedestrian, or repetitious. From unerring taste to obtuse vandalism in these matters is not such a long step. On the credit side, we may find an editor taking care not to streamline a diary's special character out of existence, by omitting everything that does not advance the 'story'; thus, in pruning away most of Ryder's notes on sermons and books, William Matthews leaves the occasional reminder of the extent of these notes in the original.

A fatally damaging editorial approach, from the point of view of this particular study, is the subordination of a diary's general interest to a specialist one, retaining only what is of use to the political or religious historian, for example. Among older editions, many were published by friends or relatives of authors recently deceased, as part of the erection of an honoured memory. Shorn of anything that might shade the reputation of the writer, or any of his surviving associates, such books are often no more than anthologies of dated observations. Their editors, who frequently destroyed the manuscripts, tend rather to conceal than to make clear their editorial habits. Another nineteenth-century practice was the dismemberment of a diary for fragments to incorporate into a biography or 'Remains'. All these factors add up to a major problem when one wishes to speak of the diarist's selective rendering of experience or consciousness—not knowing how much selective organization has been introduced by another hand.

So much for the state of the texts; what of the state of criticism in the field? Wonderful to relate, in these days of critical over-population, the territory is almost entirely uninhabited. Since the great specimen-hunting expeditions of the good Lord Ponsonby, only small-scale incursions have been undertaken, coming out with the most meagre reports. Indeed it has been the misfortune of diaries to have attracted chiefly the literary dilettante, the writer of charming ephemera for coffee-table magazines. Sometimes it seems as though a critic like P. A. Spalding has set out with the determination to come to grips with the genre in an intellectually challenging way, but has been seduced, as have others before him, by the charms of quaintness and sentimentality. His little book, *Self Harvest*, fat in comparison with Kate O'Brien's slim volume and Margaret Willy's pair of flimsy pamphlets, is hardly more than a collection of remarks, some of which, it may be added, are distinctly questionable. Much more stimulating material can be found in the editors' introductions to recent editions of diaries. Especially worthy of mention are Matthews's introductory essay in Volume I of the splendid edition of Pepys of which he is co-editor, and the introductions by F. A. Pottle and others to each volume of the 'popular' edition of Boswell's papers. In these essays one meets with minds which have *thought about* diaries and diary-writing, instead of merely smiling over them. And of course there are the diarists themselves. Particularly in more recent times, as diary-writing has become increasingly conscious of itself, they have had some very interesting things to say about the activity which has engrossed them. Anaïs Nin's two chapters on the subject in her book, *The Novel of the Future*, contain some really illuminating insights.

Looking further afield, in a couple of directions, one can find valuable critical treatment of material that lies parallel to the subject of this study. In one direction lie English-language studies of biography and autobiography; in another, French and German treatments of diary-literature. D. A. Stauffer's books on English biography, particularly his giant study of eighteenth-century productions in this field, raise many important questions about the conventions that operate in what he calls 'life-writing'. Treating biography and autobiography as aspects of one another, he even occasionally makes specific reference to diarists. Roy Pascal's *Design and Truth in Autobiography* specifically excludes diary-writing from its field, but is full of thought about the presentation in writing, more and less formal, of the materials of one's own life. Another work on specifically English autobiography, J. N. Morris's *Versions of the Self* contains a valuable section on Boswell. Among several foreign-language studies of the diary, A. Girard's *Le Journal Intime* should be mentioned. Though it deals only with the nineteenth-century French '*intimistes*' (his own term), it necessarily explores critical and philosophical questions relevant to English diary-writing. There are also several books in German on the subject of diaries, led by G. R. Hocke's *Das Europaische Tagebuch*, in which a number of English diarists are considered within a large overview of a European tradition. One other work deserves mention for its treatment of the larger subject of shifting modes of self-consciousness observable in European culture: Lionel Trilling's *Sincerity and Authenticity* appeared too late for me to take it into consideration, but its lucid and stimulating insight is warmly recommended.

Something may perhaps need to be said about the organization of the following chapters, the object of which is to integrate a thematic approach to the genre as a whole with some sustained critical discussion of particular writers. The purpose of Chapter 2 is to furnish a historical sketch of the genre, to introduce the more prominent figures and to 'place' them in a schematic relation to one another. Such an undertaking, which would hardly be necessary to the study of a more frequently trodden field of literature, will provide as it were a relief-map of the area and free subsequent discussion from the need to make constant explanatory references. It will also amplify the distinctions already proposed between the 'personal' diary and the rest, and between those diaries in which the main line of evolutionary descent is manifested and those which are merely the multiplication of species arrested at a particular stage of development. (When *Homo Sapiens* emerged, apes did not become extinct.) Chapter 3 endeavours to clarify the conceptual and procedural problems attaching to the treatment of this informal and 'non-deliberate' class of literature, while Chapter 4 examines the patterns which become apparent when diaries are considered from the point of view of the motives that have given rise to them. In Chapters 5, 6, and 7 more extended attention is given to particular diarists, in the light of three critical considerations judged to be appropriate to their character. The concern of all three chapters is with the forms of self-presentation evident in diaries. Taking them in reverse order: Chapter 7 ('Forms of Serial Autobiography') contrasts the ways in which certain long-kept diaries give to their contents the literary character of 'A Life'; Chapter 6 ('Ego and Ideal') looks at the preoccupation apparent in certain diaries with developing the self according to preconceived models; while Chapter 5 considers how a diary's style and tone contribute to the projection of a self-image.

To anticipate inquiry it is necessary to indicate some lines of possible exploration which will *not* be pursued. One is the systematic comparison of a diary with the other available sources of information about the writer's character and doings; another is the relation of the diary to other writings by the same individual—letters, published works of literature, autobiography, etc. The former could provide evidence on the question of honesty and objectivity, and on the kinds of selection and omission that operate in diaries; the latter would relate the characteristics exhibited by the diary to the writer's 'performances' in other literary conventions, and would make possible a precise isolation of those characteristics. However, in this study I seek to place diaries among other diaries, and while I am not necessarily ignorant of the author's 'real' life and other writings, I have generally confined myself to treating the diary as a self-subsisting document.

There is no denying that the attraction exerted by diaries is a peculiar one, and that it can very easily become a snare. To the ordinary reader most diaries, those which have not been edited into a concentrated narrative, present a rather unappetizing surface. Their chief characteristic is that they go on and on, filled with nonentities and non-events, an endless in-gathering of loose ends. Even the richest and most varied diaries, it must be admitted, are pretty heavy going at times. Not Haydon himself can keep us enthralled for three thousand pages. But to the devotee it is precisely the coral-like aggregations of minimal deposits that become addictive. In propagating their passion, diary-enthusiasts tend to rhapsodize over the charm of long-lost trivia. A kind of cult develops around some of the more lovably artless chroniclers of their little lives. Not only Pepys, but Kilvert and Woodforde and, I should guess, many more, have Societies dedicated to a connoisseurship of their minutest leavings.

As I have already suggested, virtually all that has been written about diary-writing has drivelled itself away in affectionate sentimentality, exclaiming over the romance of insignificant detail, the ineffable appeal of humble self-unburdening. Spalding, writing of Parson Woodforde, cherishes his diary as 'an artless chronicle of small beer, an apotheosis of the commonplace, whose charm is cumulative, depending upon familiarity'.[2] Ponsonby goes out of his way to emphasize his particular preference for trivial fond records over matters of substance: 'We prefer Pepys when he is singing with Mercer in the coach while his wife is shopping rather than when he is telling us about the exploits of the navy.' And he adds: 'All this does not mean that diary readers are frivolous minded, but that diary writers are at their best when they are just scribbling down with effortless frankness the little incidents which they are honest enough to record as having caught their attention at the moment.'³ The same taste is operative in the manner in which they bring individual diarists on to the stage. Nothing makes a more delightful quotation than a little unguarded admission of a private foible or an eccentric partiality. Somewhat patronizingly, the diarists are presented at the moments when they are most engagingly 'human'—which usually means slightly weak or silly. It is interesting to observe that this appoach reveals a subjective perception of diaries as specimens of comic art, the whole genre as a rich *comédie humaine* peopled by lovable cranks. In fact Ponsonby actually disapproves of diarists who don't render themselves (inadvertently) comic for his delectation, and calls them 'morbid'.⁴

I don't mean to imply that this approach to diaries is an illegitimate one, or that there is not indeed an irresistible appeal in the *minutiae* of these far-off lives. In fact I find myself indulging, in an equally sentimental fashion, I daresay, a sense of the pathos rather than the comedy of all those busily loquacious lives, now extinct. They were so concretely *there*, so firmly embedded in the centre of their own existences, each consciousness composing all the elements of its experience into a unique and incommunicable set of relations, with itself as the focal point of the world. One's sense of the substance of history is turned inside out. Where one habitually thought of 'ordinary lives' forming a vast background to historical 'events', now one's vision is of the great events dimly passing behind the immediate realities that comprise an individual's experience. In diary after diary events like the Old Pretender's rebellion in 1715, or the battle of Waterloo a century later, float by like rumours. Indeed, the very notion of an historical 'event' becomes obscure and begins to seem like an abstraction, a fantasy. In the foreground is the individual consciousness, absolutely resisting the insistence of future historians that it should experience itself as peripheral.

Not only in space does the diary point-of-view assert its focal position, but also in time. Every diary entry declares, 'I am Here, and it is exactly Now.' Why is it so arresting when Dorothy Wordsworth writes the following? '*6th May Thursday 1802.** A sweet morning. We have put the finishing stroke to our Bower and here we are sitting in the orchard. It is one o'clock. We are sitting upon a seat under the

---

* Rather than standardize the often idiosyncratic ways in which diarists date their entries, I have chosen to reproduce them as they stand in the quoted edition, inserting extra information where necessary [e.g. month or year] in square brackets.

wall which I found my brother building up when I came to him with his apple . . .'5 I think it is because one's bafflement and pain at the ir-recoverable immensity of the past is suddenly concentrated to a point. That 1 p.m. on 6 May, 1802, should once have been the very latest moment in time is unbearably incomprehensible. A sort of Proustian passion fastens itself on such a point, as though a sufficiently intense focus will finally compel the mystery to reveal itself. But really, what is one to do with an emotion as vacant and general as regret for the loss of all past time? Isn't there some way of experiencing This Very Moment as having the mysterious, privileged enviability of someone else's present instead of one's own?

Ultimately, however, the best diaries have a quality which must subdue any disposition on the part of the reader to be either patroniz-ing or sentimental. Such attitudes fail altogether to do justice to the energy, the vitality, the concentration of authentic human reality to be met with in these books. Like the best literature they extend our realization of what being alive is like. They are not necessarily 'truthful' —in the sense that a court of law recognizes truthfulness—but they are *actual*, true to life. Even in their disguises, evasions, and lies diarists are responding to the pressure of first-hand experience; they are being, for better or worse, themselves. In the great English diaries the reader encounters a succession of more and less remarkable human beings communicating their natures abundantly, registering the impact of the passing of days.

2

✛✛✛

Historical Perspectives

'IF we can trace no development historically in the diary as a literary *genre*, so, because it is concerned with the particular, we shall seldom, if ever, find development within the individual diary, either in what is recorded or in the manner of recording it.'[1] Spalding is wrong on both counts. The question of development within the individual diary will be taken up later. The task of this chapter is to lay out English diary-writing in such a light as will make apparent a very definite historical development, both 'in what is recorded' and 'in the manner of recording it'. Indeed, without some kind of developmental perspective to work from, no coherent presentation of the genre is possible. If the difference between the ways in which Pepys and Kilvert perceive and present their living experience has nothing at all to do with sensibility altering from age to age and language limping in pursuit, then we are back to comparing Admiralty secretaries with Radnorshire curates.

Here then already is one of the terms in which the evolution of diary-writing is to be described: as a manifestation of the history of 'sensibility'—the reflection, at the level of individual consciousness, of the succession of social and cultural epochs. Obviously it would be more surprising if diaries did *not* manifest this history, and very sensitively too. Assessed from this point of view, a diary will be more or less noteworthy depending on the range and interest of its 'symptoms'. Thus, though neither of them is especially valuable *per se*, the diary of Lady Frederick Cavendish is worth a good deal more than what survives of George Eliot's. Lady Cavendish, lady-in-waiting to Queen Victoria and wife to the man who, in 1880, was assassinated upon his arrival in Dublin as Lord Lieutenant, wrote, between 1854 and 1880, what must be a classic of gushing Victorian-ness. Covering an identical period, George Eliot's diary (1854–80) consists mainly of notes on her reading and on her health.

However, the assessment of Lady Cavendish as a major diarist will not survive the introduction of the other evolutionary factor. This is the perspective that discerns a 'literary' evolution, the emergence of new forms, new expressive possibilities, in the writings of people who have taken the diary seriously as a vehicle for the rendering of crucial experience. As is true in dealing with other genres, the critic is concerned with that work in which the impulsion to articulate the self has precipitated discovery of a fresh organization of the form's potential. The most remarkable displays of this discovery we call genius, and the diary indeed has its geniuses. Of Boswell and Anaïs Nin it may be said, to paraphrase Oscar Wilde, that they put their talent into various undertakings, and their genius into recording their lives. They are unsurpassed because they are the only ones to treat diary-writing as truly their vocation. From some of their rivals the undertaking drew a talent of which they remained largely unaware; Ryder, Sylas Neville and even Pepys are in this class. Others, such as Byron and Haydon, Fanny Burney and Scott, exercised in their diaries the talent which was second-nature to them. And still others, like Dorothy Wordsworth, Kilvert, and Alice James, possessed of a fugitive and cloistered genius, not bold enough to publish, impressed upon experience the fittest words they could encompass, and secretly wished for readers.

To speak of a 'literary' evolution, the emergence of original forms, and so on, seems perhaps to imply a movement upwards, literary history perceived as Progress, as from the primitive to the sophisticated. But the inference is as inappropriate as Spalding's opposite notion of a deterioration setting in during the nineteenth century. What might it mean to call Anaïs Nin a better diarist than Boswell—or vice versa? At any particular epoch, however, the outstanding diarist can be recognized as he who is richly expressive of contemporary sensibility while making a distinguished contribution to the art of serial autobiography. The present chapter has appointed six diarists to stand as milestones on three centuries of road, recognizing of course that their prominence is perceptible only in retrospect. The appearance of each one in the pattern is treated as the fulfilment of a phase in the evolutionary movement. Pepys, Boswell, Haydon, Kilvert, Barbellion, Anaïs Nin; it is somewhat arbitrary, no doubt, to make them stand for their generations, but not altogether unjustifiable.

Take the case of Pepys. On 1 January 1660, Samuel Pepys condemned all previous diary-keeping to be the pre-history of the genre. This is a sweeping assertion and demands some explanation. There are, without question, many interesting and even remarkable pieces of diary-writing before 1660. The body of material is substantial enough to allow us to discern 'types' of diary emerging from a variety of distinct sources, and in a moment we shall examine these early developments in some detail. The point about Pepys is that in his hands the 'personal' diary finds, from the very first entry, a form so confident and commodious as to make preceding efforts, and those for some time to come, seem like so many false starts, sometimes approaching but never finding the hidden spring that sets Pepys chiming so harmoniously. What enables him to continue for nine years with such consistency and profusion is the balance he achieves—unwittingly and by temperament, no doubt—among the tendencies to lean too far towards a particular element of the personality or a particular kind of subject matter, which result in stunted or lop-sided diaries. Most notably he balances the outer and the inner life in a very harmonious relation to one another. In a manner which appears to be simplicity itself, but is actually very rare, he renders all his experiences, from the most public to the most private, in the same key, as it were, treating all the contents of a day impartially. Perhaps this remarkable ease of demeanour, which treats no subject as either too intimate or too impersonal to be mentioned, makes for a lack of that personal intensity which appears in the more one-sidedly confessional diaries of the period; Pepys does tend to represent himself as living very much on the surface. Far outweighing this possible limitation, however, is the range and variety of experience that his manner of writing integrates into 'a day in the life'. The following entry, chosen more or less at random, illustrates, not Pepys at his most astonishing, but the characteristic tenor and texture of an average day.

2 [April, 1661]. Among my workmen earely. And then along with my wife and Pall to my father's by coach, there to have them lie a while till my house be done. I found my mother alone, weeping upon the last night's quarrel. And so left her and took my wife to Charing-cross and there left her to see her mother, who is not well. So I into St. James parke, where I saw the Duke of Yorke playing at *Peslemesle*—the first time that ever I saw that sport. Then to my Lord's, where I dined with my Lady; and after we had dined,

in comes my Lord and Ned Pickering hungry, and there was not a bit of meat left in the house, the servants having eat up all—at which my Lord was very angry—and at last got something dressed. Then to Privy Seale and signed some things.

So to White-fryers and saw *The Little thiefe*, which is a very merry and pretty play—and the little boy doth very well.

Then to my father's, where I find my mother and my wife in a very good moode; and so left them and went home.

Then to the Dolphin to Sir W. Batten and Pen and other company; among others, Mr. Delabar—where strange how these men, who at other times are all wise men, do now in their drink betwitt and reproach one another with their former conditions and their actions as to public concernments, till I was shamed to see it.

But parted all friends at 12 at night, after drinking a great deal of wine. So home and alone to bed.[2]

Diary-writing, as a flourishing autonomous activity, and not a by-product or outgrowth of some other regular writing habit, emerges from no single source. It is best regarded as the coalescence of a number of pre-diary habits into a form that exceeds its component elements. As these pre-diary habits performed a variety of functions, so the diaries that evolve from them fall into several distinct classes, each bearing the marks of its ancestry. I propose to distinguish four such classes, recognizing that the process is akin to the naming of colours along a spectrum: another eye may perceive quite different gradations. The four classes are: journals of travel, 'public' journals, journals of con-science, and journals of personal memoranda. (It should be noted that the word 'journal' is being introduced here, as promised in Chapter 1, for no other reason than to vary the monotonous repetition of the word 'diary' in almost every sentence.)

A journey recommends itself to journal-keeping. It is much easier when travelling to perceive one's life as a progression by stages, than when fixed in one place in one occupation. In fact it may be claimed that experiencing life as a graduated succession of changes is an abso-lute prerequisite for writing a journal. Not infrequently a journal will be abandoned when the writer enters upon a mode of life, marriage for example, from which the kinds of change he was interested in are eliminated. It takes imagination to discover fresh and interesting diary-material in the daily round of a settled life. Thus the travel journal appears to have been one of the earliest types to achieve the status of a recognized form in which to render one's experience.

In his essay, 'Of Travel',[3] Francis Bacon gives explicit directions for the proper employment of the diary on a young man's continental tour: 'It is a strange thing that in sea voyages, where there is nothing to be seen but sky and sea, men should make diaries, but in land travel, wherein so much is to be observed, for the most part they omit it; as if chance were fitter to be registered than observation. Let diaries, therefore, be brought in use. The things to be seen and observed are: . . .' —and he proceeds to itemize a score of institutions, objects, and events deserving attention. Bacon's advice has a basically utilitarian cast; his aim is to make travel profitable. The journal-habit is treated as the physical counterpart of that mental attitude which cultivates systematic and discriminating observation. The journal is an instrument for seeing more clearly and remembering more profitably. It is to be recommended 'if you will have a young man to put his travel into a little room', and turn it to account in his growth in knowledge, judgement, and discretion. Clearly this means to prudent self-government need not be confined to use abroad. In his own country a man may equally well develop a discriminating eye for 'the courts of princes . . . havens and harbours . . . shipping and navies . . . gardens of state and pleasure . . . comedies, such whereunto the better sort of persons do resort . . . and, to conclude, whatsoever is memorable in the places where [he goes]'. The passage could pass for a catalogue of some of Pepys's particular interests. And certainly Pepys's friend Evelyn developed those habits of note-taking and information-gathering that underlie his *Kalendarium* while on his continental sojourns in the 1640s.[4] Thus it is possible to see diary-keeping, regarded as a component of the rationally-ordered life, coming into practice as an extension of its special application to the well-spent Grand Tour.

At the same time it should not be forgotten that in the sixteenth and seventeenth centuries an adventurous traveller was an important source of information to his countrymen. Government Intelligence and popular taste both sought eagerly for accounts of foreign parts. Among the travel narratives, more and less fantastical, published at this time, some are still in the journal form from which, presumably, many of the others must have been derived. William Matthews lists a number in his *Bibliography*, and their publication must be regarded as helping to establish the diary convention as a way of structuring the presentation of first-hand material. Moreover an interesting dimension is added, at a very early stage, to the question of whether the concept of the diary can include the idea of its being intended for a reader.

My second class, which I have designated the 'public' journal, comprises a range of regular-entry books, having in common the fact that the writing of them was essentially a task, whether officially imposed or self-appointed, performed for the sake of its public usefulness. The officially imposed variety includes, obviously, such things as the transactions of public bodies, ships' log-books, military campaign-annals, and so on. Writing of this kind, which never ceases to be practised, has little direct relation to the diary, except that in the 'pre-history' period under discussion the writers sometimes inject their own personalities beyond the call of duty. More interesting are the self-appointed chroniclers of their times, and the keepers of professional records. The former type is a persistent phenomenon in the diary genre. In every age there can be found men of various ranks and classes, in the stir of great events or the quiet of country parishes, who feel impelled to compile the annals of their age. Some early examples worth mentioning are Henry Machin, James Melville, Walter Yonge, and Archibald Johnston (in his public vein). Diaries of this kind are often either about to become, or appear to have grown out of, 'personal' diaries. Either the personal life and concerns of the writer become increasingly prominent, or, more commonly, a personal diarist resorts more and more to the recording of public material as being more various and interesting than his own immediate experience. A frequent cause of the latter process is the onset of Historic Events, especially a war, which confer on the diarist the self-important role of eye-witness. Henry Slingsby is a particularly regrettable case in point; as will be described in a moment, his diary was just off to a promising start when the civil war took over and suppressed for the duration the claims of the personal life.

Diaries of this sort, mainly given over to the compiling of historic material of one kind or another, are interesting in the early period only because in the general dearth of material almost any diary is an interesting document. As time goes on and the personal diary becomes an increasingly definite and developed type, so the slight autobiographical element to be found in these chronicles of the times diminishes in importance. The same can be said of the type of diary devoted mainly to recording a man's professional activities, his business dealings, scholarly pursuits, etc. They are often quaint or eccentric, and do convey a picture of life being lived from day to day, but they can be admitted as diaries only by special dispensation. Their writers were performing a routine practical function and if at times they speak of private concerns, yet we cannot pretend that they were engaged in any-thing remotely akin to that activity which Pepys called writing a diary.

In the 'journal of conscience', my third class, we arrive at a form of regular and often daily writing whose sole preoccupation is with the inner life of the writer. There can be no question that the practice of diary-writing by the Puritans, and later by the Quakers and other dissenting groups, was a prime source of the genre, and continued to feed a major tributary stream right through the eighteenth century and into the nineteenth. Something of the Puritan motive for diary-keeping, and the ensuing character of the written document, can be seen to survive in diaries which are well beyond any conscious responsiveness to Puritan spiritual discipline. In fact it may be argued that the practice of self-examination in moral terms, which is seldom absent from even the most 'secular' diaries, may derive in part from the Puritan equation of serious self-communing with strict examination of conscience. What other business has a man with his inner secret self, if not the business of improving it?

Just as explicit guides can be found, like Bacon's, to the theory and practice of the travel-journal, so there are extant detailed recommendations of journal-keeping for religious purposes. In both cases the journal is seen as an instrument to be employed as part of a regimen of self-development, though the implied ideals of the developed self differ widely. One book whose influence is widely attested to was John Beadle's *The Journal or Diary of a Thankful Christian*, published in 1656. It is not itself a journal, but an elaborate recommendation of the practice, prescribing the kinds of material to be entered and the spiritual benefits to be anticipated. Appearing comparatively late in the day it must be regarded as summing up and re-iterating precepts which were already common and had been followed for at least half a century. Beadle stresses the importance of examining oneself for the workings of sin and repentance, the rise and fall of spiritual warmth, and the evidence of God's dealings with the soul.

A significant factor to be noted here is the prevalence of a particular idea of diary-writing with which a great many people would have been familiar. While not necessarily widely practised, it would have been in many people's minds an activity to be considered and, moreover, an activity whose conventions were largely pre-established. In other words, if you undertook a diary within this tradition you would begin with already formed ideas of how to go about it, what sort of thing to include, what tone to adopt, and so forth. Instead of proceeding from the writer's own consciousness the structure of the diary is a *donnée* and actually conditions the range of self-perception to be stimulated by it. From the religious point of view this may be a desirable effect, but it is to be regretted by anyone concerned with the development of the diary as a vehicle for the enrichment of consciousness. While a positive contribution may be seen in the intensity of self-encounter generated by the Puritan diary, this is probably outweighed by the narrowness of its limits, the tendency to formalized rhetoric, and the severity of self-repression. Moreover, the conventions tend to exclude any real interest in the outer world, except insofar as it provides a theatre for God's providences.

The three examples that follow date from the end of the sixteenth century, and illustrate well the operation of the Puritan diary at a relatively moderate pitch. (For a more tempestuous style of self-disparagement one should look at Archibald Johnston, whose ravings appear the more fierce and wild in his seventeenth-century Scottish phonetic spelling.) First, a series of entries by the Reverend Samuel Ward; their obviously functional character and mechanical tone will be apparent:

> *May 22, 1595.* My prid, which I took in every little action. My negligence in stirring up my brethren in Christianity. My cowardice in Christianity, in exhorting others to the same. My fighting with S. J. as we went to bed and my *excandescentia* agaynst him in wordes before.
>
> *May 23, 1595.* How I could not gett out of my self no good meditations agaynst pride. Of my thought of prid in Mr. Pirkins chamber. The good will that Mr. Pirkins shewed me. My sleping without remembring my last thought, which should have bene of God.
>
> *May 24, 1595.* My rising without thinking on my God. My irksomnes and unwillingnes to pray. The goodnes of God to me in blessing my prayers, and in giving me grace in some acceptable manner in calling upon him. Remember this when thow feelest little effect in prayer.[5]

The second passage, by another clergyman, Richard Rogers, though dating from the same period, displays a much more developed manner, the diary providing a vehicle for self-scrutiny of a subtler kind. In a quietly rueful tone Rogers unfolds a connected meditation, and seems to be actively thinking about his spiritual condition, not merely engaging in a routine of self-abasement:

> *July 9, 1589.* . . . . I remember no such bad estat these many monthes. I have set downe oft how such distemperature ariseth, namely, by being unwil[ling]

to take paine about the weaning of my self from secret outstrainge into unlaw-
ful liberty. My purpose is, if god bless[es] us in it, to drive out this devil by
fasting and prayer. God forgev such coldnes. The particulars have been the
scurfie of all the sinnes which I in this book set my self against, leaning too
much and inclineing towardes them, but not abideing in any, onely this except,
that knowledge seeking hath been for the most part neglected, except
study for sermons. There is still fear of the losse of liberty. Reading the write-
inges of an other brother about his estat an houre and longuer, I was moved to
write, and to bring my hart into a better frame, which in the beginning was
impos[sible] to me, but, I thanck god, I feel a sensibl chaung of that, and will
set downe after how myne hart groweth better seasoned. In my iorney to
London I went and came indifferently stayed. There is litle hope of any better
stat to the church. Sodaine daungers are greatly to be feared. We are gener[ally]
so secure and so litle dreaming of them. Of many thinges, this presently greev-
eth me, that I, seeing so much cause to mislik the grosse course of many
preachers, should my selfe be so unprof[itable] lik and out of savore.[6]

The following entry by Lady Margaret Hoby very accurately represents her characteristic manner, which uses the diary not as a direct
occasion for spiritual exercise but rather to render an account of each
day's stewardship. As recorded, her life appears to consist of nothing
but work and godly exercises, which it is the barren function of the
diary to enumerate:

Tewsday 28 [August, 1599]. In the morninge, after priuat praier, I Reed of the
bible, and then wrought tell 8: a clock, and then I eate my breakfast: after
which done, I walked in to the feeldes tell: 10 a clock, then I praied, and, not
long after, I went to dinner: and about one a clock I geathered my Apeles tell
:4:, then I Cam home, and wrought tell almost :6:, and then I went to priuat
praier and examenation, in which it pleased the lord to blesse me: and besiech
the lord, for christ his sack, to increase the power of his spirite in me daly Amen
Amen: tell supper time I hard Mr. Rhodes read of Cartwright, and, sonne after
supper, I went to prairs, after which I wrett to Mr. Hoby, and so to bed.[7]

It will be observed that Lady Hoby was using Pepys's most famous
contribution to English idiom sixty years before he began to write.

I have called my fourth class of proto-diaries 'journals of personal
memoranda'. If the Puritan examination of conscience can be considered the forerunner of the *journal intime*, then these memoranda are
the ancestors of its counterpart, the journal record of things done and
seen and heard. They do not constitute a diary *per se*, being no more
than accumulations of jottings, but they contain the germ of one. They
are put down in response to the same impulse that leads another man

to write out the day's events in connected, if casual, prose. If any dif-
ferentiation can be made, it should perhaps be between recording
things you may *need* to remember, and recording things you *want*
to remember. As the habit grows more elaborate and comes to take
itself seriously, so does the rationale become more pretentious. At its
most primitive the habit is no more self-conscious than noting the
despatch of a letter in a square on the calendar. And in fact Evelyn's
earliest notes were written in the dated blank spaces in almanac books.[8]

A very early and primitive example of this notes-of-occurrences
type of writing is the so-called *Private Diary of Dr. John Dee*, philosopher to Queen Elizabeth. Dee mingles notes on his health, family,
visits, and so on, with records of business transactions and meetings
with the Queen. Entries are dated but quite scattered, and certainly do
not give the impression of having been brought up to date regularly
as a habit. Here and there he makes notations in Greek characters,
including the periodic entry, 'Ιανε ἀδ θεμ'. In an entry dated 17 June,
1587, he observes: 'αφτερ θις ψυλ μονθ, ιανε ἀδ θεμ νοτ.'[9] On 28 February following he notes the birth of another son to his wife, Jane. On
the scale that rises to Pepys, Dee just barely registers.

A diarist typical of those for whom the noting of personal concerns
has become a regular habit, though of a pretty pedestrian character
on the whole, is Adam Eyre, a Yorkshire yeoman writing in the
1640s. While Eyre seldom rises much above a routine account of com-
ings and goings, and money received, spent, and lost at bowls, he does
at least furnish a continuous summary of how his days are spent, and
occasionally fleshes out his skeleton with a personal reflection or expression of feeling. He points forward to Pepys, and is valuable in
helping us to locate Pepys in the convention within which he raised
his autobiographical monument. The following entries come from
December, 1647:

22.—This day I rested at home all day, and cast up the accounts of my ex-
pences for this yere; and I find them to be nere hand 100£., wheras I have not
past 30£. per ann. to live on; wherefore I am resolved herafter never to pay
for any body in the alehouse, nor never to entangle myselfe in company so
much again as I have done; and I pray God give mee grace that, sleighting the
things of this life, I may looke up to Him.

23.—This morne I gave my wife 5s., and then I went to Peniston on foote
and bought a quarter of mutton of Woodcock, for which I gave him 3s.; and
then I went to the shopp and bought mustard seed 2d., and then to Ernshawe's,
where I spent with Capt. Shirt and Capt. Rich 9d.; then wee went to Robuck's

to see Mr. Ward; but because I was on foot I stayd not, but came home again; in all 4 myle; and as I went I spoke to Willm Rich, of Hornthwayte. It this day snowed very tempestuously. It thundered yesternight allso.[10]

Of one apparently remarkable diary of this class, from the first decade of the seventeenth century, only a single fragment survives. It is enough to indicate two things: first, that the habit was well established as early as 1606, and secondly, that some people regarded it as a ludicrous symptom of mental debility. Here is the surviving specimen, undated:

> 'Notandum,
> A rat had gnawn my spur-leathers: notwithstanding,
> I put on new, and did go forth: but, first,
> I threw three beans over the threshold. *Item*,
> I went, and bought two tooth-picks, whereof one
> I burst, immediately, in a discourse
> With a Dutch merchant, 'bout *ragion del stato*.
> From him I went, and paid a *moccenigo*,
> For piecing my silk stockings; by the way,
> I cheapened sprats: and at St. Mark's I urined.'

The diarist is, of course, Sir Politic Would-be in *Volpone*.[11]

One more pre-Pepysian is deserving of mention. Begun in 1638, the diary of Sir Henry Slingsby might perhaps have become a work to rival Pepys, had it not, as previously mentioned, spent itself in chronicling the passage of the civil war through Yorkshire. (Slingsby was a Royalist gentleman and was eventually executed under Cromwell in 1658.) Its particular claim upon our interest is the high degree of consciousness of the diary-writing practice shown by the writer. Both in his performance and in his often-quoted declaration of intent he shows an interest in the secular diary-for-its-own-sake far more sophisticated and developed than those of his contemporaries who were sleepwalking their way into the habit. His rationale, with its acknowledgement of a literary and philosophic model quite distinct from either the Puritan or the travel-for-profit theory of the diary, contains the promise of a book urbanely and comfortably dedicated to pleasing itself. Having mentioned 'the pattern of Michael de Montaigne a frenchman' in relation to his son's education in Latin, he goes on: 'I do likewise take his advise in Registering my daily accidents which happens in my house.' He repeats almost verbatim Montaigne's account of how his father 'kept a journal Book, wherein he day by day registr'd the memories of the historys of his house; a thing pleasant to read, when time began to wear out the Remembrance of them', and declares his own intention 'to sett down in this Book such accidents as befall me, not that I make my study of it, but rather a recreation at vacant times, without observing any time, method, or order in my wrighting, or rather scribbling.'[12] The insistence that his book shall be a 'recreation' rather than a 'study' strikes a rare note among early diarists, but one which becomes increasingly common. For Slingsby there is a recurring pleasure to be had in simply describing something or expatiating upon some theme that has risen in his mind.

If a disproportionate amount of space has been given to the period before Pepys, this is because it has seemed important to make clear the working division into categories which, I am arguing, may be seen to derive from the several distinct sources of the diary habit. These categories will continue to function as terms of reference in the following survey of the evolutionary tracts that lie between my chosen 'milestones'. In the milestones themselves the categories lose their distinctness and merge. Probably no 'major' diary is possible which draws its character from only one of the sources of impetus I have proposed. A diarist as resourceful and various as James Boswell draws on all of them. For his first-published travel journal he earned the *soubriquet* 'Corsica' Boswell; his painstaking coverage of celebrated people, chiefly of course Johnson, puts him among the ranks of the 'public' diarists, recording what posterity may be glad to know; the Puritan diary finds a descendant in Boswell's constant self-examination— though its terms are by no means always ethical; and as for the 'personal memoranda' component, it was Boswell who remarked: 'I should live no more than I can record... There is a waste of good if it be not preserved.'[13] Boswell's journals subsume all their precursors, transcend them, and raise serial autobiography to new levels of achievement.

Surveying the crop of diaries that have survived from the century that separates him from Pepys, one receives the impression of relative poverty until the suddenly rich harvest at the very end of this hundred-year period. Whether—to flog the agricultural metaphor—this is the result of adverse conditions of soil and climate, or should rather be attributed to the haphazard reaping of what was in fact abundantly cultivated, cannot be easily decided. One tentative speculation may be put forward: it appears from the evidence, and is anyway not unreasonable to think, that diary-writing was a habit to which the dissenting bourgeois mentality was particularly drawn; it was less conformable to the ethos we think of as high Augustan. As the century wore

Samuel Pepys
Portrait of 1666 by John Hayles

James Boswell
Portrait of 1765 by George Willison

on, and variations of cultural tone began to manifest themselves in new valuations of experience and new modes of apprehending the self, so the diary became, as it had not been, a viable form of expression for the sophisticated élite. In particular the emergence of a taste for that style of responsiveness conveyed by the term 'Sensibility' might have made the diary an attractive medium for self-encounter. This sort of suggestion, however, based on such tenuous social generalizations, is extremely suspect. Perhaps the sudden plenty after about 1760 is merely an optical trick of the rear-view mirror.

The tradition of the Puritan diary continues through this period. At one end there is a figure like Henry Newcome, a dissenting clergy-man in Lancashire, writing daily in the 1660s of his religious minis-trations and spiritual struggles. A consummate embodiment of the Puritan autobiographical ethos, Bunyan's *Grace Abounding*, was pub-lished in 1666. It is unquestionably based on a diary, and expresses the tradition at its visible height, giving it fresh impetus. Further along in time the example of a man like Richard Kay might be cited to show another stage of the diary as a register of the religious life. Son of a medical practitioner in Lancashire, and later a doctor himself, Kay started writing in 1737 at the age of twenty-one, continuing until shortly before his death in 1751. The initial impulse to write appears to have been some kind of conversion experience and self-dedication, the anniversary of which (his 'Espousals', as he calls them) he observes every 11 April. For years his entries exhibit a formal pattern of ac-counting for his expenditure of time and composing a little prayer. There is none of the self-abasement or desperation over sin that agi-tate the more turbulent diarists, but rather a continual referring of his life to God.

September 13 [1738]. This Day hath been observed as a Day of Prayer here, by Father and some of our Christian Friends, we have had a comfortable Day, and a considerable Number of praying Friends; I've been endeavouring to join with them in Heart Service, and to engage God's Presence, Blessing and Assistance, and Success to attend me in that great Work I shall in a little Time engage in. Lord Joyn Issue with our poor tho' sincere Endeavours for the Good both of Soul and Body.[14]

Toward the end of the diary some particularly distressing experiences draw from Kay entries of anguished and arresting eloquence, of which mention will be made later (see Chapter 5).

Quakers contributed substantially to the religious diary convention

and so in their turn did the Methodists. Indeed, the journal of John
Wesley is one of the epics of the genre. Sustained for sixty-six years,
from 1725 to 1791, it carries an inexhaustible narrative of travelling,
preaching, and travelling on again, punctuated by reflections on numerous subjects, and acknowledgements of Divine assistance. Simply on
account of its magnitude one is almost tempted to regard it as a
'major' diary, but its range is really not sufficiently wide. Wesley is
documenting the unflagging performance of a vocation. He *is* his
work; he has no personal life. In a career so staggeringly busy it would
be amazing to find a diary serving as a vehicle for any expansive self-
preoccupation. As it is, the energetic flow of his narrative is astounding
enough.

The fervour of each dissenting sect gives birth to an identifiable set
of spiritual conventions within which the religious experiences of the
adherent take place. Along with the forms of prayer and of public
self-declaration, the special 'tone' of religious meetings, and so on,
the spiritual diary—prescribed by devotional manuals and embodied in
celebrated models—continues to standardize for the devotee the
rhetoric of self-encounter. As an example one may take the early pages
of the diary kept for over forty years (1777–1821) by William Jones,
curate and subsequently vicar of Broxbourne in Hertfordshire. In his
student days Jones was an ardent Methodist with special adherence to
Whitefield, extracts from whose journals had been published before
and shortly after his death in 1770. Jones's diary actually falls in the
Boswell-to-Haydon era, and its later years, which are quite different
in character, will be discussed in another context. But its early pages
illustrate very clearly the stamp of Methodism on the manner in which
experience is rendered. Here he is during his student days, aged twenty-
two:

> *July 19 [1777].* I am not without reason astonished at the Long-suffering of
> my God! After all my Indifference, Deadness, Unfaithfulness, & numberless
> Iniquities, which come not under the cognizance of mortal eye, I am still out of
> Hell! . . .[15]

The following year he goes as tutor to the children of the Attorney
General of Jamaica. His diary continues to be the receptacle for bouts
of exclamatory self-loathing, together with his testimony, in tones of
Righteous Witness, to the depravity of almost everything Jamaican,
his patron's family excepted. Very interestingly for this present context he quotes 'the Revd. Mr. Hervey's directions for keeping a Diary'.

James Hervey (1714–58) was a popular devotional writer who had come under Wesley's influence at Oxford. His prescriptions for the conduct of a journal of conscience indicate that the old puritan employment of this means to salvation has lost little of its savour:

Compile a secret History of your Heart and Conduct. Take notice of the manner in which your Time is spent, & of the strain that runs through your Discourse, how often the former is lost in trifles, how often the latter evaporates in vanity. Attend to the Principle from which your actions flow. Minute down your sins of Omission. Observe the frame of your spirit in religious Duties, with what reluctance they are undertaken, with what indevotion performed; with how many wanderings of thought, & how much dulness of desire. Register those secret Faults, to which none but your own Conscience is privy, & which none but the all-seeing Eye discerns. Often contemplate yourself in this faithful Mirror.[16]

The trouble with contemplating oneself in this particular mirror is that it will reflect with disproportionate prominence just the features one is looking for. Seek indevotion and dulness of desire, and ye shall assuredly find.

A figure whose place in the history of the genre deserves mention in this context is Dr. Johnson. He is important not so much as a diarist in himself, but as the cause that diary-writing should be in other men. His own intermittent efforts, carried on for over thirty years, have left a miscellaneous collection of prayers, notes, resolutions, and a couple of scanty travel-diaries of his tours with the Thrale family to Wales (1774) and France (1775). Yet he regarded the keeping of a journal as a valuable practice, primarily for its contribution to the spiritual life, and frequently chided himself for failing to pursue it. Thus, for example, in 1773 in the course of his annual Eastertide self-examination, he writes, 'My general resolution to which I humbly implore the help of God is to methodise my life; to resist sloth and combat scruples. I hope from this time to keep a Journal.'[17] Though never able to sustain for long this aid to 'methodisation', he consistently recommended to others the profit and satisfaction to be derived from regular self-scrutiny (see Chapter 4).

An activity of the 'public' diary in the eighteenth century was scrutinizing, not oneself, but other people. Chronicles of the age persist, eye-witness, day-to-day accounts of the '15 and '45 rebellions abound, but a special interest seems to develop in fascinating 'personalities', especially in high life. People with access to court or political circles assiduously document their inside stories, as for instance does

Mary, Countess Cowper, Lady-in-Waiting to George I's queen, and
wife to the Lord Chancellor. She opens her diary, upon her arrival at
court in 1714, with an explicit declaration that, in view of all the lies
one hears, she is 'determined . . . to write down all the events that are
worth remembering',[18] and proceeds to carry on an almost breathless
account of the rumour-ridden manoeuvrings of Whig and Tory that
constituted political life. Her style one would be inclined to call 'journal-
istic', and it is worth observing that, much later in the century, Fanny
Burney speaks of herself as 'your journalist' in the diary account of
George III's court that she kept for her sisters' entertainment and
interest. Other lady 'court-reporters' exhibit the same quality, from the
Duchess of Northumberland in the mid-eighteenth century, through
the gossipy, not to say scandalous Lady Charlotte Bury in the 1820s,
to the Lady Frederick Cavendish mentioned earlier in this chapter.

An apparently new growth and a peculiarly eighteenth-century
phenomenon is the taste for anecdote which pervades autobiographical and biographical writing in this period. Diarists both public
and personal tend frequently towards the anecdotal manner of retailing
events, while some go all the way and make the gathering of anecdotes their presiding interest. The taste expresses a definite attitude to
life. An anecdote is a human tit-bit, a bite-sized morsel of the human
comedy, to be relished by the connoisseur. It is not a property of experience itself, but presupposes a selectively structured observation of
behaviour. The anecdote is in the eye of the beholder. What is recognized is the connection, in every miniature episode, between the
unique occurrence and the general nature it inevitably illustrates. It
may be the general nature of mankind that was ne'er so well exemplified, or the character of a well-known individual or type. In either
case each new anecdote is like a specimen, more or less fine and rare,
to be prized for its contribution to knowledge of the species. Among
anecdote collections the *bon mot* appears under two complementary
guises. Either it ranks as a verbal performance throwing light upon its
speaker, or it has the qualities of an anecdote in encapsulating with
neatness and economy a point well taken.

In 1776 Mrs. Thrale began to fill the six blank volumes presented
to her by Mr. Thrale with collections of memorabilia that she herself
entitled *Thraliana*. Though she writes of the enterprise disparagingly—
'strange Farrago as it is of Sense, Nonsense, publick, private Follies'[19]
—still she kept the practice up for many years, launching only occasionally during periods of stress into the habit of personal diary-writing.

Anecdotes, epigrams, scraps of verse, gossip, philosophic reflections, quotations from her reading—all are gathered into her scrap-book of the sophisticated social life. Her general tone addresses itself unmistakably to a public, though this does not automatically indicate that she intended to publish; some portions indeed are extremely private. Rather it means that her unloading of quasi-literary souvenirs, including scores of pages of 'Johnsoniana', is conducted as an extension of a conversational habit.

One other piece of writing that might be mentioned in the context of public diary-writing in the eighteenth century, because of the stature of the author rather than the importance of the book to this study, is Fielding's *Journal of a Voyage to Lisbon*. It will serve also to represent the category of travel-journal. Fielding, on his last journey, in pursuit of health, is writing for immediate publication. His prevailing concern is to compose a lively book out of materials that come to hand day by day. Unlike the travel-journal as Bacon recommended it, Fielding's book aims to benefit the reader rather than the writer, to instruct while pleasing, you might say. He exercises his powers to divert, to entertain, and to discourse upon a variety of subjects with spirit and sense. His authorial manner may be sampled in the following (*à propos* of an apprehended danger):

Can I say then I had no fear? indeed, I cannot, reader, I was afraid for thee, lest thou shouldst have been deprived of that pleasure thou art now enjoying; and that I should not live to draw out on paper that military character which thou didst peruse in the journal of yesterday.[20]

In effect Fielding is not so much writing a diary, as using the diary as a convenient catch-all format for a book.

Turning to the fortunes of the personal diary: it has already been suggested that the diary was more in use among the non-conformist bourgeoisie than among the gentry or the *literati*. In its secular aspect, too, the dissenting tradition contained a valuation of the self and an attitude to the conduct of life that would have made diary-keeping a natural embodiment of the personality structure. The habit of accounting for time spent and of engaging assiduously in systems of self-improvement operated as a powerful incentive on a young man like Dudley Ryder, the one surviving year of whose early diary (1715–16) stands as the most remarkable piece of serial autobiography between Pepys and Boswell. A law-student who eventually became Chief Justice of England, Ryder undertakes a more systematically introspec-

tive diary than Pepys's, while not by any means omitting the record
of daily activity. He is not engaged in the Puritan exercise of self-
examination, but rather in a constant assessment of his own ego that
points forward to Boswell, though he quite lacks Boswell's protean
volatility. Let the mind dwell for a moment on the word 'conscientious', with its suggestions of consciousness, conscience, and scrupulous
self-application. Ryder's is the conscientious diary of a highly conscientious young man.

As an extreme contrast to Ryder's diary, and almost an exact contemporary of it, there stands the *London Diary* (as its editors call it)
of William Byrd of Virginia. Written daily in shorthand by a colonial
gentleman-about-town, it promises at first glance to add just that
element of hearty candour and pleasure in London life which would
allow it to share with Ryder's the joint-inheritance of Pepys. But precisely because he lacks the quasi-moral incentive to keep a diary that
Ryder's value-system contained, Byrd cannot rise above the most
mechanical record of his actions. He clearly has no vital rationale for
his journal, and hence resorts to plain summaries of each day's doings
so nearly identical as to give the impression of a simply automatic habit.
Even his sexual candour which, be it confessed, will go far towards
redeeming an otherwise unremarkable diary, soon turns out to be a
dull regimen of 'committing uncleanness', 'rogering', and 'polluting
himself' ('God forgive me'). Even so, a sexual encounter is about the
only thing that could elicit from him such an expression of personal
response as the following: '. . . rogered her three times and found her
very straight and unprecocious and very sweet and agreeable.'[21]

To return to the dissenting tradition: one of the last 'major' diaries
by a dissenting bourgeois, and a very singular and interesting one at
that, comes from Sylas Neville, who was born (one year after Boswell)
in 1741, and wrote between 1767 and 1788. Of the diarists regarded
as major by this study on account of their range of originality, Neville
is undoubtedly the obscurest figure, historically speaking. Ryder may
not have rivalled Lord Mansfield for legal eminence, but to historians
of the eighteenth century at least he is a person of some consequence.
But Neville's ninety-nine years of struggle with untoward circumstances left hardly a trace. His nominal occupation was the practice of
medicine, but unlike the heroic Richard Kay, Neville regarded himself
as a gentleman and never quite reconciled himself to the fact that having
neither money nor connections he was obliged to work. This role-
conflict is one of several that give his diary its exceptional interest as a

psychological document. While it cannot be judged 'great' on the milestone scale, yet the self-portrait it contains displays so many features, wittingly and unwittingly revealed, as to warrant extensive consideration.

A type that seems to emerge distinctly in the eighteenth century as a fertile and various sub-genre is the diary-of-a-country-parson. Probably Parson Woodforde comes to mind, but the type is actually far better represented by contemporaries of Woodforde who did not have the luck to be so energetically puffed at a propitious moment in publishing history. Where Woodforde does little more than present himself with an itemized bill each day for forty years, men like George Ridpath (writing 1755–61), William Cole (1765–7), and the aforementioned Jones (whose country parson days lasted from 1780 to 1821), make their diaries registers of their lives. They are not religious diaries, however, and what they have in common as parsons is not a spiritual disposition but a social situation. The tenor of the regularly turning seasons and the progressions of the Church's calendar imprint themselves upon these diaries, in which men with Oxford or Cambridge degrees combat the process of vegetation with the exercise of words upon their environments. Of the four I have named, Ridpath is the most sophisticated and Jones the most eccentric. Into the nineteenth century country parsons continue to resort to diary-writing until, in 1870, the stem blossoms into Robert Francis Kilvert.

Two more pieces of writing should be noticed in the context of personal diary-writing in the eighteenth century. The first is Swift's *Journal to Stella*. In considering whether or not to include it in such a study as this one is confronted again by the arbitrary nature of any dividing line between diary and not-diary. It was written for a specific person to read and was posted at regular intervals—but so, at some periods, was Boswell's journal. Yes, but Swift writes as a means of direct communication, he addresses his reader constantly, whereas Boswell writes as though he is alone. A book which aims to examine the varieties of discourse produced within the convention of writing of oneself, by oneself, for oneself, has to exclude material forming part of a reciprocal correspondence. A more difficult case is presented by Sterne's *Journal to Eliza*, written between April and August 1767, which again addresses a specific person but is not posted and does not depend upon answers. However, his lachrymose effusions certainly have little in common with a diary in the accepted sense of the term. He is concerned not so much to register experience as to give vent to, and inci-

dentally to regenerate, a rather grotesque emotionality. Here is part of
the entry dated 16 April:

5 in the afternoon—I have just been eating my Chicking, sitting over my
repast upon it, with Tears—a bitter Sause—Eliza! but I could eat it with no
other—when Molly spread the Table Cloath, my heart fainted within me—one
solitary plate—one knife—one fork—one Glass!—O Eliza! twas painfully
distressing—I gave a thousand pensive penetrating Looks at the Arm chair thou
so often graced on these quiet, sentimental Repasts—and Sighed and laid down
my Knife and fork,—and took out my handkerchiff, clap'd it across my face,
and wept like a child.[22]

The sharpest distinction between what Sterne is writing and a 'conventional' diary is that if Eliza (Mrs. Draper) were to return, the pretext
for the journal would automatically disappear. In other words, it is
not a self-sustaining piece of autobiography but the written equivalent
of a Moan.

In one important way the *Journal to Eliza* serves as a most appropriate introduction to the next stage of this historical survey, the
period crowned by Benjamin Robert Haydon. With the emergence of
what may justly be called the Romantic diary an unmistakably new
characteristic enters the genre, and Sterne is one of the first to display
it. It is the appearance for the first time in a non-religious context of the
rhetoric of immediate emotion. Until this time diarists have written
about their emotions, often very affectingly, but they have not written
emotionally—except when addressing God and hence engaging in the
rhetorical conventions of prayer. The impression has therefore been of
secular diary-writing as dispassionate, carried on in a neutral moment
in which emotion is suspended in order to be spoken of considerately.
Now, late in the eighteenth century, there develops the tendency to
write while emotion is at its height, so that the energy of that emotion
flows directly into language. Needless to say, there is not a complete
substitution of one manner for the other; plenty of diarists continue to
express themselves in the 'neutral' manner, while even the most
extravagantly histrionic have temperate periods. But the dramatization
of the self as an emotionally-charged creature of prompt sensibility
grows increasingly fashionable, and the capacity for self-abandonment
to passion becomes an asset, not a liability. As the following chapters
take up aspects of self-presentation and the cultivation of roles, this
subject-area will be considered at length.

A good illustration of the rhetoric of 'sensibility' entering the diary

can be drawn from the *Thraliana*, which were introduced earlier as
an example of the socially-oriented eighteenth-century ancedote
collection. However, the emotional crisis leading up to her marriage
to Gabriel Piozzi in 1784 elicited from Mrs. Thrale passages of histrionic rhetoric such as the following:

What! die in my Piozzi's Arms, & leave him a Pledge of my unbounded, my
true Affection! No! let me indulge no such Dreams of fantastic Delight,
contented to see him once more, and assure him of my faithful Love.[23]

One cannot help remarking on the peculiarly 'literary' quality of this
sort of outburst, as though a more natural vehicle for the carriage of
strong emotion was not yet accessible.

The close of the eighteenth century also marks a definite end to
the ascendancy of the dissenting bourgeois ethos over the diary. What
this means is the appearance of 'major' diaries committed not to conscientious self-assessment but to manifold self-realization. Again there is
of course no complete switch. Diaries of scrupulous introspection
continue to be written, but the genre now expands to include luxuriant,
self-gratifying overflows of personality. It is tempting to place Boswell's diary at the fork in the road, embodying a tension between the
claims of rational self-government and the allure of exultant self-
proliferation. Not many years later the tension would probably have
been resolved in favour of the latter inclination, the diary steeping itself
in one role after another instead of maintaining a surveillance over them.
And note the distinction: Boswell the man tries on roles like a child in
a theatre wardrobe, but Boswell the diarist stands back and discusses
the fit. Haydon, on the other hand, sits down to write his diary still
wearing his Conquistador hat.

For nearly forty years (1808–46) Haydon, the self-appointed saviour
of his nation's Art, ranted and wept, boasted and prayed, declaimed,
whined, argued, and rhapsodized on to the pages of his staggering
diary. Striking every pose in the repertoire of the Romantic Artist,
intoxicating himself with the most monstrous self-deceptions, though
capable at times of a fearful honesty, he hurtled on through deepening
disaster, indulging to the last the fantasy that his gigantic canvasses of
historical and biblical subjects would be acclaimed by critics and popu-
lace as the apotheosis of English painting. In every project, every belief,
every relationship and every subsequent disenchantment he invested
an unbated fervour. His diary received it all in an astonishing torrent of
language. Finally, at the age of sixty, he composed his studio into a

suitable setting, wrote a dramatic farewell to the world, and shot himself. If Haydon had not existed, it would have been impossible to invent him.

Before Haydon's contemporaries are introduced, three diarists should be mentioned, one of them of major stature, who fall into that strangely blank period of English literary history, the last quarter of the eighteenth century. As with the literature of this period, one covers one's sense of their indeterminate character with the term 'transitional'. Fanny Burney, Eleanor Butler, and William Windham are the three in question. Fanny Burney began to write in 1768 at the age of sixteen. She actually continued to keep a diary of sorts until 1833, but it is the period prior to her marriage in 1793 that establishes her rank as a diarist. While it is a 'personal' diary that she keeps, in the sense that the material is her own first-hand experience, at the same time she seldom engages in introspection and can in fact be highly reticent. (Of course it must be remembered that she edited her own writings later in life.) She employs the diary chiefly to savour the pleasure she takes in 'society', revelling in its gratifications, especially during her years of fame, and sharpening her skill at capturing its incongruities. While the eighteenth century must undoubtedly be credited with having created Fanny Burney, she deserves the 'transitional' label in that hers is the prototype of a host of well-bred-young-ladies' diaries in the century to come. Eleanor Butler, better known as one of the 'ladies of Llangollen', apparently wrote a diary for many years, as did her companion Sarah Ponsonby. The surviving portion covers the years 1788–90, and is a sprightly production of the sentimental-genteel variety. The third 'transitional' diary briefly introduced here, that of William Windham the great parliamentarian, will be cited much later in this study as an example of conscientious self-assessment in the light of another ideal than that of the bourgeois dissenter. The 'significant' years of Windham's diary run from 1784 into the 1790s.

It is now time to point out a gradual development which, by the beginning of the nineteenth century, has become sufficiently pronounced to be regarded as a major change in attitude. This is the growing consciousness in the mind of the diarist of diary-writing as literary composition, a process in which the writer has an eye on himself writing, and in which increasingly he invests a deliberate 'literariness'. This is not to say that diarists prior to this time have not responded to prevailing conventions of literariness, but that they did so by absorption, it being impossible to write or even speak without participating in current styles of expression, which themselves embody social and philosophic dispositions. Nor is it to overlook the care taken by Pepys in composing his entries and his book, which Matthews has so impressively demonstrated,[24] or his special attention to the celebrated account of the Great Fire, 'written-up' some months later. For all this, Pepys could not have regarded his secret compilation as a *literary* activity in the sense in which Boswell, in a measure, and Fanny Burney certainly, and Haydon and Dorothy Wordsworth ('Grasmere Journal' 1800–03) and Scott (1825–32) in their various fashions, are consciously relating themselves to criteria of literary accomplishment in their writing.

Several supporting observations should be made: first of all, it may be objected that (unlike Pepys) all these diarists are actually writers by vocation, or close to it, which is more than sufficient to account for the literary nature of their private writing. True enough, but in fact this quality of 'literariness' is common to virtually all nineteenth-century diaries of any substance, from Francis Kilvert's to Queen Victoria's. The reason for this shift may be put as follows: as, with the waning of the Augustan cultural ethos, creative literature tends increasingly to draw on the intimate emotional life of the writer as a primary resource; so, conversely, does that mode of writing whose substance has long been the personal life come to regard itself as 'literary', and to adopt literary conventions. This is by no means the same thing as writing for publication, although in the early nineteenth century personal diaries are beginning to appear in print. Scott cites Byron's diary, which Moore showed him prior to publication, as the proximate reason for his own adoption of the habit;[25] and this period also sees the publication of Evelyn (1818) and Pepys himself (1825). Perhaps it would be truest to say that by this period few serious diarists any longer write in the certainty that they will *not* be published, posthumously at least. Inevitably this consciousness must have its effect on the manner of self-presentation, just as the most casual attire will develop a certain *je ne sais quoi* when there's a possibility of guests dropping in. Oscar Wilde, in a sly commentary on the culmination of this development, has Cecily in *The Importance of Being Earnest* refuse Algernon a look in her diary with the words, 'Oh no. You see, it is simply a very young girl's record of her own thoughts and impressions, and consequently meant for publication.'

Besides the 'personal' diary, there continues to be written throughout the nineteenth century the kind of 'public' diary which eschews intimate concerns and gives its attention to one aspect or another of life in society. One variety of the type, common in Haydon's time and beyond, is the dairy dedicated to recording conversations, or the sayings of individual raconteurs and coiners of *bons mots*. Henry Crabb Robinson, for example, spent a lifetime in conversations with famous personages, and recorded the gist of them voluminously. Celebrated wits like Sheridan, Lamb, and Sydney Smith are captured in many a diary, while everyone who ever heard the Great Duke discoursing, as he was wont to do, was impelled to write down as much as could be retained. A good deal of the indefatigable Greville's inside-view of political life consists of reported conversation; while ladies as various as Lady Holland, Lady Frances Shelley, and Miss Caroline Fox fill a considerable portion of their diaries with what other people said.

In the Victorian era diary-writing, as a conventional habit among persons of culture, seems to have reached its apogee. While the variety of recorded experience lends a natural variety of interest to the copious volumes that have survived and been printed, nonetheless the 'Victorian diary' may be recognized as a type with certain regular features. Faithfully and earnestly penned by hosts of respectable people—ladies and travellers, intellectuals and politicians, clergymen and soldiers, and the Queen—these diaries contain an enormously detailed picture of life within the Victorian social fabric, and reflect contemporary attitudes and values with great fidelity. And yet one misses, in the majority of them, the autobiographical energy and individual accent that would make them remarkable. With their accomplished fluency and their respect for decorum, they display the talents of a practised essayist. But in their descriptions of Alpine scenery and rural English customs, their reports of an evening with Ruskin or a day at the Crystal Palace, their sober ruminations on the truth of *Genesis* and the extension of the franchise, they tend to sound very much alike.

To claim pre-eminence for Kilvert among Victorian diarists is not to assert that he transcended his cultural milieu, for in fact he expressed a Victorian sensibility with exceptional completeness; rather it is to acknowledge that, in a time when diary-writing was becoming a genteel literary sideline, he brought to it a creative autobiographical fervour. With much less intelligence, subtlety, and sophistication than many of his contemporaries, he conveys with a kind of sentimental luxuriance the texture of his life as a country curate in the 1870s. Earlier in the century, the diary kept briefly (1831-2) by Elizabeth

Barrett, later Browning, is remarkable for its passion and its vehement self-scrutiny, while the diary which Alice James, invalid sister of William and Henry, wrote in the years immediately prior to her death in 1892 will be considered later for its wry, courageous humour. Another Victorian diarist, published only recently and fascinating for his subject-matter, is Arthur Munby. A Cambridge M.A., civil servant and minor poet, on familiar terms with most of the literary notables of the mid-century, Munby documents a lifelong secret preoccupation with the qualities and conditions of working-class women. In particular he ruminates endlessly on the incongruities of his concealed marriage to a semi-literate maid-of-all-work, Hannah Cullwick. However, while his situation and interests are undoubtedly unconventional enough, his mode of recording them does not particularly distinguish him from the conventional diarists of his epoch.

If one of the processes traced through this short history has been the diary's evolution towards literary self-consciousness, then it is appropriate that W. N. P. Barbellion should have a prominent place. Barbellion's book, *The Journal of a Disappointed Man*, is almost excruciatingly conscious, both of its author's psychological intricacies and of itself as a book. Running from boyhood entries made in 1903 through to October 1917 it registers the struggle of a young biologist and aspiring writer against desperately bad health and its attendant frustrations, and concludes with a note of the author's death on 31 December 1917. However, as is well known in diary-reading circles, Barbellion (B. F. Cummings) had prepared the diary for publication himself and survived until 1919. As the diary shows, he had been planning for years to publish what he felt would be regarded as an epoch-making work of fearless self-revelation, and investing in the writing and editing of it all the literary ambition that had so far been thwarted by editorial rejection slips. He several times acknowledges Marie Bashkirtseff as his literary precursor—a rare case of one diarist being 'influenced' by another—and engages in the same sort of labyrinthine self-analysis.

What Barbellion's book represents is the importation into English of the conventions of the *journal intime*, the serious exploration of the life of the psyche. By the beginning of the twentieth century the *journal intime* in French had become an acknowledged mode and offered a somewhat un-English intensity of self-preoccupation.[26] Its characteristic manner embodies the kind of high-strung, mercurial responsiveness to stimuli that used to be thought of as 'the artistic temperament', a cultivated capacity to vibrate to the slightest touch. It contains also a passion for literature and music as sources of intense experience, of transfiguration or despair. Pater is at the back of its English appearances, Pater dyed in the colours of Bohemian emotional recklessness. Two diaries which register this temperament very poignantly, especially in their early years, are those of Katherine Mansfield (written 1904–22) and Ivy Jacquier (1907–26). Almost exact contemporaries, born 1888 and 1890 respectively, both women flung themselves into the life of 'the artist', Katherine Mansfield of course as a writer and Ivy Jacquier as a painter. Their diaries, begun in adolescence, show a similar progression from ardent adolescence to a painful maturity inflicted, as on so many, by the first world war. Either might challenge Barbellion's claim to be the diarist representative of their era, by virtue of their intensity and flair, only they lack, in their published state at least, his organic consistency. The book compiled by Middleton Murry as *The Journal of Katherine Mansfield* contains relatively little deliberate diary-writing, but a considerable collection of undated autobiographical fragments, material for stories, notes on her reading, snatches of verse, 'unposted letters', and so forth; while Ivy Jacquier reduced her own diary to an edited selection of entries, sometimes comprising only a few pages a year.

Two other diarists of this period who provide an interesting contrast to one another are George Sturt and Arnold Bennett. Bennett, who needs no biographical introduction here, was writing a diary from 1896 to 1929, a thorough record of the novelist-in-progress, from his literary apprenticeship through years of relentless productivity to the plateau of wealth and fame. It presents an image of a man who rationed himself very efficiently and who always let his diary go slightly hungry. Not that he ever starved it, supplying as he did an unfailing diet of facts about his literary plans and output, but the living material that really nourishes autobiography he doled out very grudgingly. On the other hand, George Sturt (not much better known as George Bourne, novelist, essayist, and correspondent of Arnold Bennett) wrote between 1890 and 1927 a journal which, while extremely uneven, is a receptacle for some of the most vital components of his consciousness, especially in the earliest years when he sometimes wrote several times a day. Sturt owned a wheelwright's shop in rural Surrey and sought to fashion a philosophy and a literature that would incorporate traditional rural values without being anachronistic or sentimental. He used his journals to cultivate his first-hand awareness of his environment and to work out the ideas that were germinating in his mind.

By 1930 Freud and Proust and Lawrence and Joyce—to name only these—had made it a formidable task to say who you are and what you did today. By 1930 the diary that really counts must express in the complexity of its organization and texture a creative response to this challenge. One who ignores it, like Harold Nicolson, may very well write something entertaining, full of interest and personal truth, but cannot have any importance in the development of the genre. Similarly the volume of extracts from Virginia Woolf's diaries (1918–41), edited by Leonard Woolf and entitled *A Writer's Diary*, while it is a rich and valuable collection of her ideas and impressions, does not make a significant creative contribution to the art of serial autobiography. However, the promised edition of the complete diaries may well prompt a radical revision of this judgement.[27] To cite a third example: the recently published diaries of Evelyn Waugh, fascinating as they are for their abundance of mordant observation and laconic wit, remain essentially a collection of anecdotes and *obiter dicta*; they are not the field on which Waugh strove to encompass the complex realities of his life, with the resources of language and analysis that the evolution of culture had made current and accessible. Now to introduce Anaïs Nin in this fashion is not thereby to suggest that she systematically applies a Freudian, or more precisely a Jungian, analytical structure to the record of her life. But in her the consciousness which organizes experience into words has taken account of the radically new languages of psychic life, absorbed their syntax and been enriched by their perspectives. She manifests also a still more acute awareness than any before her of the *form* of the diary and its function in the life of the one who writes it. For her it is a creative process which confronts her with both an aesthetic and a personal conflict. Existing in an intermediate zone between living experience and the formal work of art, the diary threatens to encroach upon both, becoming a substitute for life and a deflection from art; the resolution of this problem is one of her central themes.

Thus far has the diary come—from the unconscious by-product of some other activity to the crucible of consciousness itself. As the activity of registering experience daily varies in importance in the life of the writer, so does the value to be placed upon the gathering book, until Anaïs Nin makes of the diary the medium through which experience may be realized, may discover its design and intricate unity, may clarify itself and flower; while the growing book, edited by Anaïs Nin the writer of fiction, becomes her greatest work of art.

3

✤✤

The Diary as Literature

THE question of whether the diary can or should be regarded as a form of literature has given rise to a number of persistent confusions. In a sense the question is an artificial one, a form of words, like the rather tiresome discussions of whether the motion-picture is an art form, or whether *Death of a Salesman* is a tragedy. But, as with these other questions, the asking of it may be a fruitful enterprise, especially if one can resist the urge to reach an answer. Moreover, if critical discussion is to be conducted in terms acceptable to the interested parties, some degree of clarification and agreement is essential. Writers on the diary have hitherto tended to shield their adopted genre from the judgements of literary criticism, arguing that such judgements would distort the qualities of diaries and assess them according to irrelevant standards. Not that they believe that diaries should be exempt from all critical judgement; on the contrary, they write very freely of 'good' diaries and 'poor' diaries, and Arthur Ponsonby, in his little book *British Diarists* (a digest of his other books), devotes a whole chapter to his choice of the nine all-time best.[1] At the same time, as will be shown below, the criteria that produce these assessments are explicitly distinguished from literary valuations. In fact the implication is that the more 'literary' a diary appears, the less it deserves the name of diary. I believe, however, that confusion has arisen from the ambiguous use of the terms 'literary' and 'literature', and from an interesting and quasi-moral ambivalence about what constitutes a 'pure' diary. Furthermore, to make 'diary' and 'literature' into opposing terms is to treat the great diaries as deviations from a norm established by the mediocre. For it is the contention of this chapter that the major achievements in diary-writing—as singled out by Ponsonby, Spalding, and others—have been produced out of a conscious respect for the diary as a literary form, and that the criteria which they explicitly aspire to meet are by far the most appropriate and rewarding to apply to all writing within the genre. In the following pages I propose to assemble from a number of diarists a body of criteria, explicitly formulated or expressed in their practice, in the light of which they value their own performances. From them may be drawn the unifying conceptions that will give coherence to critical discussion of diary-writing as a whole.

Here, from Lord Ponsonby and Kate O'Brien, are two characteristic general statements of the case:

People of all ages and degrees who may never have ventured to write a line for publication and may be quite incapable of any literary effort, are able to keep a diary the value of which need not in any way suffer from their literary incapacity. On the contrary, literary talent may be a barrier to complete sincerity. Diaries may or may not be called literature, some undoubtedly have literary value, but this has nothing to do with their merit as diaries.[2]

A good diary is not necessarily literature; for of its nature it must be free of most of the disciplines and tests of a work of art. Vision, imagination, passion, fancy, invention, scholarship, detachment, and the steely restraints and consciously selected embellishments of form and of design—none of these has a vital place in diary-writing.[3]

Miss O'Brien goes on to require only a readiness to 'set down everything', plus a little help from the reader, '. . . and out of a minimum of effort and a maximum of self-indulgence, something which is almost a work of art may be observed to grow, to have grown'.[4] Most people, I think, would be disposed to assent to the notions expressed here—that 'merit' in a diary is not earned, and may even be sacrificed, by the exercise of literary talent; while recognition as a work of literature is most likely to be accorded to the humblest and least pretentious writing, the meek, as so often, inheriting the earth. The attitude is comparable to that taken towards primitive art. Ideally the simple peasant should be discovered patiently chipping away at his soapstone or driftwood, marvellously reproducing scenes from his obscure environment. Protect him if possible from the corrupt sophistications of conscious artistry. Similarly the true diarist, immersed in the eddies of his days and ways, innocently dashes down whatever comes into his head and all unknowingly fashions a masterpiece. Thus Kate O'Brien again:

So we may fall upon the irony of the little man of little talent and less ambition accomplishing, in conspiracy with time, such strokes of illumination, of irony or of sheer, true life as the great imaginative ones have always had to wrestle for in uncertainty and pain, and with all their faculties on the stretch.[5]

The trouble with this romantic archetype of the untutored genius of the diary is that it ignores the reality. Very few indeed of the better-known diaries were written as naïvely as the model implies, and most of the 'major' diaries, as will be shown, were composed with a high degree of consciousness. Moreover, the same commentators who propound the doctrine of the artless diary actually devote most of their attention to the least naïve practitioners—naturally enough, since there really isn't much to say about a succession of Parson Woodfordes. Ironically, Kate O'Brien even admits to finding Pepys boring, pedestrian, and somewhat disgusting. Since she (erroneously) takes him to be the naïve chatterer *par excellence*, one would expect her to prize him above all others. Clearly there is a radical contradiction between what she is supposed to value in diaries, according to her principles, and what in fact appeals to her. How does such a situation come about?

The answer, I think, is that most theoretical considerations of diary-writing proceed deductively from the assumption that its defining characteristic is an unpremeditated sincerity. On the face of it this seems unexceptionable; the idea of a premeditated and insincere diary hardly makes sense. But when this quality is made out to be the essential attribute of the species, so that to swerve from it is to appear some-what disreputable, an ethical standard is coming into conflict with literary considerations and asserting a rigid and unrealistic scale of merit. To endeavour to write well, to consider the formal structure of the book one is writing, to address oneself to a putative reader or think of publication, to edit or rewrite one's own entries—all these practices must appear to corrupt the pure spontaneity of utterance that should mark the 'true' diary. When Ponsonby remarks that 'literary talent may be a barrier to complete sincerity' he refers primarily to style. He implies that a 'literary' style must be by nature contrived, artificially striving for effects, easily seduced from the straight and narrow by the lure of a fancy turn of phrase. Perhaps, in 1922, it is a delayed reaction against the elegant insincerities of Oscar Wilde that causes him to regard art as a liar and plainness the only dress for truth. Whatever the reason, it leads him into an awkward dichotomy in which sincerity and conscious, premeditated utterance are opposed to one another. Such an over-simplified notion of self-expression—one which should cause him incidentally to regard all poetry as 'insincere'—is obviously unequipped to deal with the more complex renderings of experience to be found in some of the very diaries that he most prizes. He declares that the 'literary value' that some diaries may have, 'has nothing whatever to do with their merit as diaries',[6] as though the wealth of self-articulation that makes a diary great is entirely separable from the fertile expressiveness in which it is embodied.

Another aspect of the diary-as-literature question is succinctly introduced by William Matthews. The remarks come from his 1948 preface to the *Bibliography*, and in fairness to him it should be stressed that his essay 'The Diary as Literature'[7] contains a much more sophisticated treatment of the subject. He is quoted here only as having expressed a generally held notion. Distinguishing the diary from the autobiography, on the grounds that the latter form tends to present an organized and consistent version of the self, he writes:

But a diarist rarely maintains one view of himself, and a diary which has a consistent pattern is a literary work and no diary at all. Any true diary includes a multitude of details about daily thoughts, emotions, and actions which would be pruned out in the careful topiary of the biography or autobiography. The diarist can see only the pattern of a day, not the pattern of a lifetime; if he is a true diarist, one day is likely to be at odds with another . . .[8]

Two observations might be made here. First, in distinguishing the diary from the 'literary work' in terms of structure and design he presupposes a very rudimentary level of consciousness on the part of the diarist who 'can see only the pattern of a day' and who starts each morning with a *tabula rasa*. As we shall see, one of the most important effects of keeping a diary is the awareness thereby generated of patterns and processes at work in the life of the writer. Channelled back into the diary, this awareness becomes the source of structural 'themes' that may give to the work a highly sophisticated design. When he wrote this pronouncement Matthews cannot have known of Anaïs Nin's diary, in which this process is most richly apparent; but Boswell, Haydon, and Barbellion manifest it quite sufficiently and he should have been able to consider the possibilities of the diary in a highly developed state instead of basing his remarks (as writers on the subject frequently do) on the common or garden variety. Which leads to the second observation: he speaks of the 'true diary' and the 'true diarist' in such a way as to imply a corresponding 'falseness' whose stain spreads the further we get from the regular, naïve, what-I-did-today formula. Obviously there comes a point at which what I have been calling 'serial autobiography' ceases to have much connection with the term 'diary'. But it is as limiting to make plainness, 'sincerity,' and quotidian formlessness the standard from which Boswell and Anaïs Nin depart, as it would be to regard, let us say, *Mucedorus* as the model of Elizabethan drama.

The prime reason for the persistence of a critical account of diary-writing so riddled with inconsistency must be the monumental predominance of Pepys. His name is almost synonymous with English diary-writing, and his manner is taken to be the absolutely natural, pure, and unadorned model—the diary as God intended it. All other diarists either fall short of his copious regularity or go past him into extravagance and excess. Ponsonby introduces him thus: 'By general consent the diary of Samuel Pepys may be awarded the first place among English diaries. It fulfills all the conditions of what a diary should be.'[9] Ponsonby forgets that it is from the traditionally received image of Pepys and his practice that 'the conditions of what a diary should be' are actually derived. How ironic, then, that recent scholarship should have demonstrated that Pepys was not nearly so Pepysian as had been fondly believed.

The popular idea of Pepys the diarist has been that every night for nine years he was to be seen 'just scribbling down with effortless frankness the little incidents which [he was] honest enough to record as having caught [his] attention at the moment.'[10] Using shorthand for speed and secrecy, he seemed to be indulging a habit almost as natural and unselfconscious as talking to oneself. Lately, however, the picture has undergone considerable alteration. Introducing the Latham–Matthews *Pepys*, William Matthews presents an account of the diarist's habits of composition which must revise the general estimate of the work from miraculous to masterly. As he says, 'the manuscript makes it fairly certain that Pepys's way of writing was more complex than is usually assumed, and consequently that his great diary is no simple product of nature, thrown together at the end of each succeeding day. In part at least, it is a product fashioned with some care, both in its matter and its style.'[11] Matthews's most significant conclusions are as follows: the entries are by no means always made daily, but adhere to the convention of seeming to be so. Nor are they the freehand improvisations they were imagined to be. Rather they are composed from notes and rough drafts, and are entered into the diary-volume with painstaking neatness in a fair-copy state. Thus Ponsonby's assertion that the diary 'is written with scrupulous regularity daily and is therefore quite spontaneous'[12] is dramatically controverted. In fact genuine spontaneity, which would have resulted in a disorderly style and a patchy haphazard presentation of material, is subordinated to Pepys's respect for the *form* of his book, which even includes a concern for its physical appearance.

In this revised appreciation of the 'art' of Samuel Pepys lies the clue to a critical conception of diary-writing that will be closer to the spirit in which the 'great' diaries were actually penned. While it would be wrong to think of Pepys's diary as a work of calculated artifice, nonetheless it is clear that he is aware of the diary format as a vehicle for autobiography rather than as merely the shape of a habit. Thus it is more important to him to maintain the day-by-day presentation of material than it is to write daily—although daily writing, when convenient, remains the ideal method. Still, it is a method and not a moral duty. Similarly the organization of material and the composition of each entry should be conducted with some care, if the growing book is to be a source of satisfaction to its author. In this connection the following typical remark may be quoted: 'Then back again home, and to my chamber to set down in my Diary all my late journey, which I do with great pleasure.'[13] When, in 1669, failing eyesight compels him to abandon the journal for good, he feels bereft of a necessary dimension of his being:

And thus ends all that I doubt I shall ever be able to do with my own eyes in the keeping of my Journal, I being not able to do it any longer, having done now so long as to undo my eyes almost every time that I take a pen in my hand; and, therefore, whatever comes of it, I must forbear: and, therefore, resolve, from this time forward, to have it kept by my people in long-hand, and must therefore be contented to set down no more than is fit for them and all the world to know; or, if there be any thing, which cannot be much, now my amours to Deb. are past, and my eyes hindering me in almost all other pleasures, I must endeavour to keep a margin in my book open, to add, here and there, a note in short-hand with my own hand.

And so I betake myself to that course, which is almost as much as to see myself go into my grave: for which, and all the discomforts that will accompany my being blind, the good God prepare me![14]

In these expressions of active pleasure in its maintenance and bereavement at its termination, we have the image of the diary as the passionately cherished Book of the Self, the essential imprint of a man's being-in-the-world.

The idea of the diary as the *book of the self* and as *imprint* yields a complementary pair of concepts upon which I propose to base my critical approach. Care must therefore be taken to formulate the notions and to justify them by reference to the major diarists' theory and practice. First, the 'book of the self': it is generally held that the diary, unlike almost any other kind of writing, is necessarily unconditioned by a governing idea of a formally completed whole. A diary which does appear to have been written or edited (even by the author) in the light of a formal conception is even thought to violate the conventions of the genre. What I wish to suggest, on the contrary, is that as a diary grows to a certain length and substance it impresses upon the mind of its writer a conception of the completed book that it might ultimately be, if sustained with sufficient dedication and vitality. If, having written regularly and fully for, let us say, several months, he were to abandon the habit, he would be leaving unwritten a book whose character and conventions had been established and whose final form is the shape of his life. Not all diarists by any means feel or respond to this attraction exerted by the book-that-might-be. Casual diarists and those who take up the habit for particular purposes are usually untouched by it. Even those people who consider publishing their own diaries are not necessarily recognizing the aesthetic form so much as the public interest of their lives. Nor are the most assiduous diarists always the most responsive to the conception of the finished book. There are many who express their commitment to the *exercise* of diary-writing—William Windham, for example, frequently berates himself for letting the salutary practice lapse—but the commitment of the major diarists is to the *book* that their living nourishes.

　　Abundant quotation might be furnished in support of these assertions. Almost every substantial diarist may be found referring to his diary as 'this book', taking care over it, bringing it up to date and wondering how and by whom it will be read. Sometimes a writer will take considerable care over the physical condition of the manuscript, transcribing it, making an index, having it handsomely bound—thereby expressing its importance as an *oeuvre*. Pepys encased himself in six leather-bound volumes, each so neatly penned as to make it seem, as Matthews observes, 'that he intended it to have some of the qualities of a printed book'.[15] Eleanor Butler gave herself an elegant title-page with an epigraph from Marvell's poem 'The Garden'. Beatrice Webb bought a typewriter early in 1917 and spent some time 'copying out and editing my Mss. diaries so as to make a "Book of my Life".'[16] It is particularly common to find a diarist discovering in retrospect the book that he has been creating almost unwittingly; the diary so to speak becomes conscious of itself, and the writer grows to appreciate the shape that his own image and likeness have taken. Ivy Jacquier experiences this phase and it moves her to the next consideration: 'I wonder if the publishing of my diaries would be at all possible and of interest? The difficulty is that until it is complete it cannot be judged, as the sole interest lies in the development. I work therefore in the dark.'[17] The prompting to publish comes not from personal vanity but from the recognition that a book has been in gestation.

It is rare, however, for a 'great' diary to be written unwittingly. The mighty Boswell knows quite well that he is constructing an astonishing autobiographical epic, and he discusses with himself—and his readers—many of the aesthetic considerations he encounters. In February 1763, expressing regret at the 'inconsistent fancy' which has lately assailed him of abandoning his military ambitions in favour of the Scottish bar, he says:

I am vexed at such a distempered suggestion's being inserted in my journal, which I wished to contain a consistent picture of a young fellow eagerly pushing through life. But it serves to humble me, and it presents a strange and curious view of the unaccountable nature of the human mind. I am now well and gay. Let me consider that the hero of a romance or novel must not go uniformly along in bliss, but the story must be chequered with bad fortune. Aeneas met with many disasters in his voyage to Italy, and must not Boswell have his rubs?[18]

The explicit comparison of himself with a fictional hero—actually a whole succession of them—is a central feature of Boswell's journals and will be taken up later. The point to note here is his concern for the thematic integrity of his book and the peculiar way in which this imposes upon the man living a responsibility towards the man writing, to maintain a supply of workable material. Another aspect of this relationship arises later in the *London Journal* when his friend Temple 'said he imagined that my journal did me harm, as it made me hunt about for adventures to adorn it with',[19] a charge which Boswell thoughtfully repudiates. All the same, he knows a rich lode when he sees one: in a memorandum dating from the period of the lost *Holland Journal* he reminds himself to bring his journal up to date, adding: 'You have great materials.'[20] And a chance remark years later shows how a habit of mind persists. In July 1769 his friend Douglas suggests that Boswell accompany him on a continental jaunt. 'I was, for a while, very fond of the thought, which pleased my roving fancy and would

furnish a good chapter in my life.'²¹ As conveyed by the journals many
of the episodes in his life do have the air of being 'chapters', and he
manages them with a sharp eye to their literary effectiveness. Thus,
writing weeks after the event, he will maintain an artificial suspense in
telling a story whose outcome he already knows. The most famous
examples of this practice are the inglorious 'Louisa' episode over the
winter of 1762–3, and his account of his siege of Rousseau at Môtiers
in 1764.²² In both cases he composes entries full of uncertainty as to
what the morrow will bring, when in fact the morrow in question is
already long past. The diary format becomes an artfully employed
narrative device.

It is hard to tell whether Haydon's narrative *coups* are the products
of art or life. Either way he doesn't let them slip by unnoticed. In
an entry dated 21 April 1843 he expresses desperation at his chronic
financial plight, but proclaims his faith in God's providence. The next
day:

Now Reader, whoever thou art—young & thoughtless, or old & reflecting—
was I not right to trust in God? Was it Vanity? Was it presumption? Was it
weakness? Today—*this very day*—I have sold my Curtius [a painting], when
only yesterday I had no hope, & my heart beat, & my head whirled, & my
hand shook at my distress. I had taken the butter knife off the Table to raise
13/-.²³

The effect is characteristic of the extravagant way Haydon casts his
'book of the self' in the form of a breathless saga in which the Hero
strides undaunted through triumphs and catastrophes, exhorting the
reader to keep up. Here, in 1820, he concludes the 'chapter' (which
has lasted for years) culminating in the successful exhibition of his
painting 'Christ's Entry into Jerusalem'. 'The day was indeed glorious,
& I retired home oppressed with a roar of sensations. To the reader
who in various parts of this journal will see what I have suffered & gone
through, it will be romantic . . .'²⁴ By 'romantic' Haydon certainly
means 'like something out of a romance'. He continually expresses a
sense of the stranger-than-fiction quality of his crowded volumes, exclaiming occasionally such things as: 'I shall read this again with
delight—and others will read it with wonder'²⁵ and 'A new Journal—
Vol. XIII! What a mass of character do these volumes exhibit.'²⁶
Need one say that his final act, before he ended his life, was to end the
book of that life by (literally) writing 'Finis' to his story?²⁷

Barbellion's *Journal of a Disappointed Man* also provides itself with that most appropriate of endings for a 'Life'—the subject's death. It is perhaps the most notable example of a formal consideration governing the literary practice of a diarist. Barbellion himself explains in his *Last Diary* (which actually *was* published posthumously) that 'no man dare remain alive after writing such a book' and that he had not expected to survive till its publication,[28] but the requirements of form constitute a more pressing necessity. For some years prior to his 'death' in December 1917, the composition of his 'book of the self' is Barbellion's most engrossing occupation, and for much of that time, though only in his late twenties, he (B. F. Cummings) is indeed dying. As early as 1912 he writes: 'My own life as it unrolls day by day is a source of constant amazement, delight, and pain. I can think of no more interesting volume than a detailed, intimate, psychological history of my own life.'[29] By December 1914 he is determined 'to prepare and publish a volume of this Journal'.[30] In the concluding year he is an invalid engaged in the twin processes of furbishing and editing the psychological history of his own death. Along the way an extraordinary exchange of priorities has taken place. Where the journal once served to register his living, now his living is in the service of the journal.

February 6 [1917]
Am busy re-writing, editing and bowdlerising my journals for publication against the time when I shall have gone the way of all flesh. No one else would prepare it for publication if I don't. Reading it through again, I see what a remarkable book I have written. If only they will publish it![31]

Barbellion's book raises in its most aggravated form the problem of a diarist's tampering with his own work. Obviously from the point of view of the spontaneous-sincerity school of thought the diarist has no more right than anyone else to edit or recast what he has written. He may even be seen to have *less* right, since his motives will be suspect. Where a disinterested editor seeks only to abridge, standardize, and make accessible the original document, the diarist cannot be trusted not to alter it, cutting out or polishing up what no longer suits his self-image. The result of such a process is a sort of forgery, rendered all the more despicable by the fact that it is masquerading as the most candid of productions. How can one say anything with confidence about the diarist's mode of self-encounter and self-presentation when all or any of the text may be spurious? A problem already exists in comparing a Ryder, who appears to write without a trace of self-consciousness, with a Haydon who buttonholes posterity; but at least with these two one is dealing with their original utterances.

The reply to this has of course been adumbrated by the preceding discussion. The ideal of unrevised, unpremeditated speech, unmodified by any consideration of an auditor can ultimately be fulfilled only by a tape-recording of a person talking in his sleep—and there are difficulties with this too, when one stops to think about it. That direction is a dead end. The alternative is to regard the diary-format as a literary structure for embodying subjective experience in a manner that approximates the actual passage of future into past. Some writers, and Ryder is probably one, have employed this structure very naïvely; it never occurred to them to do otherwise. Some other writers have *chosen* to write in the unpremeditated manner, preferring to be represented (to themselves and perhaps to others) by the words that came of their own accord. Thus Sir Walter Scott, whose mode of expression could hardly be called naïve, vows never to erase a single word.[32] And so along the spectrum to the 'book of the self' that has employed all the creative ingenuity at the writer's command, using the original entry as raw material to be refined, developed, brought to a fuller realization.

What all such books have in common is that they are written in the first person as a discontinuous series of more or less self-contained responses to the writer's present situation and recent experience. To relate them to one another, to contrast ways of expressing a sense of life, ways of projecting the self as narrator and as actor in the narrative, kinds of self-concern expressed or exposed, it is necessary to set them in a common framework. Primarily one must make a mental distinction between the first-person narrator who speaks in the diary and the historical personage who held the pen—in the same way that one would think of 'the narrator' in a first-person novel, or 'the poet' in Shakespeare's Sonnets. In relation to one another the diarists should perhaps be accorded the common status of characters in fiction. Thus a statement such as, 'Ryder is inhibited by a constant anxiety about the adequacy of his personality, whereas Kilvert tends to give himself quite unselfconsciously to his emotions', will not refer to the law student and the clergyman whose bones lie somewhere in England, but to the characters who live in the pages of an eighteenth-century and a nineteenth-century book. Needless to say, nearly all statements made about the diary-narrator will apply exactly to the historical personage as well, although there may be no independent means of verifying this correspondence. But any given statement may *not* so apply—and from the point of view of this study it doesn't matter.

To carry a stage further the question of the conscious and creative adoption of the diary format to render the texture of subjective experience we must turn to Anaïs Nin. As always, to enter her pages after a journey through the volumes of other diarists is to encounter a transfiguration of the form. Nothing in the diarists that precede her prepares one for an awareness of life so intense and manifold, flowering into language of such luxuriant finesse. It is not the least of her gifts to the reader that she explores continually the process of diary-writing itself, 'living in terms of immediate phraseology' as she says,[33] and its function in the organic life of the woman and the artist. (Chapter 4 of this study takes up this question.) A theme she returns to many times is the complex relation in which her diary stands to actual life on the one hand and the transformations of art on the other. Its legitimacy challenged as it were on these two fronts, the diary is sometimes on the defensive against the charge that it is a neurotic retreat from the demands of both into a compensatory dream. The following passages are dated June 1934 and August 1936; as edited the diary does not appear in the form of daily entries under a date, but as collections of passages in gatherings of a month or a season.

This diary is my kief, hashish, and opium pipe. This is my drug and my vice. Instead of writing a novel, I lie back with this book and a pen, and dream, and indulge in refractions and defractions, I can turn away from reality into the reflections and dreams it projects, and this driving, impelling fever which keeps me tense and wide-awake during the day is dissolved in improvisations, in contemplations. I must relive my life in the dream. The dream is my only life. I see in the echoes and reverberations the transfigurations which alone keep wonder pure. Otherwise all magic is lost. Otherwise life shows its deformities and the homeliness becomes rust. My drug. Covering all things with a mist of smoke, deforming and transforming as the night does. All matter must be fused this way through the lens of my vice or the rust of living would slow down my rhythm to a sob.[34]

Confronting the other face of the dilemma:

Conflict with diary-writing. While I write in the diary I cannot write a book. I try to flow in a dual manner, to keep recording and to invent at the same time, to transform. The two activities are antithetical. If I were a real diarist, like Pepys or Amiel, I would be satisfied to record, but I am not, I want to fill in, transform, project, expand, deepen, I want this ultimate flowering that comes of creation. As I read the diary I was aware of all I have left unsaid which can only be said with creative work, by lingering, expanding, developing.[35]

But at other times the diary re-asserts itself as the synthesis between the rawness of the actual and the frozen crystallizations of art. From the wretched compromise of being too literary yet not literary enough, the diary becomes the reconciler between incompatibles, literary enough yet not too literary. Expressed this way the issue perhaps seems to be an artificial one, but in her pages the problem of form appears, as it always should, as a vital problem of consciousness—what to do with the human capacity to apprehend aesthetic patterns in experience. Is it to be cultivated at the expense of authentic immediacy, or suppressed at the sacrifice of its power to enrich and transform awareness?

My father is talking about the marvels of the microscope, about the scorpion he saw and studied, about the minerals, the gold dust. And meanwhile I ask myself about the novel I wrote [*Winter of Artifice*], was it the truth? Henry deformed June in his novel, did I deform my father? Art is a microscope, as you examine one aspect of a human being, you cannot give the whole, the entire picture. The diary is closer to the truth, because it paints my father each day anew, with changes, paradoxes, contradictions, growth, and in these oscillations lies the truth. *Here* alone is the human vision restored. The novel is an act of injustice.[36]

Here, almost paradoxically, an artistic motive, the desire to render the reality of her father truthfully and responsively, leads her to abjure the 'art of the novel' for the formless form of the diary. To surpass the self-inflicted limitations of the novel, artlessness must serve as a strategy for subverting the tyranny of art. 'No consciousness of perfection must enter the diary.'[37]

However, from the pen of Anaïs Nin artlessness is a very different thing from casual simplicity. Rather it is a literary discipline vital to the book's essential quality, its receptiveness to all the voices of the self, all the multiplicity of experience. The discipline dictates that she should write rapidly and freely, out of the impressions of the present instant, with no inhibiting respect for consistency or continuity. Descriptions, mood-pieces, conversations, dreams, recollections, sketches for the portraits of her great 'characters'. Henry Miller, June Miller, Artaud, Gonzalo, Moricand, her father—she must admit everything, recognizing that the unity of the book will be a more complex harmony whose principle is not an aesthetic design but the interrelatedness of all that passes through a single consciousness. As an extended series of photographs composes a portrait that incorporates the many facets of the present and the progressions discernible over time—horizontal and vertical multiplicity—so the quality of the diary is to compose the life of the writer out of innumerable fragments, each one the imprint of a momentary state of awareness. The daily or dated entry disappears, as the mechanical division of a life into numbered units gives way to a more organic aggregation of states of being.

A passage from the diary of Virginia Woolf, dated 20 April 1919, furnishes such an exactly corresponding sense of the form that the 'book of the self' should take, that it must be quoted at length:

Moreover there looms ahead of me the shadow of some kind of form which a diary might attain to. I might in the course of time learn what it is that one can make of this loose, drifting material of life; finding another use for it than the use I put it to, so much more consciously and scrupulously, in fiction. What sort of diary should I like mine to be? Something loose knit and yet not slovenly, so elastic that it will embrace anything, solemn, slight or beautiful that comes into my mind. I should like it to resemble some deep old desk, or capacious hold-all, in which one flings a mass of odds and ends without looking them through. I should like to come back, after a year or two, and find that the collection had sorted itself and refined itself and coalesced, as such deposits so mysteriously do, into a mould, transparent enough to reflect the light of our life, and yet steady, tranquil compounds with the aloofness of a work of art. The main requisite, I think on re-reading my old volumes, is not to play the part of censor, but to write as the mood comes or of anything whatever; since I was curious to find how I went for things put in haphazard, and found the significance to lie where I never saw it at the time.[38]

The correspondence is the more remarkable in that both women are experimenting with forms of prose fiction to render the texture and flow of consciousness in ways beyond the reach of the conventional novel. Emphasizing the complex delicacy of emotional states, the nuances and dreamlike discontinuities of the psychic life, they resort to the surrealist disciplines of unprogrammed associativeness, letting patterns and connections form of their own accord. Both recognize in the nature of the diary an intrinsic capacity to reflect this aspect of selfhood. Virginia Woolf, however, continues to be a novelist, whose diary incidentally draws on her aesthetic theory, whereas Anaïs Nin makes her diary the matrix and at last perhaps the supreme achievement of her work as an artist. In 1941 she writes of the 'Joy of the realization that I am completing a work, not just making notes, the joy of discovering that this is not a sketch book but a tapestry, a fresco being completed.'[39]

In one sense these 'sophisticated' diaries seem to be endorsing the views of William Matthews and Kate O'Brien, quoted earlier, that the true diary will be made up of inconsistencies and ephemeral details, and that its aesthetic character, if any, will be perceptible only in retrospect. As with a spiral, we come full circle but to another level, the difference being that these diarists know what they are doing, have in fact a clearer view of the aesthetic paradoxes of the form than do the commentators. In cultivating an openness to the 'loose, drifting material of life' they are not opening their pages to the price of hay or the doings of a neighbour's pig, but endeavouring to preserve the fluctuating quality of an individual responsiveness to life. Moreover, they are very much alive to the role of the editor. In adopting what one might call an actively indiscriminate attitude to what goes into the book, they envisage, if they do not actually undertake, an editorial process that will bring the work to fruition, not eliminating contradiction and variety but enhancing them and exposing their patterns. Thus it is that each published volume of Anaïs Nin's diary (edited by Gunther Stuhlmann in collaboration with the writer) exhibits the thematic intricacy of major art, as her 'characters' assume symbolic proportions, embodying mutually opposed modes of being among which Anaïs seeks to harmonize her divided self.

In the foregoing pages the phrase 'book of the self' has been used to suggest the tendency of the diary to lean towards acknowledged literary forms. So far reference has been made only to those diarists who are most aware of the literary dimensions of their work, or rather who make that awareness explicit in the work itself. Thus, for example, nothing has been said about Kilvert, who devotes elaborate and loving care to the picture of his world and the expression of his joys and yearnings, sympathies and fears, but who very seldom writes about the diary itself. However his practice makes it abundantly clear that he was composing with intense literary ardour a sort of true-life sentimental novel (see Chapter 7). Scenes are narrated with a novelist's concern to establish atmosphere, convey visual detail, unfold events dramatically and develop an emotional rhythm in his re-creation of them. In the following passage a literary imagination has transformed a chance meeting into a passionate drama. Abandoning himself to the romantic suggestibility of the situation, Kilvert flings his whole narrative stock-in-trade into the episode:

But there was an attractive power about this poor Irish girl that fascinated me strangely. I felt irresistibly drawn to her. The singular beauty of her eyes, a beauty of deep sadness, a wistful sorrowful imploring look, her swift rich humour, her sudden gravity and sadnesses, her brilliant laughter, a certain intensity and power and richness of life and the extraordinary sweetness, softness and beauty of her voice in singing and talking gave her a power over me which I could not understand nor describe, but the power of a stronger over a weaker will and nature. She lingered about the carriage door. Her look grew more wistful, beautiful, imploring. Our eyes met again and again. Her eyes grew more and more beautiful. My eyes were fixed and riveted on hers. A few minutes more and I know not what might have happened. A wild reckless feeling came over me. Shall I leave all and follow her? No—Yes—No. At that moment the train moved on. She was left behind. Goodbye, sweet Irish Mary. So we parted. Shall we meet again? Yes—No—Yes.[40]

With its 'big scenes' of fallings in love, sad partings, encounters with the beauty of nature, and so forth, set in the quiet continuum of village existence, his book reflects a literary model of what constitutes the story of a life. And in the middle of the narrative of his love for Daisy Thomas, and her father's kind but firm prohibition (a situation which calls forth his most heart-felt languishing manner), he muses: 'I wonder if Daisy and I will ever read these pages over together. I think we shall.'[41] He foresees a happy ending and an indulgent reader for the unfolding tale of his life.

A diarist whom one might expect to have had a strong sense of 'the shadow of some kind of form which a diary might attain to' (in Virginia Woolf's words) is Fanny Burney. In reality, however, while she exercises her literary art unceasingly in the narration of individual episodes, she does not appear to have responded to a conception of the book as a whole entity. True, in her early journals she introduces a new volume (for 1773) with the mock-serious title of 'My Life and Opinions',[42] and the following year, after a considerable lapse, resumes the practice with this extravagant flourish:

What will become of the world, if my Annals are thus irregular? Almost two months have elapsed without my recording one anecdote! I am really shocked for posterity! But for my pen, all the adventures of this noble family might sink to oblivion! I am amazed when I consider the greatness of my importance, the dignity of my task, and the novelty of my pursuits![43]

But this rather aggravating literary pose is symptomatic of her whimsical game of being an authoress, a game which she plays with redoubled enthusiasm after the publication of *Evelina*, rather than of a commitment to the book of the self. Moreover, since her journals soon cease to be private and become family property, they increasingly assume the character of letters designed to entertain an immediate audience with the latest exercise of Fanny's gift for social comedy. And certainly they contain many long and intricate scenes in which her ear for the verbal grotesqueries of stupidity and ill-breeding has overheard some choice performances. In later years, during her arduous period of service as a lady-in-waiting to Queen Charlotte, she writes long and often fascinating descriptions of life at court, including accounts of the King's distressing bouts of insanity. But still it is not her own life so much as the scenes to which she happens to be a witness that continue to be the staple of her diary-letters.

That Fanny Burney makes no distinction between keeping a journal and writing serial letters is borne out by the evidence of her novel *Evelina*. The long epistles which the heroine addresses to Mr. Villars are very close indeed in tone and subject-matter to Fanny's journal for her father and sisters, the main difference being the layer of naïvety that the author has bestowed upon her surrogate. Moreover Evelina several times refers to her epistles as 'journals' and on one occasion, when overcome with emotion, writes: 'I cannot journalise; cannot arrange my ideas into order.'[44] Obviously if Fanny's own journal were going to approach the form of a literary model it would be the epistolary novel. Indeed, her record of the first taste of celebrity in 1778 is in many ways a 'History of a Young Lady's Entrance into the World', as *Evelina* is sub-titled. But as she increasingly concentrates on the world rather than the young lady's entrance, so she disperses the focus of interest in the self-as-protagonist that can give the book of the self concentration and unity.

Starting a new journal of his own (only fragments of which have been published) the essayist and critic John Addington Symonds remarks, 'Yet I think there needs unity of subject to keep up the interest of a journal.'[45] Elsewhere he notes, 'Mrs. Clive might have made a most powerful novel out of Haydon's Diaries.'[46] The estimate of the diary form that prompts these two observations provides a useful vantage point from which to view the diary of Elizabeth Barrett as a contrast to that of Fanny Burney. Though written apparently with little or no consciousness of being 'an author', Elizabeth Barrett's diary dis-

Sylas Neville aged twenty-nine
Engraving after the portrait by Edward Miles,
mentioned in the diary

William Windham
Portrait of 1788 by Sir Joshua Reynolds

Lord Byron
Portrait of 1813 by R. Westall

plays in considerable measure the quality of a novel, which it derives from the predominance of a unifying pre-occupation. Kept up with great fidelity, sometimes two or three times a day, it runs from June 1831 to April 1832. Throughout this time Elizabeth (aged 25) is in love with the classical scholar and religious controversialist Hugh Stuart Boyd, a man twice her age, married with a grown-up daughter, and blind. Boyd is a near neighbour of the Barretts at their Herefordshire home, Hope End, and Elizabeth visits him every few days to read Greek with him and give him some intellectual companionship. While she never describes her feeling for him as love, her consciousness is entirely dominated by an intense demand for confirmation of his need and regard for her. Her position is made the more painful by the fact that financial reverses have driven Mr. Barrett to advertise the Hope End estate for sale, so that unless Boyd decides to follow the Barretts when they move, the days of the relationship are numbered.

The situation colours the whole diary. While Elizabeth writes with spirit and intelligence of the people and events that fill her quiet days, her book is essentially the place where she scrutinizes every meeting with Boyd and every clue as to the sale of the house for auguries of hope or despair. It is not a deliberate essay in serial autobiography; she is too involved emotionally in her situation to be interested in its 'literary' possibilities, the way other diarists are. Nonetheless what emerges has in many ways the quality of an integrated work. If it were a piece of fiction one would commend the portrait of a remark-ably developed sensibility prompted into complex self-encounter by a situation artfully contrived for that purpose. (This same consideration—what sort of an achievement would it be if it were an imaginative creation?—provides an illuminating perspective from which to assess any diary's character as a book of the self. How successfully and within what conventions has life imitated art?)

Introduced earlier (p. 43) as complementary to the idea of the 'book of the self', the term 'imprint' refers to the horizontal dimension of the diary. To consider a diarist in terms of his imprint is to ask: regard-less of whether he is deliberately or unwittingly composing a book that will contain his life, how much of him, how wide a range, will we find if we cut a cross-section? The word was chosen in order to convey the dual power of a diary-passage to carry the writer's delib-erate self-expression together with unintended and unconscious as-pects of his personality. Unlike the concept that relates diaries to one another as books it is equally applicable to brief, sporadic, or fragmentary diaries as to the longest and most regular. The imprint is the mark on the page left by a person living. At one extreme it may be no more than a succession of bald notations—'headache, J. called p.m.'—the minimal register of a human existence. With increasing length, density, variety, linguistic expressiveness, personal individuality, the imprint gains in value to the point where, in the diarists one wishes to call great, the experience of being a person, living a life is really vitally conveyed.

Barbellion has an image for the operation of the diary which might be developed into an illustration of the 'imprint' idea. In common with other diarists he notices how the diary resembles an accumulation of data, recorded at regular intervals, from which a picture may be built up of the behaviour of some natural or scientific phenomenon:

> In this Journal, my pen is a delicate needle point, tracing out a graph of tem-
> perament so as to show its daily fluctuations: grave and gay, up and down,
> lamentation and revelry, self-love and self-disgust. You get here all my thoughts
> and opinions, always irresponsible and often contradictory or mutually ex-
> clusive, all my moods and vapours, all the varying reactions to environment of
> this jelly which is I.[47]

With modern technology to draw upon Barbellion might have found the electro-encephalogram a more versatile image for his purposes. The electro-encephalogram, as everyone no doubt knows, records the activity of the brain, in the form of electronic signals picked up by receptors planted in the head of the subject. The signals are passed to a set of pens which trace out on paper profiles of the subject's 'brain waves'. Having one's mental life recorded in this way one might describe, in a paraphrase of Anaïs Nin, as 'living in terms of immediate linearity'. The value of such an imprint varies according to the number and placing of the receptors and the sensitivity of the whole instrument. Similarly, considering diary-writing as a medium through which being-alive is registered on paper, one may think of diaries as instruments whose conventions constitute a structure to record from the subject an imprint more or less intricate, variegated, and comprehensive.

At the risk of beating this unlovely image to death, one may go on to imagine some of the diarists as actively interested in adjusting the sensitivity of the instrument, eager to improve the quality of the imprint. Barbellion, for example, notes that:

The most intimate and extensive journal can only give each day a relatively small sifting of the almost infinite number of things that flow thro' the consciousness. However vigilant and artful a diarist may be, plenty of things escape him and in any event re-collection is not re-creation . . .[48]

Being vigilant and artful becomes his full-time occupation. Others seem relatively indifferent, content to let the imprint come out as it will. They establish their writing habits carelessly, placing their receptors as it were at random. Thus Byron affects a casual indifference to the business, and implies that indifference will be the source of its only merit:

This journal is a relief. When I am tired—as I generally am—out comes this, and down goes everything. But I can't read it over; and God knows what contradictions it may contain. If I am sincere with myself (but I fear one lies more to one's self than to any one else), every page should confute, refute, and utterly abjure its predecessor.[49]

The imprint that results from such an approach may be barren, superficial, and repetitive or, as in Byron's case, vital and abundant, almost by chance. And, finally, as the years pass, the tuning of the instrument may alter and the imprint change in character and quality.

To return from this mechanistic metaphor to a human dimension, here is Boswell expressing an enthusiast's despair in terms very similar to Barbellion's remark quoted above:

I find it is impossible to put upon paper an exact journal of the life of man. External circumstances may be marked. But the variations within, the workings of reason and passion, and, what perhaps influence happiness most, the colourings of fancy, are too fleeting to be recorded. In short, so it is that I defy any man to write down anything like a perfect account of what he has been conscious during one day of his life, if in any degree of spirits.[50]

Ironically, the kind of imprint of himself living that fails to satisfy Boswell is very much more vital and extensive than what most lesser diarists are apparently quite content with. He is actively concerned to render 'the life of man' as a *gestalt*, a rich composite of perceptions of the external world and the play of 'the variations within'. The extent to which any diarist's imprint can combine these elements is an important measure of its achievement. A diary consisting of nothing but cogitation or self-analysis presents as distorted an imprint as one which only describes things seen and done. Thus, for example, the journal fragments published in the *Remains* of Richard Hurrell Froude, Newman's ardent friend in the early days of the Oxford Movement, contain only the imprint of his tortuous moral self-examination, and very little hint of his life in the round. Arnold Bennett, on the other hand, explicitly indicates whole areas of his being-alive which are excluded from his imprint when he says: 'It is a good thing I never write down here my moods and things.'[51]

Not only are the proportions in which the elements are combined worth considering, but also the manner in which they are organized. Two quite distinguishable forms are immediately apparent. One is the ordered narrative of the day's events—the traditional diary format—serving as a frame to which the diarist can attach as much as he is inclined in the way of reflection, the expression of feeling, the re-creation of mood, and so forth. Two kinds of facts compose the frame—external facts (what happened 'out there') and facts of inner experience. The narration of these facts is the occasion for expressing whatever judgements or sentiments they may give rise to or that may be prompted by the writer's situation generally. These elements are integrated by the style and rhetorical tone into a composite presentation of the self, partly conscious of the effect it is creating, partly unconscious. The result is a day-in-the-life. Immense variety is possible within this format, so great that systematic illustration would be absurd. The relative importance of outer and inner experience, the relation of one to the other, the character and extent of the 'authorial comment', these vary enormously from diary to diary. Within a single diary, however, the configuration of the imprint tends to remain fairly constant, or to change only gradually over an extended period, so that it is possible to identify the characteristics of a 'typical' entry.

The following entries, from Dorothy Wordsworth and Elizabeth Barrett respectively, have been selected to give a token illustration of how the composition of the imprint renders the texture of experience. Each entry is 'typical' of the diary whence it comes, to the extent that the events of an average day have prompted a characteristic *gestalt* of objectivity and subjectivity. (Elizabeth Barrett's entry is perhaps rather shorter than her average.) Allowing for the fact—which is of course a substantial one—that the diarists are different personalities in quite dissimilar situations, it is possible, I think, to compare the two versions of a 'day in the life' in terms of the ingredients which are drawn upon and the ingredients which are ignored, and the recipe that combines them into a narrative.

Friday 7th May. William had slept uncommonly well so, feeling himself strong, he fell to work at the Leech gatherer. He wrote hard at it till dinner time, then he gave over tired to death—he had finished the poem. I was making Derwent's frocks. After dinner we sate in the orchard. It was a thick hazy dull air. The Thrush sang almost continually—the little birds were more than usually busy with their voices. The sparrows are now full fledged. The nest is so full that they lie upon one another, they sit quietly in their nest with closed mouths. I walked to Rydale after tea which we drank by the kitchen Fire. The Evening very dull—a terrible kind of threatening brightness at sunset above Easedale. The Sloe thorn beautiful in the hedges, and in the wild spots higher up among the hawthorns. No letters. William met me. He had been digging in my absence and cleaning the well. We walked up beyond Lewthwaites—a very dull sky, coolish crescent moon now and then. I had a letter brought me from Mrs Clarkson. While we were walking in the orchard I observed the sorrel leaves opening at about 9 o'clock. William went to bed tired with thinking about a poem.[52]

Tuesday. July 5 [1831]

I was up a little after seven this morning. So were the clouds; and to make them more decisive, the rain is *down*; & there seems no chance of my driving out with Mrs. Martin. Surely a letter, a decisive letter will come today! or else surely Papa will come!—If *it* does—or if *he* does—what will be the consequence? Nothing good, I fear, humanly speaking: but everything good, I know, by my knowledge of the providence of God. I have prayed for good—I have asked for fish, & shall receive no serpent.

The rain went off; & Mrs. Martin arrived before the letters. So I was forced to go without them. As she had heard of my visit to Ruby Cottage yesterday, she did not propose my going there; & we went *past the house* to Grt Malvern. I never thought it possible that I cd. be made to do such a thing. But as we returned, I cd. refrain no longer, & begged to be allowed to go & see Mr. Boyd for two minutes. Allowed. She was 'just thinking of proposing it'. As we drove up to the door, there was Mr. Boyd walking! I walked into the house, & he after me; & we talked for not one minute. I ran up to Mrs. Boyd who was dressing. Talked not one minute. Then went into Mr. Boyd's sitting room, & talked to him there, not one minute. Then exit. Cool—cool—cool. Warm—warm—warm!!—As I came away without hearing of the letters, & as my writing about them, by this day's post, is out of the question,—Mrs. Boyd agreed not to come here until Thursday. I am glad of it. We drove home. Mrs. Martin has agreable conversation, & is a feeling excellent person; but she has not vivida vis enough about her, to please me altogether. She left me at our nearest gate,—& I walked to the house as quickly as my trembling feet & heart would let me. Henrietta met me in front of the house. 'Any letters.' 'Yes! but no good!! He says he has waited for some good, but has none to tell us.' I got into the drawing room — & got the letter. Yes! there is no good, but it is written in good spirits. Thank God for that!—I could scarcely read it, I trembled so much.[53]

Upon comparing the two entries it is immediately apparent that Dorothy Wordsworth's being-alive is rendered as a 'wise passiveness', a responsiveness to her environment and to William, rather than as activity. Her day is composed for her by the condition of the earth and sky and by William's well-being to which she wholly subordinates her own concerns. Her own agency is minimized: 'I was making Derwent's frocks.' She draws no attention to herself as a centre of thoughts or feelings, but rather directs it towards those objects to which she feelingly responds. Nor does she advance the 'plot' of her own story, even where an obvious occasion arises. The second entry makes clear by comparison the narrative possibilities in the receipt of a letter which she refrains from exploiting. Narrative tempo would be alien to the character of Dorothy Wordsworth's imprint; a day in her life is not a drama in several scenes, but a *tableau vivant*. Elizabeth Barrett's day, by contrast, is made out of suspenses, variations upon a state of agitation. The facts of the day as she tells them are almost exclusively events which unsettled her emotions. 'Cool . . . warm'—her imprint registers the fluctuations of a fever. Compared with the first passage, hers is far more self-centred, that is to say, centred on herself. She records no interest in things in themselves. Both diarists, in different ways, achieve literary effectiveness without seeming to strive for it. Dorothy Wordsworth chooses adjectives discriminatingly ('a threatening brightness'), while Elizabeth Barrett injects tension and emphasis into her narrative to recreate the excitation of her feelings. Both entries embody rich imprints of the personalities of their authors. In these brief distillations of their days they render themselves immediately as distinct and rounded individuals. At the same time they make no pretence of offering comprehensive accounts of what passed within their ken. Of all the things that could be told they tell very few. The imprint a person leaves in a diary, like a fingerprint on the page, is a unique and intricate miniature.

The other, less common form of diary imprint ignores the structure composed by the events of the day, and consists instead of what might be called a soliloquy, an extempore effusion on anything that comes to mind. In this case the 'essential self' that the diarist registers in his book is apprehended not as individual history—what have I been doing? What has been taking place in my landscape?—but as personal orientation—who am I at the moment? what feelings, ideas, imaginings am I composed of? Instead of the linear development of a story, the imprint displays the more miscellaneous character of a scrap-book of the self, a receptacle for any movement of thought or feeling that wants to see itself in writing. Like the daily narrative, this kind of imprint can range from the extremely informal rambling-to-himself of William Jones to the highly conscious assembling of miniature essays and episodes out of which Barbellion composes a sort of cubist self-portrait. Or, in another set of terms, the type encompasses both the aimless and trivial harvesting of ancedotes and observations by the Reverend John Thomlinson and the nimbly ironic soliloquizing of Alice James.

This form of imprint is very hard to illustrate since its effect is cumulative and does not appear until a sufficient number of entries begin to reveal the patterns of sensibility, observation, and intelligence that distinguish one from another. The daily narrative form usually exhibits itself in microcosm in each entry, whereas the 'soliloquy' type of diary grows into its character like a mosaic in which each individual element is at one and the same time self-contained and meaningless. An entry may be cited as typical of its author only in the sense that it is one of the many kinds of entry he makes, not that it exemplifies in a representative way the characteristics of all of them. In some instances one can, it is true, identify a recurring tone and attitude, as with Alice James who is repeatedly prompted to write by the wry exasperation that the human spectacle rouses in her. Here are two unrelated samples:

December 11 [1889]
How sick one gets of being 'good', how much I should respect myself if I could burst out and make everyone wretched for 24 hours; embody selfishness, as they say ———— ———— does. If it were only voluntary and one made a conscious choice, it might enrich the soul a bit, but when it has become simply automatic thro' a sense of the expedient—of the grotesque futility of the perverse—it's degrading! And then the dolts praise one for being 'amiable!' just as if one didn't avoid ruffling one's feathers as one avoids plum-pudding or any other indigestible compound![54]

November 24 [1890]
The ways of Providence *is* peculiar. The substance-full Lady Rosebery dies and a rag-tag like me is left fluttering in the breeze! It must be a strangely muddled moment when it begins to dawn upon the Personage that they are not all there. I trust that matters are conducted humanely, and the poor soul let down easily. Imagine having to begin to learn there that you are simply an atom and not in your essence a future Prime-Ministress of the Great Little Kingdom.[55]

Out of a succession of such entries, over nearly three years, her voice becomes increasingly clear and distinct until, when she dies in 1892, her book can survive as primary evidence that an energetic conscious-ness calling itself Alice James persistently strove against the debilitations of several fatal illnesses.

One could argue that what we are dealing with here is only a special type of the daily narrative format in which the balance of events narrated and thoughts occasioned thereby has tilted right over to the latter component. (After all, virtually nothing 'happened' in Alice James's narrow orbit from one month's end to the next.) This notion would be borne out by the fact that the dividing line between the two formats is not at all precise. A diarist like Byron mingles his discourses upon several subjects with a haphazard account of how he spent the preceding day; while even the most resolutely non-linear diarist draws heavily on immediate occurrences for material out of which to compose his entries. But there is an important structural difference to be observed. The daily narrative conforms more or less faithfully to a standard of completeness and regularity projected on to the external world. In other words, once a diarist has established the pattern of his record, then each day in his life contains the shape of an entry, whether or not he takes the trouble to write it out. It is the recurrence in miniature of the diary's projection into the future of its own completion as a book, mentioned earlier in this chapter. The non-linear imprint, on the other hand, sets no such standards by which it can be measured or judged. It is not governed by the self-imposed requirement to account for the expen-diture of time. Rather it is inspired by the condition of having some-thing to say—a something that will expose some facet of the writer's self-at-the-moment.

It would appear that since the beginning of the nineteenth century the non-linear book of the self has tended increasingly to prevail over the more traditional format. One reason for this trend may be a Romantic preference for the inspired utterance over the regular task. Thus Haydon, while he does keep his 'story' going, does so in enthusi-astic fits rather than systematically. He and other diarists of the period tend to find a self-indulgent expansiveness more congenial than a regular record. Then, in the twentieth century, as was suggested ear-lier, unstructured, non-linear entries become the necessary concomit-ant of a sophisticated conception of ongoing autobiography. A diary nowadays that maintained the format of Pepys or Ryder or Kilvert would confine the author to an impoverished level of self-presentation.

It has been the purpose of the foregoing chapter to develop some critical approaches to the 'diary as literature' out of attitudes expressed and implied by diarists themselves. I have argued that, contrary to commonly held ideas on the subject, diarists do think of themselves as engaged in the composition of a book—a book with special conventions and disciplines to which they more or less consistently, more or or less consciously adhere. The term 'book of the self' has been employed to denote the shadowy conception of a formal whole that has impressed itself in a variety of ways upon the writers' minds, while the complementary idea of the 'imprint' has suggested a view of the individual entry which facilitates comparison among widely different kinds of writing. The examples given so far can do no more than lend some preliminary substance to the otherwise abstract terms. The whole of the study that follows must serve as the application of these conceptual notions to particular diarists, in an endeavour to 'say what English diary-writing has been like', in its prevailing characteristics and trends, as a literature of day-to-day self-documentation.

4

✛✛

Motive and Manner

ROM time to time almost everyone who writes a diary stops to
ask himself why he does so. What purpose is the activity intended
to serve? What need does it fulfil? What satisfaction or compulsion
is it that keeps a person constant to this extraordinary practice? For
extraordinary it is in many ways. Most people tell over to themselves
the day's events, ponder about things, brood on their own anxieties
and shortcomings, indulge in reverie—most people, in other words,
are conscious of their existence in relatively complex ways. Beyond this,
many people probably have fairly habitual patterns of introspection
and recollection through which their customary self-perceptions are
developed. To go further, some people may well engage in articulate
interior monologue upon recurring occasions and themes. But only a
very few actually go to the length of systematically and regularly
digesting some portion of their experience into written prose. What
part in the total economy of the psyche is played by such a high
degree of self-articulation and formal self-encounter? For surely to
extract from one's living every day its significant shape in the form
of a diary-entry is to generate an unusually definite image of oneself
out of the flux of impressions that compose the consciousness. What is
likely to be the reciprocal effect of this process upon the life of the
writer? For some diarists the habit is a deliberate aid to coherent self-
integration; others recognize the danger of insensibly trapping themselves in the lineaments of their own self-portraits. In the two quotations
that follow, it can be seen that Boswell anticipates the insight of a
diarist as unlike himself as Franz Kafka.

. . . if I keep in constant remembrance the thoughts of my head and the imagina-
tions of my fancy, there will be a sameness produced, and my mind will not
have free scope for alteration.[1]

. . . one should permit a self-perception to be established definitively in writing
only when it can be done with the greatest completeness, with all its incidental
consequences, as well as with entire truthfulness. For if this does not happen—
and in any event I am not capable of it—then what is written down will, in
accordance with its own purpose and with the superior power of the established,
replace what has been felt only vaguely in such a way that the real feeling will
disappear while the worthlessness of what has been noted down will be recognized too late.[2]

The diary is seldom an inert element in the life of its writer. To some
degree—whether to their satisfaction or chagrin, or quite unwittingly—
most diarists become what they behold in the mirrors of their own
polishing.

The argument (in Chapter 3) that diarists are affected by the idea of
distilling from their lives an autonomous, finished book does not
answer the question, 'Why do people write diaries?' It says only that
a significant influence upon the form and manner of the diary is a
responsiveness to literary considerations. It tells us nothing about the
character that each book of the self takes from the motives and needs
that prompt the individual writer in the first place. Different kinds of
diaries flow from different impulses to write. I propose in this chapter to
explore the answers that diaries themselves typically contain to the
questions of why they are written and what part they play in their
authors' personal development. It must be stressed at once, however,
that a comprehensive examination of this topic would be unthinkable.
Attempting to unravel all the clusters of motives that have kept people
faithful to their diaries would be like discussing the reasons that impel
people to marry. (Some of the reasons actually are quite similar.)
Every individual case exhibits a different blend of variables, and all
one can do is suggest the predominant configurations as exemplified
by some of the more remarkable relationships—between two people,
or one person and a book.

Most of the diarists prominent in this study return to these questions
explicitly a number of times, sometimes repeating their own answers
and echoing the answers of others, sometimes coming up with new
accounts of what it is they are doing. The question, 'Why am I writing
this diary?' may, after all, be understood in several ways; thus several
answers may be forthcoming from the same diary which need not

contradict each other. Or the reasons for writing may change as the writer's situation changes. Moreover, beyond what the diarist himself is able to answer, there is much to be discerned about the diary's function in his life from the manner of his writing, his preoccupations and his silences. Sometimes the rationale presented by the writer actually conflicts with what his manner makes clear are significant needs and satisfactions served by the diary habit. In such a case the book of the self may embody a tension between his conscious self-image and the imprint of himself which he imparts to his book.

An obvious place to start, in this reading above and between the lines, is at the diarists' own beginnings. Confronted by the blank first page of the volume intended for a diary, many people feel called upon to make a little speech. It is, after all, a rather formal occasion, one which seems to warrant a few disarming words of self-justification. So it is common to find, in those diaries which have a definite beginning and do not merely emerge, a formal statement of intent included in the opening entry. The beginning of a fresh volume or a new year, or the resumption of the diary after a break, may prompt a similar declaration. The diary that ensues may not necessarily conform to the rationale thus presented, but even so, the rationale can tell something important about the conventional attitudes which the writer feels constrained to acknowledge, or perhaps believes himself to be following. These public apologia for self-preoccupation tell only half the story, but a half whose recurring themes are worth examining.

Several kinds of categories can be perceived among the formal rationales for diary-writing, depending upon the sort of distinctions one wishes to emphasize. A primary division, to which all the others can be reduced, distinguishes profit and pleasure as basic and complementary sources of justification. They overlap of course, but as a rule the 'official' explanation will tend to emphasize either the utility of the diary as a means to an end, or gratification as an end in itself. It was suggested in Chapter 2 that until the later eighteenth century the most positive incentive to keep a diary came from the value-system of the non-conformist bourgeoisie. This incentive, under both its religious and its secular aspect, was expressed unequivocally in terms of self-improvement. What the habit might produce in the way of serial autobiography was of little consequence, except in so far as it might edify a reader. Its vital function lay in its power to intensify the writer's surveillance over the conduct of his life and the condition of his soul. Some typical recommendations of the diary as a religious exercise were quoted earlier. The following passage illustrates the dissenting bourgeois rationale in secular terms. It is the introductory statement set by Dudley Ryder as a preface to his first entry. Written in 1715 it may be considered a classic formulation of the diary's function as an aid to rational self-development.

Mr. Whatley told me the other day of a method he had taken for some time of keeping a diary. And I now intend to begin the same method and mark down every day whatever occurs to me in the day worth observing. I intend particularly to observe my own temper and state of mind as to my fitness and disposition for study or the easiness or satisfaction it finds within itself and the particular cause of that or of the contrary uneasiness that often disturbs my mind. I will also take notice especially of what I read every day. This will be a means of helping my memory in what I read. I intend also to observe my own acts as to their goodness or badness. I think there will be many advantages from this way of setting down whatever occurs to me. I shall be able then to review any parts of my life, have the pleasure of it if it be well spent, if otherwise know how to mend it. It will help me to know myself better and give a better judgement of my own ability and what I am best qualified for. I shall know what best suits my own temper, what is most likely to make me easy and contented and what the contrary. I shall know how the better to spend my time for the future. It will help me to recollect what I have read.[3]

The terms of his rationale are purely pragmatic; he is introducing a mechanism into his life—the Power of Positive Diary-Keeping—and expects to recognize measurable improvements in his condition. It is, as it were, a move to rationalize his personal economy, to increase efficiency, maximize productivity, and eliminate wasteful conflict between competing interests. The incentive 'to know myself better' comes not from a disinterested search for wisdom but from the desire to avoid errors of judgement when faced with career decisions. He seems to be a prudent young man, on the look-out for sound investment opportunities for his time. Here he is once more, representing to himself the virtues of another regimen of self-improvement:

Thursday, March 15. Rose between 6 and 7. Went to the cold bath and agreed with the mistress of it for a whole year, for which I gave her two guineas and entered my name in her book. I intend to go in often. The reason of my design is that I think it will strengthen my body, purge it of ill humours, fence me against cold, prevent convulsions which I have sometimes been afraid of by reason of those sudden startings which I have sometimes. I have heard also it is good against the stone and gravel, which I have been afraid of upon the account of those sharp pains I have had about the belly. I expect also it will cure me those rheumatic pains which I sometimes feel and secure me against the gout, which

I believe I felt something of in my health. It will also cure the laxity of the nerves which is the occasion of what they call the vapours.[4]

From the tone of his preface one would probably judge Ryder to be a relatively confident and complacent individual, whose diary might be expected to convey a good deal of self-satisfaction. In actual fact almost every entry expresses a pervasive anxiety about his personal adequacy—social, intellectual, sexual, spiritual—and a longing to discover the clue to self-mastery. Self-assessment in the light of a personal ideal of individual development is a dominant preoccupation of diaries prior to the end of the eighteenth century, and Chapter 6 of this study will be devoted to an examination of some forms this preoccupation takes. Suffice it to say at this point that anxious self-assessment is the dominant motif of Ryder's entire diary. In narrating each day's encounters he reviews his progress towards that distant goal, the person he would like to be. He notes with alternating optimism and dismay the signs of developing aptitudes and the evidence of recurring defeats. Other people's performances he assesses critically for the lessons they may contain, and discusses with himself the symptoms of his insufficiency and the remedies that might be tried. Things take a distressing turn when he visits Bath in May 1716, and becomes sadly infatuated with the flighty Sally Marshall, only to be scorned for his awkwardness. In pain and confusion he confides to the diary the excruciating ignominy of his situation, and finds in the unburdening some relief.

Sunday, June 3. I went to meeting both parts of the day. My thoughts run upon Mrs. Marshall. I wanted an opportunity to talk to her and discover something of my passion. At last she came into sister's room and I longed for an opportunity to speak to her and sister went out, but her maid was in the closet. However, I could not help taking the opportunity of speaking to her, of begging of her to forgive all the rudeness I have been guilty of in her company, especially that in the garden, but she put it off and said she did not know anything of the matter. I was so confounded that I could scarce speak a word to her and I was fain to sit mute and silent, speaking only a word now and then. I find I have run myself further into the mire, and the more I endeavour to get out the more I get in. I think I never felt so great a pain in my life before; I could almost have been willing to die, my anxiety and trouble was so great. But I find myself something better now I have writ this. I will endeavour to drive her out of my thoughts. To bed at 12.[5]

From his opening statement of intent, quoted above, one would not have expected such a direct and woebegone account of emotional dis-

tress. Clearly the book is functioning on a more intimate level, satisfying a more personal need to communicate than the conventional
opening formula would suggest. In fact from the very outset it would
seem as though the comfort of simply talking about himself, what he
has been doing and thinking, the worries that have assailed him, is
a far more potent stimulus than the rather abstract notion of the 'many
advantages' promised by Mr. Whatley's 'method'.

Another diarist who subscribes to a purposive view of the diary,
but whose practice seems more strictly to reflect his precept, is William
Windham. He especially values the self-disciplinary function of the
diary, its contribution to a more profitable concentration of the self:

... for I have no reason to alter the judgment, given in the outset of the last
volume, that this practice of journal writing leads one insensibly into a habit of
composition, strengthens the powers of recollection, and by showing how
one's time is actually disposed of, suggests the means and excites the desire,
of disposing of it to greater advantage.[6]

Windham, like Ryder, is one of those who feels keenly the gap
between the man he is and the man he aspires to be. He resorts to his
diary in an attempt to shame himself into greater efforts with the bitter
spectacle of time wasted and powers dispersed. The ideal of development he sets for himself (see Chapter 6) is impossibly high, and a note
of exasperated chagrin pervades his sporadic record. Unlike Ryder he
seldom appears to find any satisfaction in writing about himself. The
subject of his book is not what he is and what he has done, but what he
is not, what he has failed to do. The diary reflects and intensifies the
anxiety bred of his compulsion to realize himself completely, and his
compulsive fear of time. There is even a suggestion that the fear of
premature death or debility torments him with the prospect of unful-
filled potential. Yet his book of the self is not as for some other writers
a compensatory outlet for a 'real' life unlived, but part of the harness
in which he seeks to put himself to work. As a consequence his accounts
of people and situations are for the most part perfunctory, compared
with the formal and thorough investigations he conducts into his
utilization of self. Interestingly, in the following passage he attributes
to the journal habit an active, as opposed to a merely reflexive, role in
the mechanism of self-propulsion:

[April 1788]
The period of these omissions certainly confirms a remark, which I have
often before made, that whatever the connection may be, whichever of the

two is cause, or whether both result from some common principles, the
punctual continuance of my Journal, and a diligent prosecution of other
business, always go together, so that I think I may pronounce safely of any
period, in which the one has been neglected, that the other has not been well
maintained. I have accordingly been clearly sensible of a relaxation in many
parts of study and discipline, during the time above stated, in which I find this
blank in my journal. I may likewise, I think, perceive something of a relaxation
of power, to be traced directly to the neglect of my Journal, as a cause.[7]

He proceeds to confront himself with the elapse of nearly three months
with nothing to show for them, and comments: 'I perceive already the
beneficial effects of journal writing, when it brings so strongly into
my mind, the sense of my folly and the necessity of better conduct in
future.'[8]

A larger motive for keeping a regular diary is what might be described as the impulse to deal truthfully with oneself. It remains
fundamentally a moral impulse, but not in the narrow sense of serving
an obligation to engage in self-correction. The diary which is intended
to foster self-improvement will always tend to be limited in scope, un-
responsive to much of what constitutes the writer's living experience,
because its terms of reference are too selective. It is actively opposed
to registering the free play of the self as it is, working rather to align
the personality and the life it leads with a pre-established model. Dealing as truthfully as one can with the actual self, on the other hand,
may have the effect of conferring a kind of security upon the writer.
One cannot easily lose one's bearings when one's course is being carefully
charted in an objective and trustworthy personal history. Each entry
should be as meticulously truthful as one can make it, since the book is
the repository of one's clearest perception of things. If the record
becomes suspect at any point, then the whole enterprise is sabotaged
and a kind of chaos threatens. It may be that when Pepys is obliged to
abandon the diary he feels a sort of panic at having as it were to continue his journey unaccompanied, moving further and further from his
last charted position. How will he find his way back to himself when
weeks, then months and years of living become vague and confused, not
only as to external facts but as to the state of his thoughts and feelings?
Whatever his intentions may have been in starting the diary, it came
to play a vital part in his experiencing of himself, almost like an ad-
dition to his five senses. When he is deprived of it, one of the essential
modes of knowing that he really is Samuel Pepys living his life is taken
away. Without the diary, being alive will never have quite the concrete-

ness of those nine years in the 1660s—not simply because most of it will pass into oblivion, but because it will never again be tasted and digested with the same systematic care.

Probably if Pepys had ever formulated a rationale for keeping a diary it would have been primarily in terms of its usefulness, both as a record and as an activity. As a record it preserves an enormous body of material facts with great particularity and, one presumes, accuracy. For a man like Pepys an incomplete or unreliable record would be worse than useless. There is much that pertains to the business of the Navy Office and amounts to a private set of minutes of the proceedings and transactions of a group of men whose memories could go disconcertingly awry. His domestic life too he documents with habitual thoroughness, recording every detail that might ever need to be recalled. As for the activity, he would probably have rationalized its benefits in terms akin to Ryder's—profitable self-knowledge, an audit of the expenditure of time, an opportunity for moral self-assessment and correction. But beyond these pragmatic explanations of an occupation to which he undoubtedly devoted several hours each week, he would have been able to speak of the profound satisfaction of simply rescuing experience from annihilation. A century later Boswell declares: 'I should live no more than I can record. . . . There is a waste of good if it be not preserved.'[9] But Boswell is a great deal more egocentric than Pepys. What causes him chagrin is the evaporation of that extraordinary, never-to-be-repeated phenomenon, himself. Pepys never thrusts himself forward as a human prodigy whose doings are intrinsically more interesting than those of plainer mortals. He desires to cherish the events of each day, not because they are the theatre for his latest manifestation, but because they are what actually happened and as such deserve to be acknowledged. The painful and humiliating experiences no less than the delightful and gratifying ones have to be recorded in the same faithful detail. Thus, after the storm of trouble in November 1668 over the discovery of his affair with Deb, he spends a quiet Sunday settling the episode into the pages that have been waiting for it.

22. (Lord's day). My wife and I lay long, with mighty content; and so rose, and she spent the whole day making herself clean, after four or five weeks being in continued dirt; and I knocking up nails, and making little settlements in my house, till noon, and then eat a bit of meat in the kitchen, I all alone. And so to the office, to set down my journal, for some days leaving it imperfect, the matter being mighty grievous to me, and my mind, from the nature of it.[10]

(The phrase 'for some days leaving it imperfect' must mean here 'having neglected to bring it up to date', since the entries for the preceding days are unusually long and filled with most mortifying detail.) Quite possibly he never re-read his diary. The point of registering the individual character of every day in a special book is not to browse through it periodically, but simply to know that it is *there*. A day that goes unrecorded might as well have been spent asleep; by extension the same can be said of a whole life.

To most people—nowadays at least—the storing of memories probably seems the most natural reason to keep a diary. The pleasure of discovering how many memories are revived by old letters, souvenirs, and so on, saved by chance, is always an eloquent inducement to guarantee oneself a regular supply of such pleasure. So far as one can judge, however, the pleasures of recollection seem to have gained markedly in popularity towards the end of the eighteenth century and to have been a particular favourite of the nineteenth. Certainly the Romantic ethos was more receptive to the sentimental indulgence of nostalgia than the neo-classical mentality would have been. What the rational mind might judge to be a profitless and somewhat enervating waste of time, the Romantic sensibility cultivates as a source of pleasantly poignant emotions, if not poetic inspiration. Romantic poetry, indeed, helped to turn remembering into a 'poetic' activity, one of whose particular attractions is its accessibility. Unlike some of the more dramatic emotions, the sweet sad pangs of memory are available to almost everyone. Any memories will do, though some are more appropriate than others.

The effect on diary-writing of the taste for recollection comes as a mixed blessing. The wish to record enough of each day's experience to trigger recall at a later date is an easy but not very compelling motive for writing. By itself it lacks the urgency of a psychological need, and may easily succumb to loss of interest or the sense that 'nothing happened today'. Moreover, its purpose can often be served by quite perfunctory notes from which memories may be revived. A diary which takes the trouble to describe scenes in evocative detail, explain personal references and so forth, has passed beyond the domain of strict memoranda into autobiography. On the other hand, when the desire to treasure up memories exists as at least the *conscious* motive for writing, it may discernibly influence the style in which entries are composed. In the preparation of food for nostalgia certain conventions of flavouring are hard to resist. Actually the Brownie box-camera and the family album probably superannuated a good many diaries-for-recollection, a picture, they say, being worth a thousand words.

As a stated rationale for diary-keeping the prospect of future pleasure goes back a long way. Slingsby in 1640, quoting Montaigne, speaks of domestic records as 'a thing pleasant to read when time began to wear out the Remembrance of them'.[11] But it is not until the later eighteenth century that it replaces self-improvement as the main conventional justification for the habit. Naturally, like the self-improvement formula, it serves to cover a multitude of practices, of which the sentimental-nostalgic is only one. Thus Walter Scott, for example, opens his diary with disarming informality, professing to do no more than jot down such items as might be of interest later. (The terms are actually quite reminiscent of Slingsby, with whom, intriguingly enough, Scott may have felt a sympathetic kinship, for in 1806 Constable published an edition of that Royalist gentleman's memoirs—edited by Walter Scott.[12])

November 20, 1825.—I have all my life regretted that I did not keep a regular Journal. I have myself lost recollection of much that was interesting and I have deprived my family and the public of some curious information by not carrying this resolution into effect.

I have bethought me on seeing lately some volumes of Byron's notes that he probably had hit upon the right way of keeping such a memorandum-book by throwing aside all pretence to regularity and order and marking down events just as they occurd to recollection.[13]

In fact the book has something of the character of a Memoir, frankly addressing to a reader a sustained armchair soliloquy. He writes with the fluency and composed bearing of an experienced raconteur, often personal but never intimate, even at the time of his wife's death. Certain kinds of self-display he will have nothing to do with, including sentimentality which he dismisses with the following characteristic formula: 'But I must say to my *Gurnal* as poor Byron did to Moore, "Damn it, Tom, don't be poetical".'[14]

Kilvert addresses no such injunction to himself. Within a distinctively Victorian sense of the term his treasury of days is wrought in an intensely 'poetical' manner. Kilvert's response to experience is primarily emotional; he seldom intellectualizes, has almost no capacity for irony, and when he expresses moral judgements he usually does so impulsively rather than from a settled ethical view of things. His diary entries are the imprints of each day's emotional stimuli. He seldom dis-

cusses his feelings in the abstract, or makes any effort to analyse or
understand his emotional life. But in describing the countryside, a
social gathering, a parish visit and so on, he never fails to render the
encounter in language that will evoke its power to touch his heart.
The flow of feeling is so strong that the following rationale (which
comes late in the book) seems conventional and evasive:

Why do I keep this voluminous journal? I can hardly tell. Partly because life
appears to me such a curious and wonderful thing that it almost seems a pity
that even such a humble and uneventful life as mine should pass altogether away
without some such record as this, and partly too because I think the record may
amuse and interest some who come after me.[15]

A sense of propriety compels him to minimize the seriousness of the
book into which he has poured himself so unreservedly. As though to
disarm criticism he dismisses the activity as some sort of casual hobby,
when clearly it satisfies an urgent psychological need. Mention has
already been made in Chapter 3 of the literary earnestness which the
book reveals. More significantly it registers the sublimation of a passionate nature denied direct expression. The most obvious manifestations of this function of the diary can be seen in his positively erotic
treatment of subjects whose sexual content is conventionally disguised. Nude paintings, atrocities at Cawnpore, and the corporal
punishment of little girls permit him to indulge erotic fantasies with
psychic impunity. But also in a more general way the diary allows him
to release the tumultuous emotion that actual life constrains. Very
often, indeed, his more impassioned entries seem to conclude on a
note of exhaustion, as though a great tension has been able to spend
itself in words.

I had not been long in the house when Hannah's beautiful seven year old child
Carrie gradually stole up to me and nestled close in my arms. Then she laid her
warm temples and soft round cheek lovingly to mine and stole first one arm
then the other round my neck. I stroked back her fair soft curls. Her arms
tightened round my neck and she pressed her face closer and closer to mine,
kissing me again and again. Then came the old, old story, the sweet confession
as old as human hearts, 'I do love you so. Do you love me?' 'Yes,' said the child,
lovingly clinging still closer with fresh caresses and endearments. 'You little
bundle,' said her mother laughing and much amused. 'I wish I could take you
with me.' 'You would soon grow tired of her,' said her mother. 'No,' said the
child with the perfect trust and confidence of love, 'he said he wouldn't.' . . .
Time was of no account. An hour flew like a few seconds. I was in heaven.
The people of the clusters of cottages moved about their gardens before the

houses and came to draw water from the deep well close by the open door. A lodger came in and sat down, but I was lost to everything but love and the embrace and the sweet kisses and caresses of the child.

'God bless you my own love, my precious lamb.'

It seemed as if we could not part we loved each other so.

At last it grew dusk and with one long loving clasp and kiss I reluctantly rose to go. It was hard to leave the child.

When I went away she brought me the best flower she could find in the garden. I am exhausted with emotion.[16]

An emotion which Kilvert, like many another Victorian-Romantic sensibility, especially seeks to relieve and make fruitful in the diary is the ineffable anguish aroused by beauty in nature. Having learned to feel in nature a presence that disturbs him with the joy of elevated thoughts, the nineteenth-century diarist registers its influence in many pages of descriptive effusion. One late-Victorian who passes beyond this to make a more deliberate nature-responsiveness central to his diary's function is George Sturt. Over thirty-five years the motive and manner of Sturt's diary change appreciably, but in its very full early period (1890–2) it is expressly dedicated to 'growing conscious of Being Alive'.[17] As the demands of his business threaten to erode the sensitive awareness which gives rise to literature and philosophic thought, he adopts the diary as a means of intensifying perceptions and pursuing insights that are in danger of evaporation. Speaking of his engagement of a new foreman, and subsequently partner, in the wheelwright's shop, he says:

I have hopes that Goatcher will suit me splendidly, and will shortly save me much of the worry of pressing business, that has these last few months left me but little time and less energy for this diary, amongst other things. I have almost forgotten that 'Realisation of Self', that in the early winter promised so much: and forgetting that, have had few impressions, and scarce any feeling, such as reaches down into one's soul, so that he can feel that he is *alive*.[18]

Sensitivity to the rural environment is more for Sturt than merely a pleasurable indulgence. From a philosophic position for which he is consciously indebted to Thoreau he seeks to integrate in himself the rustic's quasi-instinctual being-in-touch with nature, and the intellectual's search for consciously apprehended truths. Beyond the development of his individual consciousness towards a more vital immediacy of thought and perception lies the possibility of making a valuable contribution to social philosophy. Discussing with himself the diary's multifarious purposes, he notes that, besides the immediate stimulus and satisfaction,

> ... the thing written, however ill, might eventually come to have a real scientific value, if it at all depicted my development from what I am, to what I shall be. For a true account of the formation of any person's character would be a thing of great biological importance. There are so many questions of Education and Culture, whose answers can only be guessed at, for want of reliable observations on the effects of environment.[19]

Among other things Sturt's diary also serves him as a notebook of social observation, devoted chiefly to the traditional values of the rural village, out of which he would construct a kind of 'Red-Tory' system of Folk democracy. For a period of several years he is engrossed by the view of life expressed by Grover, his gardener, in whom he sees an unadulterated folk mentality. Grover (or 'Bettesworth' as Sturt calls him in a series of books[20]) comes to serve as the focal point of Sturt's perceptions, a mask through which he tries to look on the world with a simpler consciousness than his own.

> 5 May [1898]. It rained this morning, quietly, luxuriously, with a continuous soothing shattering of warm drops. In the doorway of our little shed I stood listening: listening to the gentle murmur on the roof, on the long fresh grass before me, and on the young fresh leaves of the plum-tree and of the blossoming apple that stand over the grass, making the light greener by half concealing the sky ...
> Framed by all this, Grover stooped over his pail, careless of getting wet. His old earth-brown clothes belonged to the moistened busy little nook of orchard he was working in: so too did his occasional quiet chatter go well with the chatter of the warm rain.
> And so did the drift of what he said seem part of quiet rural country; of the sane English Folk who have been refreshed by mornings such as this.[21]

A similar use of the diary to document and develop a quasi-sociological interest of this kind may be seen in Arthur Munby's records of his systematic study of working-class women, from costermongers to colliery hands. In both cases the observations are elaborated by the diarists into a system of social relations they would like to see realized.

It is sometimes suggested that the essential impulse behind all diary-writing is some form of egotism—an estimation of the First Person as disproportionately Singular. Unless diary-writing itself be taken as a proof of egotism, in which case the suggestion is tautological, the case must be put rather differently. Some diaries are so much more egotistical than others, that to attribute them to a common psychological condition would be absurd. Moreover there is an important difference between a serious and conscious engagement in one's experience, and an interest in oneself as an engrossing phenomenon. In none of the writers so far considered in this chapter is the gratification of projecting individual personality a predominant motive. One for whom it does operate as a major and avowed incentive is, of course, James Boswell. More frequently than most diarists, Boswell discusses with himself his purposes in keeping so energetic a journal. The process fascinates him and he displays considerable insight into the workings of such a high degree of self-involvement. Two themes run through his formulations on the subject. One is the conventional rationale in terms of self-knowledge and self-improvement, the other a sheer and unabashed celebration of his own personality. In either mode the book is dedicated to an unremitting attentiveness to the manifestations of Self. Each entry is written as though in response to the question, *How was I today?*—which may mean among other things, How did I feel? What kind of performance did I give? and Was I up to my usual standard? It is a book of the self in the fullest sense, the book of Boswell, intended for readers who love a parade.

The following passage is Boswell's introduction to the *London Journal*, begun at what he regards as an epoch in his career, his departure from Scotland in November 1762. As a detailed statement of the lines along which he intends to proceed, it must be quoted in full.

The ancient philosopher certainly gave a wise counsel when he said, 'Know thyself.' For surely this knowledge is of all the most important. I might enlarge upon this. But grave and serious declamation is not what I intend at present. A man cannot know himself better than by attending to the feelings of his heart and to his external actions, from which he may with tolerable certainty judge 'what manner of person he is.' I have therefore determined to keep a daily journal in which I shall set down my various sentiments and my various conduct, which will be not only useful but very agreeable. It will give me a habit of application and improve me in expression; and knowing that I am to record my transactions will make me more careful to do well. Or if I should go wrong, it will assist me in resolutions of doing better. I shall here put down my thoughts on different subjects at different times, the whims that may seize me and the sallies of my luxuriant imagination. I shall mark the ancedotes and the stories that I hear, the instructive or amusing conversations that I am present at, and the various adventures that I may have.

I was observing to my friend Erskine that a plan of this kind was dangerous, as a man might in the openness of his heart say many things and discover many facts that might do him great harm if the journal should fall into the hands of my enemies. Against which there is no perfect security. 'Indeed,' said he, 'I hope there is no danger at all; for I fancy you will not set down your robberies on the highway, or the murders that you commit. As to other things there can be no harm.' I laughed heartily at my friend's observation, which was so far true. I shall be upon my guard to mention nothing that can do harm. Truth shall ever be observed, and these things (if there should be any such) that require the gloss of falsehood shall be passed by in silence. At the same time I may relate things under borrowed names with safety that would do much mischief if particularly known.

In this way I shall preserve many things that would otherwise be lost in oblivion. I shall find daily employment for myself, which will save me from indolence and help to keep off the spleen, and I shall lay up a store of entertainment for my after life. Very often we have more pleasure in reflecting on agreeable scenes that we have been in than we had from the scenes themselves. I shall regularly record the business or rather the pleasure of every day. I shall not study much correctness, lest the labour of it should make me lay it aside altogether. I hope it will be of use to my worthy friend Johnston,* and that while he laments my personal absence, this journal may in some measure supply that defect and make him happy.[22]

Several points about this declaration might be noted. First of all it is a highly mannered production, an urbane essay in a distinctly 'public' tone. Boswell makes no bones about the fact that he writes to be read. The journal, after all, is not merely a record of his continuous performances in the role of James Boswell, but a major performance in its own right; just as a self-portrait reveals not only the artist's interpretation of his appearance, but also his genius as a painter. Moreover, unlike Haydon who promises himself an awestruck public among generations yet unborn, Boswell likes to have his latest flights of self-delineation appreciated while they are fresh. As for the terms of the rationale, they combine the conventional expectations of salutary effects on conduct with the prospect of beholding himself very gratifyingly displayed in his own showcase. There is also a curiously cavalier attitude to the matter of truth, with the suggestion that anything too discreditable will be omitted without comment. Withal Boswell hopes that the serialization of his London adventures will prove a consolation to Johnston and an enduring pleasure for himself.

One phrase in his introduction contains a clue to the role actually

---

* This does not refer to the great Doctor whom Boswell had not yet met, but to an Edinburgh friend, John Johnston of Grange.

played by the journal, at least in its earlier years: '. . . and knowing
that I am to record my transactions will make me more careful to do
well.' This may sound like the old idea that to record one's faults is
the first step to correcting them, and Boswell may have meant no more
when he wrote it. But, as Pottle shows in his introduction,[23] it is clear
from the evidence of the daily memoranda that the journal comes to
play in Boswell's life a role something like that of Dorian Gray's picture, only in reverse. In ways that will be discussed in some detail
later in this study, Boswell is endeavouring to create from his own raw
material the character he would like to attain. A perennial topic of the
journal is the light in which his latest performance or current state of
mind exhibits the emergent hero. The following examples are from
entries dated 10 and 13 May 1763.

At the bottom of the Haymarket I picked up a strong, jolly young damsel,
and taking her under the arm I conducted her to Westminster Bridge, and then
in armour complete did I engage her upon this noble edifice. The whim of
doing it there with the Thames rolling below us amused me much. Yet after
the brutish appetite was sated, I could not but despise myself for being so
closely united with such a low wretch.[24]

I talked really very well. I have not passed so much rational time I don't know
when. The degree of distance due to a stranger restrained me from my effusions
of ludicrous nonsense and intemperate mirth. I was rational and composed, yet
lively and entertaining. I had a good opinion of myself, and I could perceive
my friend Temple much satisfied with me.[25]

But unlike Ryder, for example, who confides his gaucheries and anxieties, as well as his successes, without any embellishment or gloss,
Boswell makes his journal reflect an encouragingly positive version of
his progress. Pretexts for self-congratulation are found whenever
possible, and the inauspicious occasions are rendered breezily as little
upsets that a resilient nature takes in its stride, certainly no cause for
despondency. The evolving portrait in the attic serves as propaganda
for his own consumption, its features registering a steady development
not so readily discernible in his daily appearances.

That the imprint left on many thousands of pages by the activity of
'being Boswell' should be a highly intricate one follows naturally from
the complexity of motive and also the restless energy that went into
the making of it. Many diarists, when they have found the channel
that allows them satisfactory scope, flow on casually for years. Not so
Boswell, who is constantly re-animating the journal, probing himself

with it from new angles. Like an indefatigable reporter assigned to accompany himself through life he continues to invent fresh interview techniques to keep the flow of copy coming. Touring through Europe in the years 1764–6 he marches into an amazing series of encounters—with princes and philosophers, vagabonds and whores—and comes out asking, How was I today? Sometimes the answer is most gratifying, as after his intoxicating successes with Rousseau and Voltaire; at other times there is matter for discomfort or chagrin. One truth abides, however, and becomes the ruling justification for the journal. As he puts it to himself with a simplicity that transcends conceit, 'I have one of the most singular minds ever was formed'.[26] Asking himself what 'use' the journal serves, he cries rhetorically:

Does it not contain a faithful register of my variations of mind? Does it not contain many ingenious observations and pleasing strokes which can afterwards be enlarged? Well, but I may die. True, but I may live; and what a rich treasure for my after days will be this my journal.[27]

Always susceptible to the opinions of others, Boswell seeks approval for his journalizing passion and defends himself against censure. Not surprisingly some natures find the habit strange and distasteful, savouring of perversion. Temple's disapproval was quoted in Chapter 3. Here is Lord Auchinleck in a letter dated 30 May 1763, passing on to his son a view of the subject with which he evidently concurs:

When I thereafter came to the country, I found that what I represented would probably be the consequence of your strange journals actually had happened. Mr. Reid came here, informed us he had seen them, and, having a good memory, repeated things from them. He made these reflections, that he was surprised a lad of sense and come to age should be so childish as to keep a register of his follies and communicate it to others as if proud of them.[28]

Many years later Boswell meets with an attack from Mrs. Boswell, whose trenchancy on the subject he is compelled to acknowledge:

I thought that my son would perhaps read this journal and be grateful to me for my attention about him, for I was twice out speaking to his nurse. My wife, who does not like journalizing, said it was leaving myself embowelled to posterity—a good strong figure. But I think it is rather leaving myself embalmed. It is certainly preserving myself.[29]

One authority whom Boswell has on his side, however, would repulse an army of detractors.

He advised me to keep a journal of my life, fair and undisguised. He said it would be a very good exercise, and would yield me infinite satisfaction when the ideas were faded from my remembrance. I told him that I had done so ever since I left Scotland. He said he was very happy that I pursued so good a plan. And now, O my journal! art thou not highly dignified? Shalt thou not flourish tenfold? No former solicitations or censures could tempt me to lay thee aside; and now is there any argument which can outweigh the sanction of Mr. Samuel Johnson?[30]

This is in 1763. Ten years later Johnson is still urging him, as if urging were needed, to write down 'the state of your own mind'[31] and to write promptly and unselectively while impressions are fresh. In 1775, at a time when he is three weeks behind with his entries, Boswell cites Johnson's precept as though it were the law by which he operates. He confesses that he is 'guilty of the *dilatory notation* which Mr Johnson censures' (Boswell's italics), and goes on, 'I find that I do not enough mark the state of my mind and its changes. I shall try to do better.'[32] It is doubtful whether Johnson, whose recommendations of keeping a journal as an aid to rational self-mastery were also to influence Windham, would have acknowledged the monument to Boswell's egomania as quite what he had in mind. And if he had chanced to read the following admission (made in reference to Mrs. Boswell's advice to hide some confidential letters) he would probably have echoed the concluding judgement: 'But really I have a kind of strange feeling as if I wished nothing to be secret that concerns myself. This is a weakness to be corrected.'[33] Yet it must be emphasized that a growing moral seriousness manifests itself in Boswell's determination to confront all the proliferations of his nature. As the years pass the celebration of his originality gives way to an anxious surveillance of alarming symptoms. From about 1774 onwards, the question How was I today? comes increasingly to have a clinical ring: Was there anything in my conduct or frame of mind to warrant unease, or was I pretty satisfactory? The diary performance in these latter years is played less to the gallery of actual or imagined readers, and more for his own private benefit.

A disadvantage of the format adopted for this study is that distributing the treatment of each major figure under several headings causes them to reappear rather predictably, like horses on a merry-go-round. Thus, on the subject of self-projection as a motive for diary-writing, when Boswell comes Benjamin Haydon is not far behind. Haydon's avowed adoption of the diary as a vehicle for immortalizing his story has already been commented upon. Later in this study the character of his titanic self-dramatization will be examined at length. At this point, however, something needs to be said to distinguish Haydon's impulse to project an image of himself from Boswell's. Obviously their motivations have much in common. Each has a sense of himself as a rare and singular being in whom the workings of human nature appear with exceptional interest. Each prides himself on the bold originality of his self-presentation. But whereas Boswell is sharing with the reader his fascination, exuberant or grave, with the bewildering phenomenon named Boswell, Haydon expects his vision of himself to be received at face value. He is projecting his official identity, an authorized self-portrait in a guise that will unify and transfigure the jarring realities of his existence. As things get worse the story told by the diary resorts to increasingly obvious and bizarre shifts to put them right, until it is operating almost on the level of fantasy. The following is characteristic of the kind of interpretation he salvages from his wreck:

I have never suited my labour to existing tastes. I know what is right & do it. So did the early Christians, & so do all great men. Suffering is the consequence but it must be born. Should I have shaken the nation if I had [not]?[34]

It is the premise of this chapter that the constant process of rendering a version of oneself to the silent audience of the diary plays a significant role in the 'psychic economy' of the diarist, and that tenor and the selective presentation of material reveal that role at least as clearly as the diarist's explicit statements on the subject. Proceeding through a gamut of motivations we have come to the diary's function as compensatory self-projection, illustrated by Haydon (especially as he grows older), and in an interesting way by poor Sylas Neville. To judge from the diary Neville was an unlovable person—envious, censorious, self-pitying, pompous and mean—and his misfortunes, which were many, both flowed from and contributed to the sourness of his nature. But the notion that character is destiny seldom occurs to the unfortunate. To outward appearances Neville was impoverished and insignificant, struggling to maintain the rank of country gentleman (having found London too expensive), disdaining the medical profession to which he had turned in desperation, and ignominiously entangled with his housekeeper, by whom he had several children. It really is not the scenario one would choose in which to project oneself to advantage, and the function of the diary is to provide a compensatory outlet for that valuation of himself which circumstances conspire to thwart.

Two of the most obvious effects of this are the suppression of the more humiliating details of his situation, and the adoption of a tone of pained and condescending superiority. Compared with Pepys's commitment to truthfulness and candour, the entries that follow display a curious evasiveness:

Mon. July 17. [1775] Something very disagreable happened. I wish it may not be attended with any bad consequences. O Lord, strengthen me to put my trust in Thee!

Sun. July 23. I have reason to believe that the above will not be followed by anything.[35]

What peculiar conflict of impulses leads a person to make a record like this? Most likely the 'something very disagreable' was sexual in nature. Neville habitually evades direct reference to his sexual life, to the extent of eliminating almost all mention of 'Russell's' pregnancies, the offspring of which are farmed out. The diary thus acts as a selective and ameliorating memory, mitigating the less palatable aspects of experience. It projects the 'real' Sylas Neville whose nature and qualities, as he himself perceives them, have always been obscured and misrepresented by his outward embarrassments. Thus it contains the expression of sentiments so incongruous, given his situation, as to suggest (to a reader less sympathetic than himself) a seriously impaired sensibility. Here he is speaking of 'Russell's' daughter by an earlier liaison, whom he allowed her to bring to live with them:

Thursd. Nov. 22. Evening. Having corrected R's girl rather more severely (I confess) than I ought to have done, her mother used me most vilely calling me all sorts of bad names. The kitchen was full of people, who, I am afraid, heard all that passed. I have taken much pain to make this little creature love me, but in vain, as her mother never chid her when she behaved ill to me. I wish I was fairly rid of both. How miserable is the situation of a bachelor, exposed to all the bad humours of low life, deprived of those real joys which a virtuous and well-educated wife affords![36]

Far from keeping him in touch with a realistic self-estimate, the function of language here and throughout the diary is to make still more opaque the righteous self-justification through which he perceives his relations with the world. He persistently refers to Russell as 'my housekeeper', and exclaims, after one of her bursts of resentment against him, 'O God, give me a woman of some principle!'[37]

Neville displays an insatiable need for approbation, and reports innumerable instances of golden opinions he has bought or begged.

Returning from a jaunt in the south and west of England in 1768, he tells his diary:

My character & principles (the principles of a true Englishman & zealous friend of liberty) have been approved by all sorts of people at most places where I have been on this tour, except the passengers in the Fly from Tunbridge, high-church enemies to Liberty. But I refuted all they could say.[38]

Commendations from any source are carefully recorded, especially the flattering remarks of his medical professors at Edinburgh. On one occasion he feigns sleep among his friends in order to learn 'that they were pleased with my behaviour'.[39] At the same time, feeding his self-image as a man of rigorous and discerning judgement, he expresses sharp disapprobation of almost everyone and everything. His tottering self-esteem, so little re-inforced by actual life, reaches after crumbs. In registering so carefully the quality of a little scene like the following— with the landlord's daughter in a Newcastle pub—he savours anew the rare gratification of having been able to relate to someone on thoroughly satisfying terms:

She has much good nature & sweetness of temper in a degree of good-sense rarely to be met with even among Ladies of superior birth & I most sincerely believe that she has virtue. As there was a probability of my sailing in the night I took an opportunity to tell her that I had a regard for her & wished her every kind of happiness—that tho' I was not fond of speaking of myself, I thought it right to tell her I was a person of some condition. She answered she was not blind to merit, tho' it had been unattended with superiority of rank. On hearing my name she honoured it by saying it was a mighty pretty one & I did it justice by informing her it was one of the most ancient and honourable in England.[40]

Whereas Boswell might record such an encounter as an interesting episode in which he played a gratifying part, Neville comes across as a self-satisfied prig who would like to convince himself (and the reader) that this would be his natural manner, if only *other* women were more like Miss K. of Newcastle. Returning home to Russell he tells himself 'I find her faithful, the generosity of my nature will not suffer me to be ungrateful.'[41] A few days later this 'person of some condition', uncertain of poor Russell's fidelity, puts a pistol to her head and makes her swear to it on her life![42] It is plain to the reader that the man is slightly off the hinges, but only very occasionally does his air of aggrieved superiority give way, to let the desperation come through:

I think I am not treated with so much respect by some people as I used to be. Whether it is imagination or that they begin to suspect the badness of my situation, I know not. Rode home by moonlight in bitterness of soul—cried almost all the way over my poor horse, which I may perhaps never ride again.[43]

A quite different aspect of the compensatory function performed by a diary is illustrated by the cluster of motives behind Barbellion's writing. The task of the disappointed man's journal is to compensate for the fact that actual intercourse with the world almost wholly thwarts his longing to project himself as the passionate, brilliant, fascinatingly complex—dare he say genius?—that he encounters in his self-communing. Yearning to burn with a hard gem-like flame, he is condemned by a sickly constitution, pusillanimous temperament and lowly station to flicker like a starving gas-lamp. What makes him exceptional among self-compensating diarists is that he is all too aware of his condition and his need. His most constant dwelling-place is in the recesses of his own psyche, observing himself observe, deriving satisfaction from the ingenuity of his introspection, and knowing that he derives such satisfaction. And since the knowledge that a good part of his life is spent in compensatory gratification is a bitter knowledge, he writes of the matter with studied formality:

Of course, to intimate friends (only about three persons in the wide, wide world), I can always give free vent to my feelings, and I do so in privacy with that violence in which a weak character usually finds some compensation for his intolerable self-imposed reserve and restraint in public. I can never marvel enough at the ineradicable turpitude of my existence, at my *double-facedness*, and the remarkable contrast between the face I turn to the outside world and the face my friends know. It's like leading a double existence or artificially constructing a puppet to dangle before the crowd while I fulminate behind the scenes. If only I had the moral courage to play my part in life—to take the stage and be myself, to enjoy the delightful sensation of making my presence felt, instead of this vapourish mumming—then this Journal would be quite unnecessary. For to me self-expression is a necessity of life, and what cannot be expressed one way must be expressed in another. When colossal egotism is driven underground, whether by a steely surface environment or an unworkable temperament or as in my case by both, you get a truly remarkable result, and the victim a truly remarkable pain—the pain one might say of continuously unsuccessful attempts at parturition.[44]

So the journal serves to relieve this pain caused by the pressure of unexpressed self. It becomes a surrogate existence into which he projects all that he values of himself. The following passage, reminiscent of Pepys's last entry, is prompted by the fear of Zeppelin raids, and dated 2 January 1915.

> These precious Journals! Supposing I lost them! I cannot imagine the anguish it would cause me. It would be the death of my real self and as I should take no pleasure in the perpetuation of my flabby, flaccid, anaemic, amiable puppet-self, I should probably commit suicide.[45]

The imprint of his 'real self' is a patchwork of various elements as he alternately rails against his lot, bitterly relates the experience of manifold frustration, 'shows off' in passages of self-consciously clever discourse or description and in reports of his conversational sallies, and tells of the agonies and ecstasies of his marriage in the shadow of death. Introspection is a recurring self-indulgence:

> Every man is an inexhaustible treasury of human personality. He can go on burrowing in it for an eternity if he have the desire— and a taste for introspection. I like to keep myself well within the field of the microscope, and, with as much detachment as I can muster, to watch myself live, to report my observations of what I say, feel, think.[46]

Barbellion's particular taste is for the introspection that searches out motives within motives, the offspring of the psychological novel.

Another dimension of his journal's compensatory role, already mentioned in previous chapters, comes with his determination to publish it. From early youth he has coveted fame, but with the onset of ill-health the prospect of making a name for himself as either a scientist or a *littérateur* fades quickly. By September 1914 he is saying, 'For a long time past my hope has simply been to last long enough to convince others of what I might have done—had I lived.'[47] Cheated by circumstances of the recognition which his talents and his singular nature deserve, he wants to believe that it will not all have been in vain. 'But I am trying to give myself the pleasure of describing myself at this period truthfully, to make a bid at least for some posthumous sympathy.' [48] Increasingly it is his own personal tragedy which must be the grounds for his fame, and the journal becomes the medium by which it will be made known. Not unlike Haydon he solaces himself with the prospect of the respectful commiseration he will one day earn. 'It gives me a kind of false backbone to communicate my secrets: for I am determined that some day some one shall know.'[49] Baring the soul becomes a performance put on for a stranger whose anticipated wonder assuages Barbellion's anguish. But as his condition worsens he is tormented by uncertainties:

Sir Walter Scott
Portrait of 1825 by Sir Thomas Lawrence

Benjamin Haydon
Drawing of 1816 by G. H. Harlow

November 12 [1916]

What a wreck my existence has become and—dragging down others with me.

If only I could rest assured that after I am dead these Journals will be tenderly cared for—as tenderly as this blessed infant! It would be cruel if even after I have paid the last penalty, my efforts and sufferings should continue to remain unknown or disregarded. What I would give to know the effect I shall produce when published! I am tortured by two doubts—whether these MSS. (the labour and hope of many years) will survive accidental loss and whether they are really of any value. I have no faith in either.[50]

It is to settle these doubts that he resorts to the solution of publishing the book himself and staying around, like a ghost at the funeral, to observe its reception.

The following generalization is offered, as it were, experimentally: the need to project an ego-image does not appear to be a leading motive in diaries written by women. This is not to say that the personalities of women are rendered any less vividly or variously in the diary imprint than men's, but that projection of the self as dramatic protagonist is not the mode which the imprint commonly takes. There should be nothing very surprising in this. It is the merest platitude to observe that the position of women in society has tended to preclude the assertion of individual ego. The drive to become Somebody, to establish oneself as *the* Robert Fothergill (for example), and the conception of one's personal history as 'My Development', have been masculine traits. Egotism in men and preoccupation with an effective self-image have been accepted and rewarded; in women they have been discouraged. A woman cannot easily cast herself as protagonist, when society and the controlling personal relationships of her life demand proficiency in exclusively supporting roles. Nor does it follow that she might therefore tend to project a more rather than less assertive ego in the diary, by way of that compensation process just discussed in connection with Neville and Barbellion. For whereas these two diarists are compensating for the deprivation of a role which their conditioning as males has led them to expect, a woman diarist begins with no such expectations. Hence one simply does not find in past centuries women diarists who strut and perform and descant on their own singularity. I shall argue, however, that the diaries of women in the present century who have had a strong self-concept in the role of artist do display the interest in individual development that has been at the centre of male diaries for centuries.

At first sight it might seem that Fanny Burney, the earliest 'major' woman diarist, is immediately an exception to the general rule just propounded. But it was suggested in Chapter 3 that despite the impression she gives of eager vanity, her diary is not propelled by a conception of the emerging self whose story must be told. It is impossible, for instance, to imagine her adopting the terms of Boswell's rationale for his journal. When she does speak of her impulse to write, it is usually in terms of the need to confide her secret thoughts, to 'unburthen myself'[51] to a sympathetic listener. Her early diaries, undertaken at the age of sixteen, begin with the well-known 'Miss No-Body' passage, from which the following is taken: 'To Nobody, then, will I write my Journal! since to Nobody can I be wholly unreserved—to Nobody can I reveal every thought, every wish of my heart, with the most unlimited confidence, the most unremitting sincerity to the end of my life!'[52] These opening flights of whimsy soon give way to the regular social and family narrative, yielding a satisfaction which she describes as 'the pleasure of popping down my thoughts from time to time on paper'.[53] Even during the years of fame when she delightedly chronicles her celebrity it is a passive role—the receiving of attention—that she projects. Her own part, as she describes it, is to be overwhelmed with compliment.

In keeping with the self-effacing manner in which she proceeds, Dorothy Wordsworth introduces her *Grasmere Journal* (begun while William is absent on a trip into Yorkshire with their brother John) with the following consideration: 'I resolved to write a journal of the time till W. and J. return, and I set about keeping my resolve because I will not quarrel with myself, and because I shall give Wm Pleasure by it when he comes home again.'[54] The pleasure that it gives William, and also the help in composition, continue to supply her with motives for writing, but it is possible to speak also of the personal need that the habit of the journal satisfies for her. True to the dictum concerning women diarists, she makes no use of the journal as a mirror for her individual self-image. Rather it seems to give her an outlet for the intensity with which she apprehends experience. The constantly changing beauty of her surroundings bewitches her sometimes almost painfully and only the finding of fit words will deliver her from the spell;

Earth and sky were so lovely that they melted our very hearts. The sky to the north was of a chastened yet rich yellow fading into pale blue and streaked and scattered over with steady islands of purple melting away into shades of pink. It made my heart almost feel like a vision to me.[55]

These are her intensest moments, but the journal is not of course confined to them. In a sense this whole period of her life with William at Grasmere is a privileged moment. They are sharing very intimately the same sensibility, the same attuned responsiveness to nature, to the condition and character of rustic folk, and to the quality of life lived simply. Dorothy's journal is one of the instruments of this sensibility, an intermediary stage between sheer experience and the poetry William is distilling from it.

Elizabeth Barrett's diary is the imprint of an intense emotional life compelled to find in writing the expression and relief denied to it in action. Far indeed from desiring to project herself as a tragic heroine or to indulge in reflections of her personal originality, in her opening entry she explicitly fears the self-display that might be fostered by the habit:

Saturday. June 4th 1831. Hope End.
I wonder if I shall burn this sheet of paper like most others I have begun in the same way. To write a diary, I have thought of very often at far & near distances of time: but how could I write a diary without throwing upon paper my thoughts, all my thoughts—the thoughts of my heart as well as of my head? —& then how could I bear to look on *them* after they were written? Adam made fig leaves necessary for the mind, as well as for the body. And such a mind as I have!—So very exacting & exclusive & eager & head long— &— strong— & so very very often wrong! Well! but I will write: I must write— & the oftener wrong I know myself to be, the less wrong I shall be in one thing—the less *vain* I shall be![56]

Her need is to express openly the turbulent conflicts of feeling which her situation obliges her to repress. In the diary she can speak in her own voice, and talk over her experience in relation to the concerns which constitute its meaning. Equally important, however, is the compulsion to deal truthfully with herself. Unlike Kilvert, for example— in many ways the most feminine of diarists—she cannot abandon herself to luxurious tides of sentimentality, but must struggle against the surrender of her critical intelligence and her moral will. To allow self-deceptions to flourish would be perilous and contemptible. The very intensity of her emotions demands a strenuous effort to see things as in themselves they really are, if she is to keep her balance and her self-respect.

On reading what I have written . . . I am more than half ashamed of it. I have certainly *no reason* for accusing Miss Hurd of being as much liked by Mr. B as I am; & if I had the *reason*, I should still be without the *right*. And as to coldness—Mr. Boyd used not to be cold to me! Had he been so, I should not have thought him so on Tuesday. The fact is—the greatest regard, *far* the greatest, is on my side:—or rather the fact is—my disposition is far too exclusive & exacting. Both those facts are *operative* facts. When will they cease to be so?— Read, as I do every day, seven chapters of Scripture. My heart & mind are not affected by this exercise as they should be—witness what I have written today. I would erase every line of it, could I annihilate the *feelings*, together with the description of them; but, since I cannot, let the description pass! That Friendship should fade away before my eyes, as Fame did in my poetical vision, is too painful! And that the 'skeleton' of Friendship . . . but I am getting wrong again! Oh I never never should have begun this journal!—No one should write journals, who is not wiser, on a hundred points, than I am! & stronger, on a thousand![57]

Another woman diarist, Alice James, expresses a reason for writing which, it could be argued, must be shared by all diarists to some degree. The following is her opening entry:

May 31st, 1889
I think that if I get into the habit of writing a bit about what happens, or rather doesn't happen, I may lose a little of the sense of loneliness and desolation which abides with me. My circumstances allowing of nothing but the ejaculation of one-syllabled reflections, a written monologue by that most interesting being, *myself*, may have its yet to be discovered consolations. I shall at least have it all my own way and it may bring relief as an outlet to that geyser of emotions, sensations, speculations and reflections which ferments perpetually within my poor old carcass for its sins; so here goes, my first Journal![58]

Of Alice James's 'loneliness and desolation', at least at the moment of starting the journal, there can be no doubt. She was existing between wheel-chair and bed in the provincial town of Leamington, with neither her brother Henry nor her companion Katherine Loring within call. But is loneliness a necessary pre-condition for all diary-writing? Certainly there are some diarists who express intense loneliness at times—Barbellion, for instance—and many more for whom writing is a substitute for the kinds of intimate communication with others which their circumstances are not affording them. As examples of this latter type one may cite Elizabeth Barrett, Katherine Mansfield, Fanny Burney (at certain periods), Francis Kilvert, perhaps Walter Scott. But is it legitimate to argue that diary-writing *per se* is proof of an un-

fulfilled need for intimate relationship? In one way the assertion seems
irresistible; whatever is communicated to the diary has failed to find
an outlet elsewhere. According to this line of reasoning, even the most
sociable or most married of diarists are compensating for a thwarted
impulse to relate themselves more totally to other people. I think,
however, that a distinction should be made between loneliness, considered as an actively felt deprivation, and a kind of psychological
solitude which may be cherished as a luxury. The one is painful and
limits one's power to experience oneself. The other is a pre-condition
for an interior life. If every diarist is to be judged an essentially lonely
individual, then so is everyone who thinks. Like egotism, whose claim
to underlie the diary-habit was discussed earlier, loneliness is a condition
which the diary will register and may assuage. In the case of Alice
James, who has known the companionship of her brothers William
and Henry, confinement to the company of no one but a simple-minded
little nurse is a living death. The journal permits her to experience herself intermittently as a lively intelligence instead of a bundle of ill-
health.

In August 1923, as if to mark an epoch in the diary's discovery
of itself as a genre, Ivy Jacquier is reading Lord Ponsonby's newly
published work, *English Diaries*. It is a peculiarly appropriate encounter
since she is at this time reading through the sixteen years of her own
diary and wondering at the image there presented. After the raptures
and despairs of her early life as an artist in Dresden and Paris during
which she sought 'to grow by everything and feel myself evolving',[59]
after the tense attrition of the war, she finds herself, at the age of
thirty-three, married, with a daughter, and settled in Worcestershire.
With a sense that the journeying has ended and that for better or for
worse she has arrived somewhere, she looks back to see where and what
she has been.

Aug 2.
Ponsonby's book brings up the question why one keeps a diary. I think now
and for many years it is that I realize the fluctuations of self. One never is, one
has been or is becoming. Years ago I knew more, had read more, seen
more, and known more emotions than now. It seems to me in 1912 in Paris I
was altogether a richer person. Now I am tamed and disciplined. So much of
vital importance is forgotten. I cannot recapture the past. Yet, as Ponsonby
says, 'We think we know ourselves better than others know us. But the truth
is we only know the inside half.' To recapture the whole atmosphere of a past
day—that has a charm. Today—so uneventual. Shopping, visiting a young

Swede staying at the Deanery, watching for ten minutes a cricket match
(what a game!), lying reading Ponsonby all afternoon while the rain stormed;
then Sally came in.[60]

It comes as no surprise that she is reading Proust avidly at this same
period. Her sense of Time and Changes, of the self as a pattern of
continuities recognizable only in retrospect, takes its colouration from
Proust. Needless to say Proust did not invent or discover the poignancy
of *le temps perdu*, but in expressing it so totally he gave it back to the
European consciousness in a more sharply realized form. What has
always been one of the leading motives for diary-keeping receives a
distinctive new flavour from the Proustian alchemy. For Ivy Jacquier
the original purpose of the diary—to intensify the impact of those
experiences that make for growth as an artist—yields to the subsequent satisfaction of providing a route back into what she has been.
Her meditation quoted above is like a transposition into a subtler, more
evocative key of Boswell's boisterous shout: 'Does it not contain a
faithful register of my variations of mind? . . . what a rich treasure for
my after days will be this my journal.'[61]

With Anaïs Nin the question 'Why does she write the diary?' has
two aspects. Chapter 3 dealt at some length with the aesthetic dimension
of the question—diary *versus* fiction. The other aspect, which constitutes a major theme in her writing for several years, concerns the psychological function of the diary. It is such an integral part of her psychic
life, and has been since she was thirteen years old, that her struggle to
come to terms with its operation amounts to a radical re-assessment of
herself as a person. Between 1932 and 1934 she undergoes psychoanalysis, first with Dr. Réné Allendy, then with Otto Rank. A crisis comes
at the end of 1933 when, at Rank's insistence and with extreme pain,
she gives up the diary. It has been identified as the focal element of a
neurotic condition, and the therapeutic idea is to redirect the energies
that have been absorbed by a compulsive dependency. When after a
break of several months she resumes the habit, it is with a changed
perception of her relation to it.

To appreciate the traumatic nature of her separation from the
diary one has to realize that for a number of years it has been not
simply a regular routine but a consuming addiction. She writes it almost
continuously: '. . . on café tables while waiting for a friend, on the
train, on the bus, in waiting rooms at the station, while my hair is
washed, at the Sorbonne when the lectures get tedious, on journeys, on
trips, almost while people are talking.'[62] It is part of the very texture of

her experience to be always extracting herself from participation and engaging in the weaving of words. Deprived of the habit she suffers definite withdrawal pangs: 'The period without the diary remains an ordeal. Every evening I wanted my diary as one wants opium. I wanted nothing else but the diary, to rest upon, to confide in.'[63] Aware as she is that, in so far as her condition is regarded as maladjusted, the diary is symbolically if not actually the crucial symptom, she makes repeated attempts to understand its source and its place in her economy. Of its origin on the voyage to America with her mother and brothers when she was thirteen, she has this to say:

The diary began as a diary of a journey, to record everything for my father. It was written for him, and I had intended to send it to him. It was really a letter, so he could follow us into a strange land, know about us. It was also to be an island, in which I could take refuge in an alien land, write French, think my thoughts, hold on to my soul, to myself.[64]

Before long she has switched to English—a language which her father could not read—and ceased to consider it as literally a communication to him. Yet she continues, so it seems to her, to project in it an image of herself whose unconscious aim is to win her father's admiration and love. As Rank articulates this motivation to her: 'Revealing yourself to your father, you thought he would grow to know you, love you. You told him everything, but with charm and humor.'[65] At the same time the diary serves her as a protection and a retreat from the abrasions of the external world. It is the domain of subjectivity. Outside herself she encounters a hostile world to which she is compelled to relate through roles which seem to her illusory and inauthentic. The task of the diary is to reverse this subordination, to recompose experience into dreams of her own dreaming, a mythopoeic function. From its cost in psychic energy and its failure to do more than avert the realization of her anxieties, she herself recognizes the diary as a neurotic solution to the problem of living.

A central tenet of Rank's psychoanalytical theory at this period is that neurosis should be seen as a malfunction of the creative imagination. In asking her to give up the diary he wants her to take deliberate possession of her mythopoeic imagination and create artistic fictions instead of fantasies and dreams. In contrast to Allendy he encourages her to become more energetically imaginative rather than less so, to inherit herself as an artist rather than to devolve into a 'normal' person.

This means writing more strenuously and purposefully than before. Of the period without the diary she says in retrospect:

I went to my typewriter and I worked on *House of Incest* and *Winter of Artifice*. A deep struggle. A month later I began the portrait of Rank in a diary volume, and Rank did not feel it was the diary I had resuscitated but a notebook, perhaps.

The difference is subtle and difficult to seize. But I sense it. The difference may be that I poured everything into the diary. It channeled away from invention and creation and fiction. Rank also wanted me to be free of it, to write when I felt like it, but not compulsively. 'Get out in the world!' Rank said. 'Leave your house at Louveciennes! That is isolation, too. Leave the diary; that is withdrawing from the world.'[66]

The novel, *Winter of Artifice*, that she refers to tells the story (also told in part in the diary) of her prolonged reunion with her father during 1933. The encounter is a crucial one in her development, for it enables her to come to terms with and pass beyond the psychological sub-jection to his image which has confined her for many years. It is symbolically fitting that the novel she works on during her liberation from the diary-compulsion should have as its subject her liberation from its source. When she resumes the diary she is able to affirm it as a creative activity and to encounter the problems arising from it in aes-thetic rather than personal terms. As she says later, 'The diary was once a disease. I do not take it up for the same reason now . . . Now it is to write not for solace but for the pleasure of describing others, out of abundance.'[67]

It would be absurd to pretend that the preceding discussions could exhaust the subject of motive in diary-writing and its effect upon the character of the imprint. The aim has been to demonstrate the rele-vance of the question among critical approaches to the genre. No two diarists are prompted by identical impulses; at the same time no diarist writes for reasons unique to himself. The tendency of this chapter has naturally been to isolate the distinct motives that each diary seems to exhibit in particular. Before leaving the topic, therefore, it should be emphasized that the operation of a dominant impulse to write does not exclude other motives common to many or all of them.

5

++

Style, Tone, and Self-Projection

PEPYS, KAY, JONES, SCOTT, BYRON, JAMES, MANSFIELD

WHETHER or not a diary contains explicit discussions of the writer's personality—his qualities, shortcomings, and contradictions—it inevitably establishes an autobiographical persona or self-presentation more or less complex, more or less controlled. Any piece of writing, as it adopts out of a multitude of tones and stylistic conventions its own particular formula, defines a relationship with the putative reader. A diary is especially interesting in this regard since the reader to whom it is addressed is seldom a precisely identified individual. Some diaries, of course, as we have seen, do have actual recipients. In such cases the communication may be little different from that of a letter, the style of self-presentation being governed by an already existing relationship. Then, on the other hand, there are diaries like Scott's (to be considered shortly) for which 'the public' is the intended reader, 'the public' being an entity with which Scott has had prior relations. In general, however, it might be said that a diary is addressed not to a specific figure but to a certain kind of responsiveness. Diarists themselves usually recognize the anomalous nature of this communication and comment on it rather self-consciously. Here is William Jones, writing from his country parsonage in 1800:

... yet had I nothing to do, but to submit, & that peacably too, I assure you.

I have just observed that I ended the last sentence with 'I assure you.' I suppose I may have frequently used the same form of expression, as if appealing to some listening friend, some person at least attentive to my lamentations & woes.[1]

What this simple little reflection epitomizes is the way in which the diary, unlike most forms of communication, creates its own reader as a projection of the impulse to write. Whether identified as a listening friend, future generations, or God the Father (Jones goes on to add, 'To Heaven I appeal'), the reader is literally a figment of the writer's mind, a completion of the circuit.

To refine one's sense of the particular character of a diary-persona it is thus useful to ask: what kind of reader is presupposed here? what sort of response is the presentation calculated to elicit? to what extent does the diary-persona try to impose a controlled impression of himself, instead of simply allowing an impression to be formed? to what extent is the diary-monologue a performance in a role? At the same time another set of questions arises as to the effects upon individual self-projection of prevailing conventions of style. The common analogy between language and dress suggests itself here, a writer's style being comparable to a costume which expresses his self-image and conditions the manner in which people will relate to him. A costume may be consciously selected as suitable to a role, or it may be thrown together without deliberate consideration—either way it expresses the wearer. Likewise a costume may be conventional or idiosyncratic, but must in either case partake of a limited range of current alternatives. So, in any given diary, what kind of transaction takes place between personal individuality and received structures of expression? Such questions cannot be answered categorically. Their function is to alert us to the varieties of self-projection to be discerned in diaries, and to add fresh terms to the attempt to perceive the formal characteristics of the genre.

To illustrate these general considerations I propose to analyse the styles of self-presentation of a number of major diarists. Selected for this treatment are diaries which, compared with those discussed in the chapter to follow, may be said to express Being rather than Becoming. This is an imprecise but suggestive distinction. Some people, maybe most people at certain stages of life, perceive their identity in terms of change, see themselves as engaged in a process of becoming, or of oscillating between opposing poles in their own nature. Others, at other times, experience themselves as having become, having settled in a coherent identity that can speak in the first person singular without misgivings. Without making any hard and fast categories, one may therefore group diaries according to whether they primarily express one or the other identity-consciousness, or whether, like some of the great serial autobiographies, they register the transition from one to the other. In this chapter attention is given to diaries which present a relatively settled self to the reader.

A consideration of Pepys comes first. To introduce him in this context is not for a minute to deny his book a place among the serial autobiographies of Chapter 7, but only to acknowledge the fact, previously observed, that his style of self-presentation seems so irresistibly 'natural' as to provide a universal standard for comparison. In part, of course, this impression is due to nothing more than familiarity. One feels almost that one could recognize Pepys's voice across a room, his cadences are so well known. Yet the impression is not merely fortuitous. Reading a good many other diarists and then returning to Pepys seems to confirm that the quality of his diary one wishes to call 'natural' is not only in the ear of the listener, but is also an intrinsic feature of his self-projection. But what can this really mean? How can one person's way of conducting himself in a diary appear more 'natural' than another's? Is it a quality of the man that one responds to, or of the conventions observed in his manner of talking about himself? Of course it is both, although *le style* is not *l'homme même* to the extent that they cannot be considered separately. As a man, Pepys allows himself to appear in terms which make a reciprocal relationship an open possibility. His account of himself and his activities displays less affectation, less posturing, less verbal self-dramatization than any other diary of comparable density. As a writer he offers a way of answering the all-encompassing question, 'What happened today?' that the reader feels he too might adopt. The styles of most other major diarists embody more individualistic self-projections, so that to imitate them would be to flaunt another man's costume. But, to express the case paradoxically, Pepys's distinguishing characteristic is his lack of singularity. His manner of writing has the air of being accessible to anyone sufficiently conscientious and free from petty pride to avail himself of it. Describing it tends to involve one in lengthy negative comparisons, as one lists all the mannerisms of other diarists that Pepys eschews. Added to these two aspects there is perhaps something one could call the moral appeal of Pepys's self-projection. Surely to be able to articulate the best and the worst of oneself with such unreserved directness must be a kind of sanctity.

Consider how he puts himself across in the dual role of Samuel the writer of the diary and Samuel the participant in the events described. In either aspect of the role he has the stage to himself. Any narrative manner, any style of discourse he chooses to indulge is free to him; any representation of his performance in daily life will pass without question. Yet he is content to abstain from any kind of stylis-

tic ostentation, and to exhibit his conduct in a light that seldom especially distinguishes him. Nor is this mode of self-presentation merely
automatic. As Matthews emphasizes,[2] in official papers and correspondence Pepys could garb himself in elaborate formality. When he wanted
to exert a power of language over reader or hearer he knew how to
do it. So, in divesting himself of grammatical symmetry (though
seldom of correctness), of verbal flourish, rhetorical cadence and so
forth, he is making a choice among genuine options. By the analogy
of dress, he favours for the role of diarist a costume that carries with it
the least possible suggestion of a role-model, rather than one which
involves some degree of self-dramatization. His manner of address
draws no attention to itself for elegance or wit, inventiveness or originality. He quotes no Latin or Greek, cites no learned *exempla*; he
expands into no fine images, nor condenses himself into any neat
sententiae; he never writes amusingly or cleverly, though he appreciates
and takes note of amusing and clever things. His style never insists,
'Be interested in me, Samuel the writer', but constantly serves the
subject-matter and the reader.

A phrase which might aptly characterize his report is 'politely
informative'. Samuel the writer has a helpful and considerate way of
keeping his book up to date on what he has done and seen and learned.
He takes unusual pains always to be clear and thorough, explaining
obscure references and apparent anomalies, correcting errors, identifying people and locations with a parenthetical note. He writes as though
for the benefit of a reader who lives abroad or in seclusion, with whom
he stands on a footing of friendly courtesy, and whose lack of first-
hand familiarity with Pepys's world and involvements makes frequent
elucidation a necessity. Perhaps it is an elderly person, retired from active life, who has known Samuel from a child and who encourages
his young friend to feed his sympathetic interest in everything there is
to tell. In keeping with the tone of such a relationship Pepys's ubiqui-
tous comments, judgements, expressions of satisfaction and the
reverse, are also made as it were informatively. He seldom neglects to
register a personal reflection on what he has to relate, noting it as
something 'which pleases me very well', 'which methought was so
noble', 'which did vex me to hear', 'which appears to me very ominous', 'of which I am glad'—examples drawn from a five-page span.[3]
But invariably his own reaction comes at the end of the report, clearly
labelled as a personal opinion. It is an important component of the
narrative but not the subject of it.

For Pepys's book doesn't set out to be a 'faithful register of his variations of mind' (in Boswell's phrase), but a discursive history of what
passes daily through his ken—from a pain in the left testicle to the
Great Fire, from a passing lust after the book-seller's wife to a confer-
ence with the king—the Life & Times of S. Pepys. As compiler of this
private history he incorporates into the skeleton of each day's occupations a mention of whatever was out of the ordinary—news, a novel
sight, developments in office politics, some special pleasure or annoy-
ance, an entertainment, fresh knowledge, an idea, an unaccustomed
inclination—any of which may prompt an observation or a judgement
in the telling. He very seldom engages in moral or philosophic generalization; when he does so it is often no more than a modest platitude
like the following: 'But though I am much against too much spending,
yet I do think it best to enjoy some degree of pleasure, now that we
have health, money and opportunities, rather than to leave pleasures to
old age or poverty, when we cannot have them so properly.'[4] No
pretentiousness or assumption of superiority enters into his relationship with the reader. Nor does he make his own psychology a subject of any special interest. An astonishing feature of his daily report is
the capacity for simple admissions of discreditable thoughts and deeds,
presented with neither extenuation nor self-abasement. A fit of anger,
a lie, a sexual attempt, if it is one of the facts of the day, finds its way
into the record as such. True he will often express remorse or embarrass-
ment at aspects of his behaviour, and note his intention to amend,
but there is no 'confessional' air to these passages. He does not come to
the diary to bewail or, alternatively, to gloat over his sinfulness. As for
his habit of recording sexual encounters in a peculiar concoction of
French, Spanish, and Italian, it seems to proceed from a wish to
delude the eyes of a few poor household spies, rather than from the
kind of moral discomfort that prompts Sylas Neville into cryptic
notations.

A major achievement of Pepys's style is its avoidance of self-preoccupation and the appearance of conceit. It takes phenomenal tact to
be able to tell a nine-year story of himself without seeming egotistical.
His manner is so consistently disarming. Always ready to admit himself worthy of blame he seldom claims any special credit. Without
artificial modesty he manages to make personal successes sound like
strokes of good fortune rather than pretexts for self-congratulation.
It is second nature to him to guard against the alienating effect of vanity
and against pride that comes before a fall. So, in the following passage,

he relates his prodigious triumph before a parliamentary investigation of the Navy (5 March 1668) as an example of things turning out better than expected:

But I full of thoughts and trouble touching the issue of this day; and, to comfort myself did go to the Dog and drink half-a-pint of mulled sack, and in the Hall did drink a dram of brandy at Mrs. Hewlett's; and with the warmth of this did find myself in better order as to courage, truly. So we all up to the lobby; and between eleven or twelve o'clock, were called in, with the mace before us, into the House, where a mighty full House; and we stood at the bar, namely, Brouncker, Sir. J. Minnes, Sir T. Harvey, and myself, W. Pen being in the House, as a Member. I perceive the whole House was full, and full of expectation of our defence what it would be, and with great prejudice. After the Speaker had told us the dissatisfaction of the House, and read the Report of the Committee, I began our defence most acceptably and smoothly, and continued at it without any hesitation or losse, but with full scope, and all my reason free about me, as if it had been at my own table, from that time till past three in the afternoon; and so ended, without any interruption from the Speaker; but we withdrew. And there all my Fellow-Officers, and all the world that was within hearing, did congratulate me, and cry up my speech as the best thing they ever heard; and my Fellow-Officers were overjoyed in it.[5]

Characteristically he underplays his own role as chief Actor in the business, expressing pleased surprise at having brought the thing off at all. Avoiding self-dramatizing rhetoric he emphasizes his nervousness and the efficacy of Dutch courage. His story builds up to the climactic moment—one has only to think what Boswell or Haydon would do with such a scene—and hurries on past it. The next day's entry records at length the many congratulations earned by his performance, but includes the following prudent *caveat*: '. . . for which the Lord God make me thankful! and that I may make use of it not to pride and vain-glory, but that, now I have this esteem, I may do nothing to lessen it!'[6] Of course this is something of a ritual gesture, like touching wood, but it expresses a central trait of Pepys's dealings with his fellows and with the reader—a diplomatic prudence in avoiding the giving of offence. Boswell was once described by Lord Eglinton as 'the only man he ever knew who had a vast deal of vanity and yet was not in the least degree offensive'.[7] Pepys, who would probably have found Boswell singularly offensive, is incapable of taking that kind of risk. Socially out-ranked by most of his colleagues, he knows his official position to be a precarious one demanding a politic carriage at all times. He cannot afford to be seduced from the cautious realism of his own self-estimate.

To allow others to perceive him more coolly than he perceives himself would be to enter a highly vulnerable condition.

Pepys's self-presentation embodies the politics of a peace-loving man ill-equipped for war. Contention and strife, whether at home or at the office, cause him great anxiety. The kind of relationship he most likes to secure is one founded on reasonableness and good will, rather than on the power of asserted ego. On one occasion, 'provoked by some impertinence of Sir. W. Battens', he calls his colleague 'unreasonable man'.[8] It is not a term he would like to hear applied to himself. To be open to rational persuasion, ready to admit himself in the wrong, scrupulously fair in assessing degrees of blame—these are basic elements of Pepys's disposition. Nor is this a posture which he saves for the office. Reporting his many quarrels with his wife, over such things as her domestic extravagance and his gadding about, he likes to be able to conclude, 'and so friends again'—a state usually reached by negotiation and the mutual admission of fault. Here he is reviewing one such dispute and giving the verdict about 70:30 in favour of himself:

Came home; I to the taking my wife's kitchen account at the latter end of the month, and there find 7s wanting—which did occasion a very high falling out between us; I indeed too eagerly insisting upon so poor a thing, and did give her very provoking words, calling her 'beggar' and reproaching her friends; which she took very stomachfully, and reproached me justly with mine; and I confess, being myself, I cannot see what she could have done less. I find she is very cunning, and when she least shows it, hath her wit at work; but it is an ill one, though I think not so bad but with good usage I might well bear with it; and the truth is, I do find that my being over-solicitous and jealous and froward, and ready to reproach her, doth make her worse. However, I find that now and then a little difference doth do no hurt—but too much of it will make her know her force too much.[9]

During the uproar over Deb. in November 1668 the thing that really incapacitates Pepys in the face of his wife's fury is the sense that he hasn't a leg to stand on:

... which she repeating and I vexed at it, answered her a little angrily, upon which she instantly flew out into a rage, calling me dog and rogue, and that I had a rotten heart; all which, knowing that I deserved it, I bore with, and word being brought presently up that she [Deb.] was gone away by coach with her things, my wife was friends, and so all quiet, and I to the Office, with my heart sad, and find that I cannot forget the girl, and vexed I know not where to look for her. And more troubled to see how my wife is by this means likely for ever to have her hand over me, that I shall for ever be a slave to her—that is to say, only in matters of pleasure, but in other things she will make her business, I know, to please me and to keep me right to her, which I will labour to be indeed, for she deserves it of me, though it will be I fear a little time before I shall be able to wear Deb. out of my mind.[10]

Temperamentally incapable of defending the indefensible, he has nothing to do but wait for time and good behaviour to make amends. For what reasonableness cannot do to win friends and influence people, pleasantness must. Long before, in September 1662, he noted, 'It is my content that by several hands today I hear that I have the name of a good-natured man among the poor people that come to the office.'[11] No one, of course, would suggest that his good nature is in any way a calculated front. But in so far as personality may be seen as the strategy one learns for dealing with the world, the disposition Pepys shows to like and be likeable is central to his self-presentation. The capacity to be delighted by so many things, to take such pleasure in human interchange, to be, in a modern phrase, so outgoing, is a very winning trait. Often he presents himself as an essentially simple mechanism motivated by the pursuit of cordiality and the avoidance of unease, an accommodating person to deal with.

Attempting to apply the term 'natural' to Pepys's diary seems to bring us up against a curious ambiguity. On the one hand, the term is a recognition of the all-too-human character of so many of his inclinations and reactions. The little incidental circumstances, little quirks of consciousness, little interactions with other people are irresistibly 'true to nature'—which is to say surely everyone, whether or not he is capable of acknowledging it, has experienced life in the same way. It is even possible to feel that one should try to imitate Pepys, to unlearn the tactics by means of which one evades his kind of ingenuous candour. The supposition is that everyone has a Pepysian stratum in his consciousness if only he could get back to it. However, the idea of 'getting back' exposes the ambiguity. Doesn't this 'naturalness' of Pepys in some ways appear like the persistence into adult life of a child's habit of confiding everything to God? This is not to argue that the diary consciously addresses the deity in whom the adult Pepys believes, or that the frequent exclamations, 'Lord! . . .' and 'God be praised!' are direct invocations of the Almighty. Rather it is to suggest that the guileless expression of a responsiveness to life that often comes across as childlike, in fact inherits a childhood practice of talking to God from the heart. God of course knows everything already, but likes to hear it again in a person's own words, with an emphasis on gratitude and contrition. He prefers a plain openness of manner, and can immediately detect sophistries and evasions. He welcomes the mention of current anxieties and is happy to hear of constructive resolutions for the future. Samuel the diarist preserves something of this soul-before-its-maker directness, and to recognize it as 'natural' may be to recall a confiding disposition that most people have probably passed through. Growing out of it doubtless entails a loss, but to persist in casting one's experience in that oddly simplistic fashion, to become as a little child in one's periods of self-encounter, seems like a kind of suspended development.

For a diarist who really does address himself to God we might look briefly at Richard Kay, the Lancashire doctor mentioned in Chapter 2. Kay's diary is not to be classed among the serial autobiographies, being definitely 'minor' in scope and character, but it displays some features which make it useful for purposes of comparison, and it deserves attention in its own right for the stark quality of its closing pages. For the purposes of this discussion of tone and self-presentation, Kay's regular manner will be considered separately from the rhetoric of some of the last entries.

That Kay's 'reader', the object of his address, is a personal paternal God cannot be doubted. The general tone displays to a marked degree the presentation of the self in a humbly filial role, and every entry concludes in a prayer. Each day he furnishes a polite account of his expenditure of time and expresses a renewal of his religious commitment. The entry quoted in Chapter 2 fairly represents the pattern. For some years after the diary opens in 1737, at which date he is twenty-one, Kay has no particular occupation beyond helping in his father's medical practice and composing a 'little manuscript' which he calls 'the Employment of my Youth'—apparently some kind of devotional manual. This work he solemnly presents to his parents in a rather bizarre little ceremony on 11 April 1740, the third anniversary of a formal self-dedication to God which gave rise, among other things, to the diary. On the same date in 1742 he notes that it is now five years since 'I begun this my Diary, I like it very well, and hope by God's Assistance and Blessing still to continue it very much to my Satisfaction and Improvement'.[12]

A gradual change comes over the book (though still not to the point of making it especially remarkable) when, after 1743, he takes up the practice of medicine himself, going to London to study and returning to Lancashire to join his father's work. Now the diary becomes a harrowing record of his ministrations to the injured, the diseased and the dying over a large area of the agricultural north. The entries grow longer and almost chattily informative, as he supplies particulars of 'remarkeable' symptoms and effects that come to his notice. Occasionally he describes a typical day in unusual detail, noting that the diary would become 'abundantly too tedious and prolix'[13] if he were to report every day so thoroughly. He continues in each entry to commend himself and his work to God, displaying considerable fertility in varying the form of this invocation. It becomes clear that the diary embodies, in the fullest meaning of the term, a vocational attitude to his work. The constant re-animation of his sense of religious duty, backed by immediate divine assistance, is necessary to sustain him against demoralization.

Towards the end of the diary the struggle against demoralization becomes acute and extorts from Kay an extraordinary rhetoric of religious anguish. The first blow comes with the death of his cousin Richard in 1749, to which he responds with a strange, almost incantatory dirge in the stylized language of biblical lamentation and ejaculatory prayer. Passing through a conventional *memento-mori* passage—'I must be laid speechless and motionless by the cold Wall, when I must have my Winding-Sheet thrown over me and be laid in the dark and silent Grave . . .'[14]—he concludes with a re-affirmation of faith, resigning himself to God's providence. In the following year, however, the fatal illness of his brother-in-law Joseph Baron throws him into a crisis of faith with which he wrestles in page after page of tormented rhetoric, at once highly conventionalized and painfully first-hand. During the illness he laments with passionate dismay, mixing the tones of classical threnody—'O my Brother; Alas for You my Brother . . .' —with the grotesque rhetorical question, 'Must the Stench and Appearance of a few loose Stools sensibly convince us that the Juices of your Body are stained . . .?'[15] The effort to submit to God's will struggles against the desire to clamour God into changing his determination. Acknowledging that 'Whatever is, is right',[16] he nonetheless urges all the reasons why Baron might be spared, concluding, 'Lord, I am speaking unto thee as a Man speaketh unto his Friend.'[17]

The next entry describes the actual death-bed scene, which Kay renders as a sort of moralized tableau on the theme of How a Christian Should Die. The language is formal and slightly elevated, as though Kay seeks to clothe the event in a guise in which he can reconcile it with his conception of a just Providence. The process of writing the diary would seem at this point to be a vital stage in his handling of the shock and distress—not merely an inert record but the immediate articulation of a spiritual struggle. As the following lines make clear Kay's difficulty formulates itself in the terms of a classic problem of faith:

Lord, Thou hast this Day made a great Breach upon us; the Death of our desirable good Friend and Relative is to us a mournful Dispensation; It is a Lamentation, and what I have written concerning it let it be written for a Lamentation. We must submit to thy Stroke, and say Good is the Word of the Lord: The Lord gave and the Lord hath taken away; blessed be the Name of the Lord.[18]

Yet the next day the burial of the dead man prompts him to renew his lamentation in terms which come close to reproaching God for this apparently gratuitous blow:

His Death is to us a dark Providence, we cannot see how a wise and good God shou'd cause such a Breach to be for our Good, we think Joseph Baron was One who cou'd ill be spared on a great many Accounts, there being few Persons in private Life on whom there was so great a Dependance.[19]

The diary breaks off less than a month later during an epidemic of typhoid fever. I have given it some space in this chapter, not on account of any special individuality, but because it exemplifies the kind of diary in which the attitude of the persona presupposes actual divine attentiveness.

At the beginning of this chapter William Jones was quoted to the effect that if he seemed to be addressing his 'lamentations and woes' to a 'listening friend', it was really 'to Heaven' that he appealed.[20] However, to turn to Jones from the earnest sobriety and occasional passion of Richard Kay is to discover an altogether different mode of self-presentation, one which projects the writer as a 'character', a parcel of odd humours and eccentric turns of phrase. One of Ponsonby's nine 'best' diaries, Jones's book of the self serves as a receptacle for all sorts of mental flotsam and jetsam that accumulate over the years into an elaborate imprint of an unusual man. Actually the book falls into two distinct sections. The first is a detailed, fairly regular segment (1777–80) surrounding his stay in Jamaica. After this comes an eighteen-year-long hiatus registered only in a few scattered cries of distress, followed by a burgeoning of entries from 1799 to his death in 1821.

The latter segment, to which the following discussion refers, corresponds almost exactly to his period as Vicar of Broxbourne, after nearly twenty years as curate of the same church. With the promotion comes a little more leisure and some relief from the financial worries resulting from the ten children born to his shrewish wife Theodosia ('Dosy'). One of the employments of this modicum of leisure, it seems, is the enlargement of his habit of spreading himself on paper.

As he himself presents it, the diary is part of a much larger tactical manoeuvre in the face of experience, namely, his retreat to a 'den'. This poky little amenity provided by the Broxbourne vicarage Jones prizes as though it were a kingdom. Few things could draw from him such a cheerful exclamation as this:

Wedy. Jany. 6th. [1803]. How happy, how very happy, do I feel myself in my dear little room, which some delicate folks would perhaps, rudely call a *hog-stye*! I am undisturbed, I have my cheerful little fire, my books & in short every comfort which I can reasonably desire. I read, I reflect, I write, & endeavour to enjoy, as far as I can, that blessed leisure & absence of care with which the good Providence of my heavenly Father has indulged me, particularly since my retirement into this happy cottage.[21]

But the den is more than merely a room of his own, it is a refuge and a haven. He compares it to a snail's shell that he would like to be able to carry everywhere with him,[22] and remarks on another occasion, after a distressing encounter with the outside world: 'When I reflect on my natural disposition—volatile and unguarded, I am no where so *safe* as in my own dirty study—*alias*—*dog-hole*!'[23] In his den Jones can be comfortably and securely himself; he can dawdle and potter around, and talk about anything that comes into his head without fear of rebuff or hostile indifference. The den is his asylum, the diary its house-organ.

As a vehicle for the presentation of self Jones's diary is an uncommonly ramshackle conveyance. The very opposite of Pepys's systematically informative report, its form alone constitutes a self-portrait in silhouette. The medium is the self-presentation. The book has no discernible shape or order; no standard entry-format exists to dictate a pattern to whatever Jones may feel impelled to say. Certain limitations of scope, however, are imposed by two companion volumes, the *Journal of Health* and *Domestic Lamentations* (both unfortunately lost) which siphon off their special concerns from the main stream. With these exceptions the *General Journal*, as he calls it, has no policy of discrimination. Anything at all may be the subject of his fragmentary chats. Looking back over the whole length of the journal in 1818 Jones himself remarks on its '*rambling & disjointed*' appearance.[24] To the reader the character of the book tends to impart an image of the writer as genially erratic.

The style which he pulls round himself in the comfortable squalor of his den contributes further to the image of an idiosyncratic singular sort of man. His writing is peppered with mannerisms—odd habits of expression and punctuation, peculiar emphasis, bits of Latin, stray quotations, and obscure allusions—all of which project a thorough-going eccentricity. The effect, while not actively cultivated, is one of which he is not unconscious. Just as his clothes,[25] after years of neglect, give him the appearance of a comfortable kind of old scarecrow, so he is content to let his oddities of style go forth to represent him. He counts upon the indulgence of the reader, some taciturn old friend long familiar with his meanderings. In the following sample-entry the £30 and the 'little Colonel' refer to an imprudent loan to an election candidate; the foreigners are lodgers.

Novr. 19th. 1806. I may cry out with Archimedes, the famous geometrician of Syracuse—'I have *found*! I have *found*!' He did it in Greek—I will do it in plain English.

I have *found* that the little chimney in my dirty study has a communication with the chimney of what we call our best parlour, & that, by stopping the draft of the register-stove, I am delivered from one of the two curses which harrass many poor devils of husbands. May not this furnish a hint to chimney-doctors in other parallel cases?

How rejoiced I am at this *grand* discovery! Is it not of more Value to me, in the comfort which it produces, than—say 30£,—& then may I not—(what hinders me?) cheat myself of the uneasiness arising on the score of the little Colonel?

I lent my money from the best of motives. I was *simple,* though above 50 years of age, & he, who was *knowing* at 23, took *simple* me in; but let me not repine, Providence can repay me a thousand ways—besides my smoky chimney cured, which had vexed me infinitely longer than any loss which I ever sustained, I have, at present, three foreigners. I will exert myself to keep them as long as I can; for thus I shall soon come to the right about.

Who is afraid![26]

An interesting comment on this rather self-conscious display of a 'humorous' turn of mind may be had from Jones's own pen in an entry dated 13 July 1814. Resuming the diary after a gap of nearly five years, during which time 'I have occasionally scribbled my thoughts, whether merry or sad' in large homemade notebooks, he reports finding 'that I wrote in a more free & unstudied manner in them than in these small, formal pages, which would hardly dry fast enough.'[27]

Two noteworthy elements in Jones's projection of a persona are his adoption of emphatic *attitudes* on a variety of subjects, and the character he gives himself in discussing his relations with the world. The diary gives vent over the years to a good deal of moral indignation as Jones fulminates against mercenary and indifferent clergymen, parsimonious parishioners, and nasty-minded Old Maids.[28] In 1801 he is roused to pages of fury by the '*savageness & brutishness*' of the '*rogue & villain*', '*mushroom*, or shall I rather say—*toad-stool*?'—a certain Farmer Rogers who tyrannizes the parish and attempts to block Jones's elevation to the Vicarage.[29] At the same time he expresses many humane and generous judgements and much affection for people and things. Without parading himself in the role of a Parson Yorick he displays a prompt emotional response to many of the things that befall him. The deaths of several of his children elicit from him expressions of undisguised distress. The following little passage refers to his favourite daughter Caroline; it serves simply to register a present state of emotion, to permit him to talk to someone:

½ *past six o'clock*. The passing bell has, this instant, begun for her! I have sent to the sexton, to desire him to ring it for a very short time; I cannot bear it! I am now scribbling through a mist of tears. May God prepare us all for a change so awful![30]

As for the character he ascribes to himself, it is composed of numerous details. In diaries of earlier periods it is uncommon to find a diarist discussing himself as 'the sort of person who . . .'; the relationship with the reader did not permit such a complacent attitude to the self-as-subject. The change is one aspect of the major shift in the manner of diary-writing already noticed in this study, itself a manifestation of that great transformation of consciousness to which the conditions of late eighteenth-century Europe gave rise. In their exceedingly humble ways Kay and Jones may be seen to exemplify the transformation as registered in the obscurest of cultural backwaters. Allowing for the differences in individual personality and social situation, it is still possible to assert that Jones's diary embodies elements of a mode of self-projection that really was not available to Kay. This is not to say that in the person of the Rev. W. Jones Romanticism flowered in Broxbourne, Herts. For one thing, while he writes in the early decades of the nineteenth century, Jones is the cultural product of an earlier generation. What he exhibits, in a relatively low state of development, is the disposition to be satisfied with his individuality without feeling called upon to express a need for improvement.

If Jones were to acknowledge a literary archetype for his diary-persona it might well be Dr. Primrose in *The Vicar of Wakefield*, a book which he cites familiarly on a couple of occasions.³¹ While his misfortunes are less catastrophic than those of Goldsmith's character, and his prosperity a good deal less blessed, there is enough similarity in their conditions to permit Jones to identify himself with the disposition that Dr. Primrose presents to the reader. The persistent motif in nearly all of Jones's statements about his own character is the image of an unworldly, sanguine, simple-hearted sort of man. He likes to insist on his disregard for appearances and for 'What the World may say'.³² He admits himself gullible and imprudent and an easy victim of dishonesty, but tends to regard this lack of worldly aptitude as a sign of grace:

July 26th. *[1805].* Not only as the worthy vicar of Broxbourn am I too generally cheated, but all my life through have I experienced the same lot; for having not made it any part of the plan of my life to cheat others, I have been generally credulous & unsuspecting. Thousands of others, clergymen and laymen, (if that could administer comfort), share the same fate; &, were I to hear them complain, I would kindly endeavour to silence their complainings with that consoling assurance, which (thank Heaven!) effectually quiets all my croakings & grumblings.³³

Undoubtedly the greatest cross he has to bear is Mrs. Theodosia Jones, and one of his most consistent roles throughout the diary is that of Much-Abused Husband, suffering in silence. Some early entries express married rapture and appreciation of 'sweet, lovely Theodosia',³⁴ but before long she has become his chief Domestic Lamentation whose endless bullying and contempt become the theme of a separate volume. In the *General Journal* Jones pretty well confines himself to scathing remarks about matrimony and bitterly ironic references to 'my *dear* wife', 'my *gentle* wife', and 'her *wifeship*', whose enormities the reader may guess at. It would seem from the following entry that his sufferings at her hands were considerable:

Oct. 1st, 1804. I, W. J.—the writer of too frequent 'domestic lamentations', am neither more nor less than a *paradox*!

A stranger, who might chance to read some of these *dolorous* scrawls, would imagine me to be one of the most miserable of all miserable, unhappy beings—but is it so?—no such thing.[35]

By separating the Lamentations from the main diary Jones thus preserves in his 'imprint' the image of a generally cheerful man, making the best of things and indeed periodically expressing fervent gratitude for the blessedness of his lot.

Sir Walter Scott's *Journal* (1825–32) displays in a highly developed form the diary's function as a surface on which the writer projects his own image. In his mid-fifties when he begins the journal, his reputation at its height, Sir Walter presents himself as a man who has taken confident possession of his own identity, who has very definitely 'become'. The book contains the ample and deliberate imprint of a formed self. A reader is assumed from the outset, and occasionally addressed directly. In other words there is no convention, real or pretended, to the effect that the diary is a private or secret utterance. The tone and scope of Scott's writing define pretty sharply the relationship he takes up with the reader, and make it clear that he assumes dominance in that relationship. This is the book in which he is at liberty to hold forth, to appear in the guises that please him.

Two major occurrences dominate the first year of the diary, eliciting from Scott very distinct and rounded performances in the role of Sir Walter. In January 1826 the publishing enterprise in which he was involved collapsed, leaving him personally liable for debts of over £100,000. On 15 May Lady Scott died. The first of these two calamities dictated the shape of the remainder of Scott's life. To avert the sequestration of all his property, including Abbotsford, he put his affairs into trusteeship and set himself to earn the whole amount owing by the forced labour of writing new novels, so many pages per day, and reissuing the old ones with new notes. On top of this work he continued to engage in periodical journalism, especially for his son-in-law John Lockhart, editor of the *Quarterly Review*, and to serve as a Justice on the circuit court. The diary acts as a running progress-report on pages written, proofs corrected and moneys earned. As for the death of his wife, while deeply felt it was not unexpected, and he appears to have adjusted to the loss relatively easily. Nonetheless, as friends die and his own health deteriorates, the diary takes on the character of a chronicle of a lion's declining years.

Scott's self-image at this period of his life seems to have been a singularly definite one. His manner of conducting himself in the diary abundantly reinforces the statements he makes about himself and the sentiments he expresses on men and morals. As a beginning, here he is on the subject of Sir Thomas Lawrence's portrait of him for George IV; the date is 18 November 1826:

> I finished my sittings to Laurence, and am heartily sorry there should be another picture of me except that which he has finished. The person is remarkably like, and conveys the idea of the stout blunt carle that cares for few things, and fears nothing. He has represented the author as in the act of composition, yet has effectually discharged all affectation from the manner and attitude.[36]

So determined is he to appear unaffected that he almost carries the opposite quality to the point of affectation. In normal times he favours a gruff, downright, soldierly style of talk, colourful but not painted, spiced with slang, though never vulgar; an after-dinner, masculine air. In his attitudes as well as in his style he takes care to avoid the imputation that he is any sort of literary softie. The following passage illustrates very well his growly have-at-ye manner on the subject of nothing in particular—in this case the town of Calais:

> Lost, as all know, by the bloody papist bitch (one must be vernacular when on French ground) Queen Mary, of red-hot memory. I would rather she had burned a score more of bishops. If she had kept it, her sister Bess would sooner have parted with her virginity. Charles I. had no temptation to part with it— it might, indeed, have been shuffled out of our hands during the Civil wars, but Noll would have as soon let Mons[r]. draw one of his grinders; then Charles II. would hardly have dared to sell such an old possession, as he did Dunkirk; and after that the French had little chance till the Revolution. Even then, I think, we could have held a place that could be supplied from our own element, the sea. *Cui bono?* None, I think, but to plague the rogues.[37]

This is some fellow, who, having been praised for bluntness, doth affect a saucy roughness.

Scott is a remarkably expansive diarist. For the first two-and-a-half years he writes almost daily, often several hundred words to an entry. One of his commonest subjects is the character of his acquaintances, in the appraisal of whom he projects himself as an experienced judge of men. His favourable judgements tend to express approval rather than admiration, and he implicitly congratulates himself on his own values in acknowledging the merits of another. He consistently speaks in praise of men who reflect the qualities he cherishes in himself. 'I love the virtues of rough and round men,' he says, in speaking of Robert

Cadell, one of his publishing partners.[38] Very early in the diary he devotes a lot of space to Byron and Tom Moore, the former lately dead, the latter a recent visitor to Abbotsford. (Moore's own diary gives a very full account of this visit.[39]) The light in which Scott places these men casts a far from unflattering glow upon himself. Of Moore he says, 'There is a manly frankness, and a perfect ease and good breeding about him which is delightful. Not the least touch of the poet or the pedant.'[40] He goes on to speak of similarities he detects between Moore and himself, *à propos* of Byron's having bracketed their names together:

We are both good-humoured fellows, who rather seek to enjoy what is going forward than to maintain our dignity as Lions; and we have both seen the world too widely and too well not to contemn in our souls the imaginary consequence of literary people, who walk with their noses in the air, and remind me always of the fellow whom Johnson met in an ale-house, and who called himself 'the *great* Twalmley—inventor of the floodgate iron for smoothing linen.'[41]

A similar theme appears in his remarks on Byron. After relating a number of Byron anecdotes, for the record as it were, and pronouncing some judgements on his character, he concludes: 'What I liked about Byron, besides his boundless genius, was his generosity of spirit as well as purse, and his utter contempt of all the affectations of literature, from the school-magisterial stile to the lackadaisical.'[42] As usual, in extolling the qualities of another man he communicates a satisfaction with the degree to which he himself manifests the same qualities. This may be contrasted with the diarists whose imprint renders them as 'becoming', and who tend to measure themselves anxiously against other people and to look out for role-models.

Scott's manner takes very much for granted his reader's assent to the values and attitudes which he expresses. There is nothing tentative about his stance in the role of old-fashioned aristocrat. The diary is not a place where he confides any 'human' weaknesses, or gives any indication that he is not a hero to his valet. A comparison with Pepys will make this clear. One morning in January 1661 a rumour that a group of armed fanatics is at large in the city sends Samuel hurrying home to get his gun: '. . . so I returned (though with no good courage at all, but that I might not seem to be afeared) and got my sword and pistol, which however I have no powder to charge, and went to the door, where I found Sir. R. Ford . . .'[43] Central to his presentation of this occurrence is the distinction he draws between outward show and

inward state. Pepys hastens to dispel the notion that martial prepared-
ness is with him a state of mind. Scott, on the contrary, faced with the
possibility of a duel, presents to the diary the same face that he presents
to the world. The language of his self-presentation admits no suggestion
of a gap between mask and wearer. He is referring to a letter he has
received advising discretion:

I wrote in answer, which is true, that I would hope all my friends would trust
to my acting with proper caution and advice; but that if I were capable, in a
moment of weakness, of doing anything short of what my honour demanded,
I would die the death of a poisond rat in a hole, out of mere sense of my own
degradation. God knows, that, though life is placid enough with me, I do not
feel anything to attach me to it so strongly as to occasion my avoiding any
risque which duty to my character may demand from me.[44]

To call this kind of rhetoric self-dramatizing, with its talk of 'my
honour', 'duty to my character' and so forth, is not to suggest that
Scott is faking, merely that his mistrust of *some* verbal costumes
as affectations does not prevent him from appearing in others which
might well be considered extravagant in certain quarters.

Nothing brings out Scott's self-dramatizing rhetoric so well as the
prospect of Ruin. In December 1825, when it seems to pass as a false
alarm, and again in the following month, financial disaster stares
him in the face. His response in the diary is a soliloquy of a peculiarly
theatrical nature, a speech echoing the accents of tragic heroes, full of
little touches of restrained pathos such as would be called artful from the
pen of a dramatist. Here, in part of a long entry dated 18 December
1825, he contemplates the loss of Abbotsford:

How could I tread my hall with such a diminished crest? How live a poor
indebted man where I was once the wealthy—the honourd? My children are
provided—thank God for that. I was to have gone there on Saturday in joy
and prosperity to receive my friends—my dogs will wait for me in vain—it is
foolish—but the thoughts of parting from these dumb creatures have moved
me more than any of the painful reflections I have put down—poor things, I
must get them kind masters. There may be yet those who loving me may love
my dog because it has been mine. I must end this, or I shall lose the tone of
mind with which men should meet distress.[45]

The concluding sentence with its gesture of stern self-mastery reflects
Scott's explicit identification with the Stoic disposition, an attitude
which painful situations regularly prompt him to commend. His
performance in the Stoic role involves the display of just enough

emotion to make clear the heroic fortitude required to overcome it. Without being false to the essential movements of his own spirit, his distress, finding a pen in its hand, manages to compose an exceptionally articulate imprint of the Finely Tempered Man facing Adversity. Frankly regarding his own career as potentially a *Life* he supplies his biographer with just the kind of material he himself would love to have for the *Life of Napoleon Buonaparte* he is writing—authentic records of the Great Man's actual feelings at the crises of his career. When the crisis apparently passes Scott reflects on the possible shapes his story may yet take, and on the figure the hero will cut when all is said and done:

An odd thought strikes me. When I die will the Journal of these days be taken out of the Ebony cabinet at Abbotsford, and read as the transient pout of a man worth £60,000, with wonder that the well-seeming Baronet should ever have experienced such a hitch? Or will it be found in some obscure lodging-house, where the decayd son of chivalry has hung up his scutcheon for some 20 shillings a week, and where one or two old friends will look grave and whisper to each other, 'poor gentleman,' 'a well-meaning man,' 'nobody's enemy but his own,' 'thought his parts could never wear out,' 'family poorly left,' 'pity he took that foolish title'? Who can answer this question?[46]

Given his own habit of consigning his friends to the grave with judicious, well-turned obituaries, he may well wonder what kind of verdict he can negotiate for himself.

The death of Lady Scott in May 1826 is another occasion to which the journal rises nobly. As in the face of Ruin, his performance embodies a fluent literary tact. Writing (apparently) while emotion is at its strongest he exercises a controlled and controlling power of language in which to speak of his feelings and project his state of mind. Promptings of self-pity mingle with concern for his daughter Anne; memories of happier days steal upon him, only to be banished for threatening to undermine his resolution. Characteristically he concludes the first long entry on the subject thus: 'But I will not blaze cambrick and crape in the publick eye like a disconsolate widower, that most affected of all characters.'[47] He desires that his conduct should be an example of perfectly natural good breeding, neither coldly unfeeling nor ostentatiously emotional. Of a Highland custom of speaking freely of the dead he says, 'It is a generous and manly tone of feeling—and, so far as it may be adopted without affectation or contradicting the general habits of society, I reckon on observing it.'[48] The journal too, as a form of conduct, adheres to the same decorum, exhibiting a 'generous and manly tone of feeling' as in the following extract dated three days after the announcement of the death:

May 18.—Another day, and a bright one to the external world, again opens on us—the air soft, and the flowers smiling, and the leaves glittering. They cannot refresh her to whom mild weather was a natural enjoyment. Cearments of lead and of wood already hold her—cold earth must have her soon. But it is not my Charlotte, it is not the bride of my youth, the mother of my children, that will be laid among the ruins of Dryburgh, which we have so often visited in gaiety and pastime. No, no. She is sentient and conscious of my emotions somewhere—somehow; *where* we cannot tell; *how* we cannot tell—yet I would not at this moment renounce the mysterious yet certain hope that I shall see her in a better world, for all that this world can give me.[49]

Thus does Scott deliver himself of elegiac sentiments in a manner which he would undoubtedly regard as eminently natural but which must seem to the modern reader like a product of literary artifice. This paradox, if it be one, may be partly resolved by observing the extent to which a more or less literary self-dramatization has become second nature to him. He remarks on one occasion, addressing the shade of Burns whom he has just quoted, 'when I want to express a sentiment, which I feel strongly, I find the phrase in Shakespeare—or thee'.[50] Certainly, by means of quotation, allusion or snatches of improvised verse pastiche, he very often identifies his situation with a literary archetype, frequently a Shakespearian protagonist. Haydon's diary displays the same habit, as does Byron's on which Scott professes to model his own. Thus while many of his higher flights must seem 'unnatural' in the sense that only a sensibility imbued with literary culture would or could resort to them, yet on the other hand they are 'natural' to the extent that for Scott they are thoroughly 'in character'.

Byron, to whom this consideration of the diary as self-projection now turns, was a less than dedicated diarist. His total output in this medium records only a few months of his life, notably the periods November 1813 to April 1814 (which he spent in London), and January to February 1821 (Ravenna), together with some other brief fragments and 'Detached Thoughts'. Nonetheless, as might be expected, he leaves an unusually vivid imprint of his being-alive during these times, and one which puts itself squarely among those diaries which project a strongly marked persona. More self-indulgently than Scott he avails himself of the diary's waiting page to exercise a role, to strike attitudes as though for an impressed audience rather than a sympathetic friend. Delivering a laconic monologue in a fashionable literary *déshabillé*, he never seems to invite the reader into a reciprocal relationship. Shortly after abandoning the first journal he lets Moore have it, telling him in a letter date 14 June 1814, 'Keep the journal; I care not what becomes of it; and if it has amused you, I am glad that I kept it.'[51] This off-hand manner is consistent with the tone of the journal itself—and rare among diarists.

The 1813–14 Journal, to which the following remarks are confined, projects a pretty thorough-going world-weariness for a man of twenty-five. Considered as an inter-personal manner, the style in which he presents himself is really quite disagreeable. On most subjects he expresses attitudes that veer between discontented indifference and misanthropy, relieved by spells of patronizing tolerance. A spirit of restlessness propels his brittle talk from one subject to another, mostly personalities, upon which he delivers opinions as from a great height. On literature he does indeed, as Scott says, express an utter contempt for all its affectations—and for most of its practitioners. Certain individuals, notably Moore, Rogers, Campbell, and Scott, he praises highly, but for the tribe as a whole, himself included, he affects impatient scorn. In this, as in other areas of life, his pose of bored self-contempt— one of the faces of intense pride—empowers him to wither up all those who haven't yet attained to this attitude themselves. Speaking of his indifference to criticism he says:

I rather believe that it proceeds from my not attaching that importance to authorship which many do, and which, when young, I did also. 'One gets tired of everything, my angel', says Valmont. The 'angels' are the only things of which I am not a little sick—but I do think the preference of *writers* to *agents*— the mighty stir made about scribbling and scribes, by themselves and others— a sign of effeminacy, degeneracy, and weakness. Who would write, who had any thing better to do? 'Action—action—action'—said Demosthenes; 'Action*s* —action*s*', I say, and not writing,—least of all, rhyme. Look at the querulous and monotonous lives of the 'genus';—except Cervantes, Tasso, Dante, Ariosto, Kleist (who were brave and active citizens), Aeschylus, Sophocles, and some other of the antiques also—what a worthless, idle brood it is![52]

A fair specimen of his diary manner, the passage exhibits a number of the component elements of his self-presentation: the attitude of the man of action 'a little sick' of almost everything; the indifference to considerations that preoccupy others and even preoccupied him 'when young'; the off-handedly clever style of writing. Of his own career as a *littérateur* he declares emphatically: 'To withdraw *myself* from *myself* (oh that cursed selfishness!) has ever been my sole, my entire, my sincere motive in scribbling at all; and publishing is also the continuance of the same object, by the action it affords to the mind, which else recoils upon itself.'⁵³ (The explanation for his publishing seems a trifle obscure.)

The habit of dressing in the borrowed robes of Shakespearian characters, already mentioned in connection with Scott, is so marked a feature of Byron's self-presentation as to demand special comment. As G. Wilson Knight has devoted a whole book to Byron's incarnation of Shakespeare's creations and an essay to his 'dramatic prose',⁵⁴ it is hardly possible to contribute anything new on the subject. But since this present study is concerned to connect diaries, not with their writers' other works but with diary-writing as a genre, it is appropriate to go briefly over the same ground. The first thing one notices is the variety of characters that furnish Byron with lines and phrases, quoted or adapted, for his personal use. Different moods evoke different prototypes, and sometimes two or three who will jostle each other in a single entry. Prominent among his models are Lear, Macbeth, and Hamlet, sometimes at the level of mere cliché ('Man delights not me'⁵⁵), but usually to more dramatic effect. Hamlet particularly, as might be expected, contributes to the self-image of one who has 'something "within that passeth show"',⁵⁶ and finds himself surrounded with people who ' "fool me to the top of my bent". '⁵⁷ Yet he does not draw exclusively on tragic protagonists. Richard III makes a number of appearances; attentions from several women at once prompt him to remark: ' "Since I have crept in favour with myself, I must maintain it"; but I never "mistook my person", though I think others have.'⁵⁸—interesting in view of Byron's sensitivity regarding his own deformity. And when his cynicism is in better humour, Falstaff comes to his aid. Of the despised crew of 'scribblers' he declares, ' "I'll not march through Coventry with them, that's flat".'⁵⁹

Byron's manner of using Shakespearian fragments reminds one of the customary distinction between simile and metaphor: some people quote Shakespeare *illustratively*—'as so-and-so says'—laying out a comparison between their own situation and that of the quoted character. Byron (and other diarists of the Romantic period) make the Shakespearian phrases their own, incorporating them into the structure of their own talk, telescoping comparison into identification. Until this time only biblical or parabiblical phraseology is to be found directly imported into the language of a diarist's self-projection, as biblical roles—Job,

the Psalmist, Jeremiah—provide objects for dramatic self-identification.
Now, in the Romantic period, it would seem as though a changing
style of selfconsciousness combines with a changing appreciation of
Shakespeare to make the Shakespearian soliloquy one of the primary
models—and perhaps for Byron *the* primary model—for the kind of
self-articulation represented by the diary. Byron himself remarks
that 'except in soliloquy, as now'[60] he does not generally like talking
about himself. The soliloquy, indeed, is, for him, exceptionally apt,
combining as it does the convention of private utterance with the
presence of an audience. Unlike the Pepysian style of helpful narrative,
the soliloquy is essentially *dramatic* speech, articulating present states
of feeling, changing direction as new thoughts arise, contending with
immediate perplexity or pain. In soliloquy the protagonist is supposed
to be conducting his psychic life aloud in a dynamic, figurative,
individualized language and an agile syntax responsive to the currents
of impassioned thought. Moreover, it is important to notice that
the convention is strictly a literary one. The diarist who more or less
consciously identifies his practice of diary-writing with the soliloquizing
habit is perceiving himself by definition in a theatrical situation, the
hero, *solus*. A reciprocal effect is generated, so that it is possible to see
the soliloquizing posture as both reflecting and intensifying the writer's
self-dramatization. In the following entry of Byron's, for example,
the style and tenor of the whole passage has a distinctly Shakespearian
ring, over and above the jumble of quotations and echoes that it contains. No single impersonation seems to be sustained, though Eno-
barbus perhaps comes close to being the predominant role:

Saturday, April 9, 1814.
    I mark this day!
    Napoleon Buonaparte has abdicated the throne of the world. 'Excellent well.'
Methinks Sylla did better; for he revenged and resigned in the height of his
sway, red with the slaughter of his foes—the finest instance of glorious contempt
of the rascals upon record. Dioclesian did well too—Amurath not amiss, had
he become aught except a dervise—Charles the Fifth but so so—but Napoleon,
worst of all. What! wait till they were in his capital, and then talk of his readiness to give up what is already gone!! 'What whining monk art thou—
what holy cheat?' 'Sdeath!—Dionysius at Corinth was yet a king to this.
The 'Isle of Elba' to retire to!—Well—if it had been Caprea, I should have
marvelled less. 'I see men's minds are but a parcel of their fortunes.' I am utterly
bewildered and confounded.
    I don't know—but I think *I*, even *I* (an insect compared with this creature),

Francis Kilvert

Henrietta Meredith-Brown, Kilvert's 'Ettie', in 1875 when she was twenty-six

Alice James in 1891
The taking of this photograph is mentioned in her diary

have set my life on casts not a millionth part of this man's. But, after all, a crown may be not worth dying for. Yet, to outlive *Lodi* for this!!! Oh that Juvenal or Johnson could rise from the dead! *Expende—quot libras in duce summo invenies?* I knew they were light in the balance of mortality; but I thought their living dust weighed more *carats*. Alas! this imperial diamond hath a flaw in it, and is now hardly fit to stick in a glazier's pencil:—the pen of the historian won't rate it worth a ducat.

Psha! 'something too much of this'. But I won't give him up even now; though all his admirers have, 'like the thanes, fallen from him'.[61]

Wilson Knight calls this 'the Shakespearian power speaking direct through a pinnacle of human consciousness from out of the heart of great events.'[62]

'How fatally,' remarks Alice James, 'the entire want of humour cripples the mind.'[63] The line would make a fitting epigraph for a diary containing the unique instance in the genre of a self-presentation which is almost unremittingly comic. Other diarists have wry or humorous things to say from time to time, and may even relate ludicrous episodes involving themselves. And of course it is not uncommon for the most earnest of diarists to be unintentionally very funny indeed. (This is one of the commonest features of the genre to be exploited in diary-imitations, such as Grossmith's *Diary of a Nobody*.) Alice James alone projects herself deliberately and throughout as a phenomenon which, to be seen rightly, should be seen as comical. In circumstances which would justify the bitterest self-pity she reduces the mention of her suffering to a minimum and persistently arranges that the terms on which she will be met by the reader shall preclude the appeal for commiseration.

A large part of the diary consists of ironic observations of the *comédie humaine* as exemplified in the newspapers and in her immediate vicinity. From high life and low, reported to her by the *Pall Mall Gazette* and 'Nurse' respectively, she draws unfailing instances of human, and more specifically English, inanity, hypocrisy, and cant on which to exercise her sprightly sarcasm. Into the gaps between pretension and actuality she inserts an ironic pen and gives it an indignant little twist. In serving up her almost daily samples of 'the all pervasive sense of pharasaism in the British constitution of things'[64] her role is that of an incredulous outsider, never quite able to believe that humane rationality should be so universally violated. Being an American, a Unitarian, a spinster, and an involuntary recluse, she looks at things

English, Anglican, marital, and worldly from a slightly uncomprehend-
ing distance. The role of satirist, however, can easily become ludicrous
if sustained too long—a danger which Alice James anticipates in remarking, *à propos* of lengthening gaps between entries:

These long pauses don't point to any mental aridity, my 'roomy forehead' is
as full as ever of germinating thoughts, but alas the machinery is more and
more out of kilter. I am sorry for you all, for I feel as if I hadn't even yet given
my message. I would there were more bursts of enthusiasm, less of the carping
tone, through this, but I fear it comes by nature, and after all, the excellent
Islander will ne'er be crushed by the knowledge of the eye that was upon him,
through the long length of years, and the monotone of the enthusiast is more
wearisome to sustain than a dyspeptic note.[65]

The incongruity of her delivering agitated addresses on the debased
state of English civilization is apparent to her, and she mocks herself
with the fantasy of a vast audience hanging on her words.

   This manoeuvre typifies the pattern of her comic self-projection.
In rendering itself as ludicrous the ultra-sensitive ego seeks to forestall
the alienation of the audience; this it does by presenting a deliberately
alienated image of itself, with disarming good humour. Fearing that the
audience will withdraw its sympathy, as she herself does, at the sight
of moral obtuseness, pretension, vanity, any kind of distorted self-
estimate, she hastens always to deflate her own balloon. Whenever a
danger appears of her taking herself or her opinions solemnly she is
quick to point out the irony to which she has opened herself. Thus,
after waxing indignant over Browning's son having disregarded his
father's wishes on the subject of burial, she writes:

A note just came in from H., in which he says that Browning *fils* had no choice,
that the Florentine municipality behaved so atrociously about opening the
cemetery, so the above indignation is rather uncalled for at this moment, but is,
of course, highly valuable as showing how a super-exquisite soul like mine
would be affected had the son acted just as he has not.[66]

Or again, when Henry replies to her comments on the dramatized
version of *The American*: 'I was greatly thrilled and touched by the
implication which his letter gave that he cared for my opinion as an
opinion,—the smallest flatteries of one's kin outweighing the acclama-
tions of a multitude—these last so familiar to me!'[67] Examples could
be drawn from every part of the book. Frequently a comic self-perception furnishes not merely a parenthesis but the actual subject of her

remarks. Consider the following passage; its whole function is to amuse, its style a sampler of comic tactics:

You would be amused if you saw the paces thro' which I put poor little Nurse; in the winter she has to applaud me Mind, in summer me beauty! In my moments of modesty, don't scoff, I have 'em, I consult her about my letters and you may be sure she knows too well which side her bread is buttered to do aught but admire. In the summer when we pass an old frump more sour than the last I throw myself upon her mercy and ask her if I am as dreadful to look upon as that. When she comes up to time with a reassuring negative, and I sink back on my cushions, in my black-goggled, greenery-yallery loveliness, pacified—for the moment![68]

A diarist whose situation invites comparison with that of Alice James is, of course, Barbellion. Dying without ever having had a chance to realize their potential, both are consciously performing for a posthumous audience, making a bid, as Barbellion says, 'for some posthumous sympathy'.[69] But the differences are considerable. Barbellion presents himself as a bitterly tragic figure whose unjust fate calls out for pity. By exhibiting what he is and what he endures he seeks to extort love and respect as his due. Alice James is wiser and knows the hard truth that objects of pity excite discomfort and distaste. The only way to be a popular invalid is to relieve your visitors of guilt by showing what a good time you're having. As for posthumous sympathy, it should be expressed as a regret at not having had the chance to know you personally, rather than a shudder of relief at having escaped your fate. Alice James's strategy for dealing with her condition is to represent her afflictions as comical and herself as rather absurd, like a person with the hiccoughs. The following entry is the response of the diary-persona to the news that after a lifetime of 'nervous disorders' she has, quite suddenly it seems, produced symptoms of a definitely fatal kind:

May 31st.

To him who waits, all things come! My aspirations may have been eccentric, but I cannot complain now, that they have not been brilliantly fulfilled. Ever since I have been ill, I have longed and longed for some palpable disease, no matter how conventionally dreadful a label it might have, but I was always driven back to stagger alone under the monstrous mass of subjective sensations, which that sympathetic being 'the medical man' had no higher inspiration than to assure me I was personally responsible for, washing his hands of me with a graceful complacency under my very nose. Dr. Torry was the only man who ever treated me like a rational being, who did not assume, because I was victim to many pains, that I was, of necessity, an arrested mental development too.

Notwithstanding all the happiness and comfort here, I have been going downhill at a steady trot; so they sent for Sir Andrew Clark four days ago, and the blessed being has endowed me not only with cardiac complications, but says that a lump that I have had in one of my breasts for three months, which has given me a great deal of pain, is a tumour, that nothing can be done for me but to alleviate pain, that it is only a question of time, etc. This with a delicate embroidery of 'the most distressing case of nervous hyperaesthesia' added to a spinal neurosis that has taken me off my legs for seven years; with attacks of rheumatic gout in my stomach for the last twenty, ought to satisfy the most inflated pathologic vanity. It is decidedly indecent to catalogue oneself in this way, but I put it down in a scientific spirit, to show that though I have no productive worth, I have a certain value as an indestructible quantity.[70]

She is determined that during this long 'mortuary moment'[71] her imprint shall represent her in a manner worthy of the Jameses. To preserve a humorous intelligence in the face of death, repudiating both self-dramatization and moral collapse, becomes her primary aim. She would like to die in full possession of her faculties for, as she puts it, 'a creature who has been denied all dramatic episodes might be allowed, I think, to assist at her extinction.'[72]

It would be wrong to leave the impression that Alice James's diary-persona is exclusively facetious. The comic spirit that pervades the book and confers a remarkable kind of anti-heroism on the end of it, is not a compulsive reflex trapping her in an eternal self-burlesque. On the occasions when she emerges from behind the screen of irony and fun her seriousness draws extra strength from the fact of its being worn lightly. In rare philosophic declarations, in expressions of feeling for her brothers and for her companion Katharine Loring, and in entries like the final one on 4 March 1892, in which she admits the extent of her suffering, she comes through with unabashed directness. To conclude this brief account a portion may be quoted of an entry dated 29 January 1890, on the subject of a collection of her parents' letters which she has come across. As always her manner is deft and controlled, marshalling language into a deliberate composition. Sprightly or serious, it is not her way to express herself without premeditation.

One of the most intense, exquisite and profoundly interesting experiences I ever had. I think if I try a little and give it form its vague intensity will take limits to itself, and the 'divine anguish' of the myriad memories stirred grow less. Altho' they were as the breath of life to me as the years have passed they have always been as present as they were at first and will be for the rest of my numbered days, with their little definite portion of friction and serenity, so short a span, until we three were blended together again, if such should be our spiritual necessity. But as I read it seemed as if I had opened up a post-script of the past and that I had had, in order to find them *truly*, really to lose them.[73]

From thinking of the quality of their lives she is moved to recall their deaths in 1882, less than a year apart, and concludes, 'and now I am shedding the tears I didn't shed then!'[74]

Writing about Katherine Mansfield as a diarist always presents a special difficulty. While Murry's edition of the *Journal of Katherine Mansfield* undoubtedly establishes her as a compelling and important voice whose contribution to the genre cannot be ignored, yet the miscellaneous and fragmentary form of the book makes it hard to deal with in the terms this study has proposed. It is not merely that so little of the book is in the form of regular dated entries; Anaïs Nin's diary as published dispenses with this form altogether. The problem is that much of what has been gathered into the *Journal* was not written as the conscious extension of a continuing book, but disconnectedly, without that unity of *occasion* which most diaries display. Some of the most striking passages in the book are in the form of unposted letters or morsels of short story. But if it cannot be regarded as a book of the self, its assemblage of autobiographical fragments contains the imprint of many *moments* of experience and feeling. A brief consideration of the character of these imprints will conclude this chapter on the language of self-projection in diaries.

Plainly apparent in the surviving pages of her earliest diaries is the influence of Marie Bashkirtseff (1860–84), whose diary of the impassioned artistic soul doomed to an early death was first published in 1887. This book, which Alice James managed to resist during its initial wave of popularity, imagining it to be 'the perverse of the perverse',[75] undoubtedly helped to establish an archetype of the reckless votaress of the Religion of Art. In 1906, in her late teens, Katherine Mansfield added the following line from Marie Bashkirtseff to a collection of quotations headed '*Die Wege des Lebens*', all pointing towards an ethic of heroic self-realization: 'Me marier et avoir des enfants! Mais quelle blanchisseuse—je veux la gloire.'[76] Two years later, two years of dramatic passion and struggle, she writes

Independence, resolve, firm purpose, and the gift of discrimination, *mental clearness*—here are the inevitables. Again, Will—the realization that Art is absolutely self-development. The knowledge that genius is dormant in every soul—that the very individuality which is at the root of our being is what matters so poignantly.[77]

So little remains, however, of what she later calls the 'huge complaining diaries'[78] of the turbulent years prior to her relationship with Middleton Murry (begun in 1912) that one can only guess at their tropical storminess.

From 1914 to her death in January 1923 the *Journal* comprises a rich though broken mosaic of her emotional and imaginative life—a life perpetually agitated by the fluctuations of her feeling about Murry, the struggle with her work, and the miserable state of her health. The imprint is of a tragic sense of life in which suffering is the essential mode of consciousness. As a rule she expresses herself passionately, evocatively, the impulse to write proceeding from a state of emotion rather than an idea. She renders herself as an ardent sensibility acutely responsive to currents of joy and anguish. The following passage is dated 21 January 1915; she is living with Murry ('J') but in love with Francis Carco who has written from the front asking her to visit him in France.

I am in the sitting-room downstairs. The wind howls outside, but here it is so warm and pleasant. It looks like a real room where real people have lived. My sewing-basket is on the table: under the bookcase are poked J's old house shoes. The black chair, half in shadow, looks as if a happy person had sprawled there. We had roast mutton and onion sauce and baked rice for dinner. It *sounds* right. I have run the ribbons through my under-clothes with a hairpin in the good home way. But my anxious heart is eating up my body, eating up my nerves, eating up my brain, now slowly, now at tremendous speed. I feel this poison slowly filling my veins—every particle becoming slowly tainted. Yes, love like this is a malady, a fever, a storm. It is almost like hate, one is so hot with it—and am never, never calm, never for an instant. I remember years ago saying I wished I were one of those happy people who can suffer so far and then collapse or become exhausted. But I am just the opposite. The more I suffer, the more of fiery energy I feel to bear it. Darling! Darling![79]

The sensibility that writes like this is also very definitely a *literary* one. The architecture of the passage, the selection of details to establish the air of deceptive 'rightness' in her visible outward state, the histrionic rhetoric of the climax—these are habits of expression that have been imbibed from literature.

Who is Katherine Mansfield writing to? What kind of imagined reader conditions her self-presentation? In considering this question it is necessary to distinguish autobiographical declaration from fragments of imaginative writing, though, as will be suggested in a moment, the one is always running into the other. A clue occurs in a passage written in Paris in May 1915 in which she tells of having spent the day in the imaginary company of Rupert Brooke, lately dead:

I crossed and recrossed the river and leaned over the bridges and kept thinking we were coming to a park when we weren't. You cannot think what a pleasure my invisible, imaginary companion gave me. If he had been alive it would never have possibly occurred; but—it's a game I like to play—to walk and talk with the dead who smile and are silent, and *free*, quite finally free. When I lived alone, I would often come home, put my key in the door, and find someone there waiting for me. 'Hullo! Have you been here long?'[80]

In February 1916, in a comparable though graver vein, she addresses herself to her beloved brother 'Chummie', killed the previous autumn. 'Dear brother, as I jot these notes, I am speaking to you. To whom did I always write when I kept those huge complaining diaries? Was it to myself?'[81] Expressing a sense of immediate communion with him she vows to 'write every day faithfully a little record of how I have kept faith with you',[82] and in her stories of New Zealand to perpetuate the magical recollections which they shared of even minute details of their childhood—'even of how the laundry-basket squeaked'.[83] Chummie, dead, belongs completely to her. Unlike a living friend to whom she might write a letter, he has no other existence beyond his responsiveness to her. His readiness to understand is fluid, taking the complementary shape of her need to express. It is not to be supposed, however, that all her subsequent diary-fragments are literally addressed to her brother. But the convention seems to persist whereby she is communicating to an idealized sympathetic responsiveness that has passed beyond the possibility of change, a consciousness with a distinct identity yet not alien. At a later stage, for example, it is the ghost of Chekhov, especially Chekhov the letter-writer, to whom she confides her loneliness and anguish.

As for the scraps of short story scattered through the volume, they present an interesting example of a writer's immediate experience undergoing the early stages of the metamorphosis into art. Memories, encounters, moments in a relationship, glimpses of others' lives— beyond their status as the facts of a day, are also potentially separable from this context as self-contained *aperçus* of the way life is. In a long passage dated December 1919 she describes how she is able 'to *live* over

either scenes from real life or imaginary scenes' which recreate themselves with an immediacy 'far realer, more in detail, *richer* than life'.[84]
Like Proust she recognizes the magic realism of first-hand experience
in which one is not physically present. There is a constant tension (as
for Anaïs Nin) between the roles of diarist and author; the self remembered and written about tends to become a fiction of the self remembering. In the following little paragraph the process can actually be
seen taking place; the shift from first, through second, to third person
narrative betokens the emergence of an aesthetic possibility in the situation:

I did not go to the *clinique* because of my chill. Spent the day in bed, reading
the papers. The feeling that someone was coming towards me was too strong
for me to work. It was like sitting on a bench at the end of a long avenue in a
park and seeing someone far in the distance coming your way. She tries to read.
The book is in her hand, but it's all nonsense, and might as well be upside down.
She reads the advertisements as though they were part of the articles.[85]

A really remarkable example of this practice of transposing the material
of her life into a narrative form is the passage entitled 'Anguish'
(February 1920). In it she describes the receipt of a letter from Murry
which seems to signal the end of their relationship. By casting it in the
third person, noting from the outside the behaviour of a character in a
story, she imparts to the situation an almost symbolic quality. She
puts the experience away from her and bestows it on a surrogate figure.
Now in reviving it she revives a suffering of which she has taken
the measure. The following extract is set in the nursing home at
Mentone whither the condition of her lungs has sent her:

The first bell rang. She got up, she began to dress, crying and cold. The second
bell. She sat down and steeled herself; her throat ached, ached. She powdered
herself thickly and went downstairs. In the *ascenseur*: 'Armand, cherchez-moi
une voiture pour deux heures juste.' And then one hour and a quarter in the
brilliant glaring noisy *salle*, sipping wine to stop crying, and seeing all the
animals crack up the food. The waitress kept jerking her chair, offering food.
It was no good. She left and went upstairs, but that was fatal. Have I a home?
A little cat? Am I any man's *wife*? Is it all over? He never tells me a thing—
never a thing—just all those entirely self-absorbed letters, and now just these
notes. What will come next? He *asks* if I believe he loves me, and says 'Don't
give me up', but as though *perfectly prepared* for it. She wrote out the telegram.
He is killing me, killing me. He wants to be free—that's all.[86]

In so far as a passage like this can be regarded as a diary-entry it exhibits a mode of self-presentation rare in the genre. As anyone will

discover who undertakes the exercise of reconstructing an emotional experience in the third person, it exaggerates quite strikingly the division of the self into beholder and beheld. This literary convention—describing one's feelings and actions as if they are those of another person—may be handled in a number of ways which obviously reveal one's self-valuation. It is clear from Katherine Mansfield's handling of it that she respects the emotional integrity of the 'character' she describes. She exerts no ironic knowingness into her narrative, nor implies that the emotional state depicted is anything but an authentic and appropriate response to the situation.

Seven 'styles of self-projection' have been examined in this chapter. The intention has been to exercise a way of talking about diaries which focuses attention on the special nature of the document, lying as it does in some indeterminate region between behaviour and art. In the following chapters the approach is not forgotten but yields precedence to other aspects of the genre which the diaries to be dealt with particularly exemplify.

6

✛✛

Ego and Ideal

RYDER, WINDHAM, BOSWELL

THE following chapter considers the variations on the theme of self-hood to be observed in three eighteenth-century diaries. For the diarists to be discussed, Ryder, Windham, and Boswell, the condition of the self and the direction of its development are paramount themes, the shaping concern of their autobiographical activity. In contrast to those diarists considered in Chapter 5, these three diary-personae express degrees of disengagement from the characters of which they are an aspect and from the everyday conduct of life of which they are spectators. At the same time they are preoccupied with the cultivation of a character and conduct with which they can be satisfied, which conforms to their ideal of personal development and the well-lived life. The diary frame of mind is marked by the pursuit of critically considered truth about the self, and by the disposition to will changes. Unlike the autobiography, which may tell in retrospect the history of self-development and the resolution of internal conflicts, the diary receives the actual form and pressure of these processes. In the language of the mind's encounter with itself in these regions of experience something may be seen of contemporary conceptions of the psychic life.

Many people and many diarists never seriously encounter the questions, What am I really like? In what directions would I wish to change myself? What am I becoming? What might I make of myself? In the concerns of those who do, two intersecting perspectives reveal themselves, a vertical and a horizontal axis, so to speak. From one perspective the concern is expressed as the struggle towards a goal, a state of self-development envisaged as superior to one's present condition. The alternate perspective views self-hood in terms of singleness and multi-plicity, identity being realizable either as the one authentic role among two or more contestants, or as a complex unity of dual or multiple aspects. In these latter terms, which tend to prevail in the self-conscious-ness articulated in diaries of the nineteenth and twentieth centuries, the predominant concern is to explore and be reconciled with the com-plexities of one's nature. Haydon's mirror reflects a variety of personae; for later diarists, introspection increasingly discovers a self divided. The spiritual disease of Hesse's 'Steppenwolf', Harry Haller, is manifested by many: '*Who am I?*' asks Sturt in October 1891; 'At one time Jesus, at another Judas. Nay, not so; the difference is not so well defined: but rather, at one time a survival from the last century, and at another a precursor of the next, with all manner of intermediate characters thrown in.'[1] Barbellion considers the same question repeatedly. 'It alarms me to find I am capable of such remarkable changes in character. I am fluid and can be poured into any mould.'[2] He is for ever discover-ing himself to be a hybrid—Boswell and Johnson in one person, Sir Thomas Browne and Marie Bashkirtseff, 'Christ and the Devil at the same time—or my sister once called me—a child, a wise man, and the Devil all in one.'[3] (His diary also exacerbates that 'modern' sensation of being the detached and somewhat cynical spectator of his own living, corrupting his sincerest moments into calculated performances.) Katherine Mansfield speaks of her sense of being split into 'hundreds of selves', and at the same time of knowing a 'persistent yet mysterious belief in a self which is continuous and permanent', a self which may perhaps flower in 'the moment of direct feeling when we are most ourselves and least personal'.[4] And Anaïs Nin expresses one of the primary themes of her book of the self thus:

I have always been tormented by the image of multiplicity of selves. Some days I call it richness, and other days I see it as a disease, a proliferation as dan-gerous as cancer. My first concept about people around me was that all of them were coordinated into a WHOLE, whereas I was made up of a multitude of selves, of fragments. I know that I was upset as a child to discover that we had only one life. It seems to me that I wanted to compensate for this by multiplying experience. Or perhaps it always seems like this when you follow all your impulses and they take you in different directions. In any case, when I was happy, always at the beginning of a love, euphoric, I felt I was gifted or living many lives fully. . . . It was only when I was in trouble, lost in a maze, stifled by complications and paradoxes that I was haunted or that I spoke of my 'madness', but I meant the madness of the poets.[5]

She evokes wonderfully the ambivalence inherent in this mode of self-encounter, with its alternation of promise and threat. The same recognition of one's manifold possibilities may be experienced as an invitation to know oneself in many colours, and as the harbinger of anarchy, the loss of one's bearings among incoherent, treacherous illusions of identity.

In contrast to this horizontal vision of the dual or multiple self, the vertical perspective is less concerned with *who* one is than with *how well* one is being it. One's character is assumed as a given entity which at any particular moment exists in a state of relative development on a scale that runs from personal and moral squalor up to harmonious completeness. The diaries of Ryder and Windham exhibit this orientation pretty consistently. In Boswell's self-encounter both perspectives appear, and it will be suggested that his journals register the experience by an individual psyche of the turbulent co-existence of old and new valuations of self-hood during a period of cultural transition.

As a document of dedication to an ideal of personal development Ryder's diary must be unrivalled. No other diary expresses in such detail the ideal to which its writer aspires, or documents so thoroughly the methods employed to achieve it. His aim is nothing less than to transform himself into the complete Augustan gentleman, through the power of diligent application. Not being by birth and upbringing an inheritor of this cultural syndrome, he perceives its features very distinctly but from a certain distance, as mediated to him by the *Spectator*. As the diary records it, his effort to encompass this mode of being is rather like that of an actor preparing himself for the part of a lifetime, or an immigrant seeking to be assimilated in a new culture. When the performance begins in earnest he must be so thoroughly schooled in its manners, so steeped in the frame of mind from which they flow, as to be indistinguishable from the real thing—perhaps, indeed, to *be* the real thing. For it is evident that he really longs to experience a transfiguration of his own consciousness, to feel the ineptitude, the shyness, the anxiety, the mental sluggishness dwindling away until there is no longer any need to exercise control over his performance; he will have become the kind of person to whom cultured urbanity is a way of life. If such a condition were ever to be achieved the diary would presumably die out together with the painful selfconsciousness of which it is the voice.

The ascendancy over Ryder's mind of Augustan culture as an ideal standard in all departments of life is well-nigh total. It provides him with a model against which to evaluate every aspect of his living, from external details of social behaviour to the tone and governance of his mind. In contrast to Boswell, for example, he looks towards an exceptionally coherent and positive vision of the perfected self. In his explicit formulations of ethical and social norms, in the terms in which he appraises his own and his friends' deportment and ideas, in the language of his criticism of literature, the same assumptions consistently reinforce one another. The vision is free of ambiguity and guaranteed to be attainable. Any difficulty he personally encounters in modelling himself after it must be attributed to his own inadequacy or lack of perseverance. There is something almost comical in this spectacle of a man reciting for his own edification all the tenets of his cultural moment and endeavouring to live by them. Quotation cannot begin to convey the range and frequency of his invocation of these normative values. Only a sustained reading makes clear the extent to which they possess his imagination. Yet there is this incongruity that his habitual self-presentation in the diary is utterly ingenuous and expressive of great moral earnestness. For humble transparent candour he is the equal of Pepys, taking few precautions with language to shield himself from the derision of the reader. The voice of a studious youth tells of his progress towards debonair sophistication.

Lifting himself up by the hair into his ideal character demands a complex supervision of both inner and outer man. The Augustan gentleman (like Justice) must not only exist in himself but be seen to exist. Dudley rarely shines in company, however, and is mortified at how little his virtues, such as they are, go forth from him. It is particularly unsettling when Aunt Billio ('a pretty great tattler') gives him the word on his reputation in the home town:

It was that I was not very sharp. I must confess this moved me a little. There is nothing touches a man so sensibly as what reflects upon his sense or understanding, especially because I thought I had maintained a very considerable character in Hackney in that respect. However, I am persuaded yet that I have in the general in Hackney the character of a man of good sense at least and, by some, that of an ingenious man. I believe indeed there are few persons who have so very different a character among different people as I have. Those that are thoroughly acquainted with me and see me upon all occasions, have been alone with me and are themselves of a pretty free temper and ready to raise subjects of conversation, conceive, I believe, a pretty good opinion of me, but others who see me only in a large company or assembly take me to be very stupid and dull.[6]

It may be possible to detect an unusual stiffness in his manner as he erects a little reassuring syntax between himself and Aunt Billio's stinging report. Heaven knows the pains he takes to develop his social aptitudes! Certainly no one could be more conscious of the impression he creates, or more anxious to improve it. He knows himself to be 'the worst person in the world to entertain a lady in conversation'.[7] He finds he is 'mighty apt to look silly and a little uneasy' when in company, and fears that 'something of a forbidding reserved air in me' puts people off.[8] He especially envies that freedom from anxiety about social success, the secret of which eludes him:

> I wish I could arrive at that talent of appearing indifferent in the company of the ladies. It is this that chiefly gives that life and spirit to a conversation which is agreeable and which the women especially universally like, and indeed what enters very much into the modern character of a gentleman.[9]

To advance in self-command there is nothing he would not do. To improve his conversation he reads books on the subject, and studies the *Spectator* 'with very great care and attention in order to observe the peculiar thoughts upon gallant subjects such as are proper to entertain the ladies with'.[10] He takes dancing lessons to the point where they distract him from his studies, and practises 'romping' with his sister-in-law, and 'boldness and confidence in addressing myself to persons' with whores.[11] Despite these efforts, successes at 'raillery' are few and tenuous. After one failure to 'maintain the conversation' he is moved to ask himself:

> Why cannot I be satisfied with the character of a man of sense and enjoy myself without the trifling inconsiderable reputation of a good tattler with a woman or a fine gentleman among the ladies? What I am now aiming at, the character of agreeable company to the women, when I have got it can be enjoyed by me but a little while, to lose the relish of it at last by matrimony. But yet I am strangely prejudiced in favour of this pleasure and I cannot tell how to exclude it out of my present ideas or prospect of happiness.[12]

This might appear at first to indicate a conflict of role-models, but actually there is no reason why the images of the 'man of sense' and the 'fine gentleman among the ladies' should be mutually exclusive. In Ryder's ideal self they should complement one another quite happily. What he is doing here is attempting to reconcile himself to a condition apparently beyond his power to alter, 'to reason myself into an easy state of mind', as he says in another connection.[13]

It is not surprising to discover that 'reasoning himself into states of mind' is a central process in his consciousness. Rational self-mastery is the goal towards which he strives—a state in which unproportioned thoughts and feelings will have no purchase on his mind. By clearly representing to himself the consequences of actions and the nature of his true interests, he will so reinforce the inclination towards the rationally determined good as to free himself from the sway of passion and folly. One of the special pleasures of studying diaries is finding the customary generalizations about the prevailing mentality of a cultural epoch validated in the day-to-day consciousness of a particular individual. In Dudley Ryder we have a man whose practice of self-government as he reports it, and whose mode of self-encounter as the diary directly registers it, enact almost to the letter the moral psychology of John Locke. Both in the experience of specific dilemma and in the effort to direct himself towards a general condition of mind he reflects in detail the conceptual structure of Book II, Chapter 21 ('Of Power'), of *An Essay Concerning Human Understanding*. Though the diary does not mention it there is every likelihood that he is familiar with the work, since he mentions and praises several other books by Locke, including *The Reasonableness of Christianity*, *Two Treatises of Civil Government*, and *Letters on Toleration*. In any case the question of whether he has actually read and imbibed Locke's discourse on the operations of the rationally determined will is immaterial. The point is that Ryder's conceptions of the means and ends of ethical consciousness derive their shape from the language of Locke, however received. A variety of instances of Ryder 'being a Lockean' present themselves. The following passage reports with charming self-congratulation the performance of a rational act in accordance with his own ethical ideal. The Latin phrase is a 'sentiment of Cicero's' on the proper disposition of the philosopher; Mr. Whatley has lately proposed it as a subject for discussion at the club.[14]

Came home. Found everybody but servants in bed, but I determined to sit up a while and read. My inclination led me to sit in the parlour by the fire because it was a little cold, though I was convinced it would be better to sit in my closet because I should be in danger of sleeping before the fire. However, I went into the parlour to sit down, and it came into my head that I was now a-going to break the very rule which I had laid down for myself to-day in some thoughts I wrote down upon *totus aptus ex sese*, viz. that I should habituate myself to submit to the determination of reason by taking care especially that in little matters where there is no greater temptation to the contrary but only the humour or sudden fit of inclination, I do nothing contrary to what I judge right and fit. This thought made me immediately resolve to go into my closet and sit there, which I did and I was mightily pleased with myself for this one act of resisting inclination. To bed at past 11.[15]

'Thus', as Locke says, 'by a due consideration, and examining any good proposed, it is in our power to raise our desires in a due proportion to the value of that good, whereby in its turn and place it may come to work upon the *will* and be pursued.'[16]

According to Locke (and Ryder) the good and happy man is not he who most energetically fights the good fight, but he who has least need to fight it, who is, like the angels, 'more steadily determined in his choice of good'.[17] The aim of intelligent men, therefore, must be to develop an increasingly clear perception of their true happiness, and then to concentrate on the image of it until 'we have formed appetites in our minds suitable to it and made ourselves uneasy in the want of it, or in the fear of losing it'.[18] Ryder is in full assent with this notion. He reports many examples of his endeavours to cultivate the taste and temper of his mind, and indeed much of the diary itself is an imprint of this operation. Not that it is always as easy matter; as Locke points out, mere rational assent even to the highest good of all will not suffice to fix it before the will.[19] This Ryder discovers repeatedly, as for example upon reading a sermon by Tillotson: 'I am only vexed with myself that what I hear or read in the way of religion has no more effect upon my life to assist my conduct, teach me to govern my passions, conquer my unruly inclinations and live by the rules of reason.'[20] None the less he places a good deal of faith in the salutary influence of literature upon the mind, for secular as well as spiritual benefit. Thus he reads Boileau for 'a polite natural way of thinking and writing' of which he would be glad to 'get the habit', and the *Spectator* 'to improve my style and manner of thinking'.[21] In both instances he explicitly refers to a style of *thinking* that he wishes to acquire; not merely the appearance of rational composure but the state of mind itself.

A third element in Ryder's ideal self, along with social accomplishment and a well-ordered mind, is a lively though moderated sensibility. Governing the passions doesn't mean suppressing them, and every gentleman should be able to summon up a feeling or two when a situation calls for it. Ryder, as might be expected, suffers some anxiety on this score. The following admission, which relates to his cousin Richard's funeral, is interesting not for the experience it relates, which is commonplace enough, but as yet another instance of Ryder's efforts at self-correction. (One may recall, incidentally, Richard Kay's performance in a similar situation.)

When we came there we sat down in the room where the coffin was, looked as grave and sad as we could, scarce any conversation at all. I was very much displeased with myself that I could not be much affected with such a posture of affairs, that the death of a relation made so little impression upon me and I did what I could to raise a little concern in me.[22]

However, there are many occasions on which he is able to report a quite gratifying susceptibility to appropriate emotion, as for example in response to music, literature, and religious meditation.[23] He records, too, a receptivity to nature, his sober expression of which contrasts sharply with the passages of nature-rhapsody that become *de rigueur* in nineteenth-century diaries: 'It was extremely pleasant walking in the fields, the first beginning of the spring when the sun begins to warm the earth and gild the fields and wonderfully agreeable to the mind and I feel a strong kind of cheerfulness and alacrity diffuses itself all over me.'[24]

The irruption of Sally Marshall into his life confronts him with a disquieting conflict of values. With half of his mind he experiences this futile passion as painful, contemptible, and demoralizing; the other half takes a dismal and even perverse pleasure in the role of the disconsolate lover. The diary tends to express the former disposition and reports the manifestations of the latter with concern, as though discussing symptoms of mental illness in a near relation. The lover, as Dudley learns only too well, is far from being *totus aptus ex sese*. Under Mrs. Marshall's spell he can control neither the flow of his thoughts nor even his physiological reactions, being on several occasions reduced to tears—a collapse which he is not Sterne enough to regard with any satisfaction. His better self, that is to say, the frame of mind he would generally like to cultivate, can only disapprove of this subjection: 'I could not help indulging my sorrow and melancholy and desire of her, and yet my reason tells me it will never do.'[25] Yet however earnestly he seeks to 'reason himself into an easy state of mind' the fact remains that 'there is a kind of secret pleasure in this longing and desire'.[26] When cousin Joseph Billio falls for Mrs. Marshall too, the two lovers unburden themselves to one another and endeavour to think 'this love of ours as a very foolish vain thing that proceeded from an impotency of mind and ought not to be encouraged'.[27] Though he may seek to discourage it, this same 'impotency of mind' leads Dudley

to contemplate suicide[28] and to attempt poetry. To this latter undertaking he brings his usual earnestness as well as his capacity for humble
candour. The following rueful assessment of his gift, with its claim to
at least an inkling of inspiration if not much technique, is almost heart-
rending in its respect for an acknowledged ideal:

I find I have no genius for poetry. Thoughts don't flow in easily and I am very
long in making the rhyme. But I have so much of the poetic genius as to know
what poetic fire and rapture is. I find sometimes myself carried a little away by
a little poetic fit in which I find harmonious numbers jingle in my head and
my thoughts almost naturally run into something like verses. But these fits
hold but a very little while. A little thought or study or endeavour to form and
polish my lines quite puts an end to it and then it is extremely difficult to
recall it.[29]

How, one wonders, did such an innocent ever get to be Chief Justice of
England? Certainly he cannot have reckoned very highly his own
chances of making a figure in the world when, during the worst period
of his infatuation, he has this to say of young Mr. Powell, the raffish
Oxonian whom Sally Marshall finds such good company:

He is never ruffled or disturbed by any passion and acts with ease and tranquil-
lity. Indeed I think he is of a make very fit to become a great man. He has a
taste for gallantry, but enjoys it without any of the disturbance and difficulty
that attends it and can leave off when he finds it inconvenient; even in things
that have an air of debauchery and are less justifiable he appears in them as if he
acted from judgment and consideration.[30]

One other aspect to be noted of Ryder's surveillance of his own
Becoming is the way he deals with the attractions of posing. Apart
from the role of urbane gentleman—which of course he doesn't regard
as a 'pose' at all, but as the epitome of cultivated naturalness—he is distinctly wary of affectation. He notes it as a fault to which he is particularly prone,[31] and frequently comments on the appearance of it in
others. Here he is, observing a manifestation of it in himself:

It is a strange thing how vanity and love of being observed and esteemed mixes
itself insensibly in our most ordinary actions. I could not help as I went along
pleasing myself in hopes somebody or other that knew me would meet me in
that thinking studious posture. It might give them a notion of me as a great
thinker, that knows how to employ myself alone and take pleasure in retirement. This is not the only time I have had that thought in my head and it has
made me put on a more fixed countenance than ordinary.[32]

What he fears is the dispersal of his integrity that might be occasioned by the indulgence of false self-presentations—the same integrity that prompts such candid self-appraisal in the diary. Nor would he want to become the victim of fluctuating moods, as seems to be the predicament of his manic-depressive friend Mr. Whatley. Dudley tends to look on this gentleman's extravagant performances with a mixture of wonder, sympathy and suspicion. Some of Mr. Whatley's antics are decidedly aggravating, and his attacks of melancholy incomprehensible. But in general Dudley can only pity the 'unhappy disposition and frame of soul' which, being 'so very unconstant', will likely make it impossible for his friend to 'do anything considerable in any way or profession'.[33] It is a warning to any young man to keep himself together and repel the vapours. There, but for the grace of God and some resistance to self-indulgence, goes Dudley. A stirring production of Rowe's play *Tamerlane* causes him to remark 'The play itself is good, but I find myself too much moved and affected with tragedies to take much pleasure in them. And besides they fill in and justify too much my natural humour, that I think comedy much more proper for me.'[34]

To sum up: Ryder's diary articulates the desire to unify the self, to pattern it after a socially validated norm, to feel himself rising towards a plateau of assured self-containment. 'Fluctuations of self' (Ivy Jacquier's phrase) give him no satisfaction; they only render him uneasy. In Mr. Whatley he sees, as he would no doubt see in Boswell, 'a fellow o' the strangest mind i' the world'—a condition verging on madness. To have 'so very different a character among different people'[35] he regards as a sign, not of his having a manifold personality, but of his failure to project a unitary one.

Before proceeding to Boswell, in whose diaries the theme of selfhood is so all-engrossing, this discussion will pass, as in Chapter 4, from Ryder to Windham. The progression is an appropriate one, since Windham expresses fierce dissatisfaction with a state of self-development which already encompasses everything Ryder could have dreamed of—brilliance, cultivation, success and great personal attraction. Unlike Ryder, however, whose aspirations to self-mastery had no higher goal than a respectable level of accomplishment, Windham is driven by a compulsion to be transcendently excellent. He disparages his own prodigious talents and achievements, and sets himself with perverse concentration to the study of mathematics and the translation of classical authors. The conviction that he was squandering his

life was to persist to the end of his days. Byron's diary mentions an
account by 'Conversation' Sharp of an interview with Windham in
1810, shortly before his fatal operation:

Windham,—the first in one department of oratory and talent, whose only fault
was his refinement beyond the intellect of half his hearers,—Windham,—half
his life an active participator in the events of the earth, and one of those who
governed nations,—*he* regretted,—and dwelt much on that regret, that 'he
had not entirely devoted himself to literature and science!!!' His mind
certainly would have carried him to eminence there, as elsewhere;—but I
cannot comprehend what debility of that mind could suggest such a wish.[36]

In attributing this seemingly unreasonable demand on the self to mental
'debility', Byron is in part, of course, merely repeating his affected contempt for 'scribblers'. Yet there is indeed an appearance of unbalance
in this outstanding mind's subjection to such an unappeasable dissatisfaction. For without much doubt Windham's compulsiveness is by its
nature incapable of satisfaction. A relentless super-ego enlists him
permanently on the side of Civilization against Eros, and engages him
in conspicuously useless tasks, the never-finished quality of which
cheats him of the psychic reward due to his performances in other areas.

   In terms of the horizontal and vertical dimensions of self-development proposed at the beginning of this chapter, Windham seeks to
concentrate himself into intense singleness and to raise himself to levels
of enhanced mental potency. Typical of the way he deals with himself
in the diary is the following passage, written at the end of 1786, in
which he surveys his utilization of the preceding weeks:

In the whole time I have written but about three pages of translation. I have
never, that I recollect, sat down two hours together to mathematics. If after
this I feel in myself a great diminution of power, if my faculties are perceptibly
less active, my comprehension less clear, and the command of my thoughts less
certain; if the confidence and alacrity with which I engage in any work are
greatly decreased, and a proportionate tendency is felt to relapse into my old
distrust of myself, and fear of competition; it may seem unreasonable to charge
the alteration to the effects of London air.[37]

One may note the rhetorical formality of this address, culminating in a
grimly restrained sarcasm. Passages like this are uttered in the tone of
a judge directing the jury to bring in a verdict of 'guilty'. The diary
seldom relaxes from this austere manner. Even when giving expression
to personal feelings, which he rarely does, he maintains a stiffly public
tone. In this account of an Eton reunion he twice veers from the per-

sonal to the impersonal mode in mid-sentence, as if rendered uncomfortable by the exposure of sentiment:

The presence of so many persons, all imparting the ideas of a particular period, and many of them unconnected in one's mind with any other, produced in a considerable degree the effect that one would suppose: it would have done so in a degree still greater if I had not happened to be in a state unfavourable rather to such impressions. As it was, I felt at some periods during the course of the evening sensations of enjoyment, such as one has not often known since life was in the spring, and which contributed in their turn to recall and impress the images by which they were produced. I remained there, rather enjoying one's own feelings than the conversation . . .[38]

The condition for which Windham strives may be expressed as that of a sentient instrument of fine and varied powers experiencing the satisfaction of operating at one hundred per cent efficiency. This requires of the sentience that controls the machine an unceasing vigilance against the imperfect tuning that prevents the achievement of optimum performance. Failure of this vigilance infallibly leaves Windham feeling weary, stale, flat, and unprofitable. To denote the rare experience of his faculties operating in superb unison he makes peculiar, italicized use of the word, '*feel*', in the form of a noun. Thus, for example:

Rose at twelve and continued at home till dinner, with the *feel* that sufficiently proved the importance of exertion to happiness. My mind was so light, and my powers so active and vigorous, that no undertaking appeared difficult. The activity of the mental powers awakened the feelings also, and made me susceptible of enjoyment, to which I am in general a stranger.[39]

Increasingly, it seems, the focal performance in which he makes trial of his powers is the parliamentary speech. It is a performance which calls forth all the qualities which compose his ideal self—strength of intellect, courageous self-possession, clarity and brilliance of expression, personal magnetism—all put to a crucial test. To be acknowledged as a first-rate speaker will not satisfy him. Windham's demon persuades him that he owes himself, and should be satisfied with, nothing less than consummate perfection. So he continually disparages what are evidently exceptional pieces of oratory, in such a way as to admit yet contemn the superiority. It is interesting to compare the narrative strategy of the following piece with Pepys's account of his parliamentary appearance, quoted on page 100.

. . . but somehow, by the time I got there [the House], my mind had got into some disorder, and my spirits into some agitation; and by the time Burke had finished, I found myself in no good state to speak. The same state continued,

though with a little amendment, till the time of my rising: yet I contrived somehow to steady and recover myself in the course of speaking, and so far executed
what I had prepared, that I conceive it to be the fashion to talk of what I did as
rather a capital performance. 'Tis a strong proof on what cheap terms reputation for speaking is acquired, or how capricious the world is of its allotment
of it to different people.[40]

Here is a manoeuvre prompted clearly by 'my old distrust of myself
and fear of competition'. Taken together, Windham's analyses of his
parliamentary showings reveal a conflict in his mind between an eager-
ness for fame and praise, and an almost reflex disparagement of his
achievements.

A particularly revealing little crisis of self-esteem registered in the
diary occurs while Windham is visiting the English positions at the
siege of Valenciennes in 1793. In not availing himself of an opportunity
to take part in a dangerous aggressive action he gives himself cause to
impugn his physical courage. Notwithstanding the fact that he has
accompanied the Duke of York (the English Commander) through
some 'pretty smart fire'[41] which succeeded in decapitating a sergeant
only a few feet away, he suffers a moral vexation which takes away all
the savour of his trip. Everyone assured him it would be 'absurd' to
engage in the assault, yet his conscience remains uneasy: 'Was it a
thing which would have been more praised or blamed, had it been
done? Would it, considering all circumstances, have raised the character of the actor or have depressed it?'[42] A regard for reputation looms
large in his consideration, yet, as in the case of his parliamentary
speeches, he imposes on himself a far stricter standard of what is worthy
of honour than anyone else could. A sort of aristocratic fastidiousness
pervades his valuation of his own conduct, a concern for his *areté*.
'I cannot help viewing myself in the character of a man who has fallen
in some measure below what was expected from him. Though that is,
I hope and trust, a false impression; yet, even if nothing has been lost,
it is difficult not to regret what might have been gained.'[43] It seems an
essentially barren image to which the diary-persona aspires. Despite
the relatively late date of Windham's diary there is little in it that
points forward to a Romantic valuation of the self. The appeal of roles
to the self-dramatizing imagination has little force compared with
the power over him of guilty dissatisfaction and chagrin. He keeps
himself on a tight rein, allowing himself the indulgence of few en-
thusiasms. The encounter with self is basically a struggle for supremacy
over nature.

In terms of the orientation of the developing self the diaries of Ryder and Windham are relatively uncomplex. The same thing cannot be said for Boswell's. The documenting of the evolution of Boswell *Sapiens*—for that at least is what the author hopes it will turn out to have been—weaves together a number of different elements. No really stable vision of the self-to-come illuminates the turbulent succession of shapes in which he beholds himself. Yet to trace the theme of Becoming through fifteen years of its incessant agitation is to recognize distinct patterns of fluctuation in Boswell's attitude to the question. In the section that follows an attempt will be made to expose these patterns to view and to indicate shifts in perspective that occur with the passage of time. The account is necessarily an abbreviated one; as usual the intention is to indicate the individual's place in the mosaic of the genre rather than accord each one an extensive separate treatment. In the case of a diarist of Boswell's stature and profusion it is equally impossible in a study of this kind to leave him out or to treat him as he deserves. Fortunately the injustice done to him by the relative brevity of what follows is redressed by the existence of some excellent extended studies of Boswell's autobiographical writings, most notably in John Morris's *Versions of the Self* and in the introductions by F. A. Pottle and others to each volume of the Yale edition of the Journals.

One constant fact of Boswell's self-encounter is the prodigious changeability of his own nature. Moreover, he experiences change in himself not as a graduated process but as the passage of successive states. An account which he sends to the *London Chronicle* (24 October 1769) of one of his more eccentric exploits, concludes with the words, ' "A man so various," &c.'[44]—an allusion whose context is worth quoting for the self-image it reflects:

> A man so various, that he seemed to be
> Not one, but all mankind's epitome:
> Stiff in opinions, always in the wrong;
> Was everything by starts, and nothing long;
> But, in the course of one revolving moon,
> Was chymist, fiddler, statesman, and buffoon:
> Then all for women, painting, rhyming, drinking,
> Besides ten thousand freaks that died in thinking.
> Blest madman, who could every hour employ,
> With something new to wish, or to enjoy!
> (Dryden, 'Absalom and Achitophel', 545—54)

How seriously Boswell recognizes himself in this caricature would
be hard to say, but the resemblance will certainly endure a second look.
As for the tone of the description, Boswell might be offended or grati-
fied by it, depending on the level of his spirits. The paradoxical 'Blest
madman' sums up the ambiguity of its application to him: from one
perspective Boswell views his variety as a gift, from another as an
affliction. And of course neither perspective commands his vision for
long at a time. In any case, whether he deplores or delights in being
'everything by starts', the condition is largely of his own making and
may be attributed as much to his journal habit as to any other single
cause. For the journal is dedicated to capturing 'the whims that may
seize me and the sallies of my luxuriant imagination'.[45] Every odd, contrary, or eccentric psychic manifestation that another person would
ignore as peripheral to his 'self', Boswell pursues, brings to light and
makes significant. Most people settle into conventional images of themselves, which become increasingly definitive and self-policing. Boswell
positively encourages the play of diverse inclinations, and instead of
repressing contradictory tendencies in himself he lets them contribute
to his self-concept. The same is true of the various role-models that he
adopts, either to enhance experience by stimulating his imagination
with associative fantasies, or to absorb by imitation the qualities of a
superior being. The *London Journal*, especially, records many 'characters', real and fictitious, individuals and types, whom he takes as objects for impersonation, among them the Spectator, Macheath (from
The Beggar's Opera), a blackguard, a Man of Pleasure, West Digges
(the actor), and of course Dr. Johnson. In keeping an album, so to
speak, of the different guises that have appealed to him, he promotes
his own multiplication.

At the risk of simplifying the case somewhat it is possible to see
in Boswell a perpetual oscillation between opposing codes of self-
government. By unhappiness and anxiety he is drawn towards the
need to gather himself together and exert an organizing dominion
over the chaos of his nature. An introjected authoritarianism causes
him to disapprove of the degraded and impulsive frivolity that renders
him a feather to every passing gust. In such moods he delivers vigorous
exhortations to himself and sets his father and Dr. Johnson back on the
pedestals from which they can superintend his conduct. The most
articulate expression of this state of mind is the 'Inviolable Plan' which
he draws up for himself in Utrecht in the autumn of 1763.[46] He has
come to Holland to study law, having abandoned his military ambitions

and submitted, with Johnson's approval, to his father's wishes. Lonely and insecure, his morale at a low point, he sets out in formal terms the considerations which are henceforth supposed to govern his life. Accusing himself of having been 'idle, dissipated, absurd, and unhappy' he issues a brisk injunction to take himself firmly in hand: 'You are now determined to form yourself into a man.' The 'solid principles' which he proceeds to enunciate comprise the armour of rational piety and the strait-jacket of self-control—means, respectively, to 'immortal felicity' and success at the Scottish bar. Unlike Ryder, for whom the 'pleasure of being a respected gentleman' is a truly desirable goal and one which summons him to transcend his familiar self, Boswell tends to stress obligation ('the duties of a *Laird* of Auchinleck') and the need for stoic resolution to suppress his natural bent. Discipline is the keynote, prompting a series of commands: 'attain propriety of conduct . . . avoid affectation . . . remember religion and morality . . . have constant command of yourself . . . keep firm . . . be excessively careful against rattling . . . yield not to whims, nor ever be rash.' Moreover he should govern his emotional reactions more sternly and not indulge a disposition to melancholy: 'That is the sign of a weak and diseased mind. A hysteric lady or a sickly peevish boy may be so swayed. But let not antipathies move a man. It is not sensibility. You can cure it and at all times do so.'

When, however, a spell of good fortune restores his morale and puts the swagger back into his walk, the role of a 'decent gentleman' conforming himself to the patterns of family, profession, station in life, and the established church, loses its appeal. In such periods the journal-persona (which sometimes addresses the rest of Boswell as 'you') is far more indulgently disposed towards 'wildness of fancy and ludicrous imagination'.[47] The need disappears to be continually reminding himself to be '*retenu*'—his particular term for a contained and sober deportment. His unpredictable nature promises a spectacular development and should not be confined by a pre-established model. Here he is in July 1764 at the outset of his European tour, the gloomy days at Utrecht behind him, commenting on his behaviour at a German wedding:

I was rather too singular. Why not? I am in reality an original character. Let me moderate and cultivate my originality. God would not have formed such a diversity of men if he had intended that they should all come up to a certain standard. That is indeed impossible while black, brown, and fair, serious, lively, and mild, continue distinct qualities. Let me then be Boswell and render him as fine a fellow as possible. At one we went home. I made Mademoiselle play me a sweet air on the harpsichord to compose me for gentle slumbers. Happy man that I am![48]

This is all very well, and testifies to the renewal of that ready-for-anything exuberance which sheer mobility, as much as anything, arouses in him. His enthusiasm makes him infectious company and successive encounters reflect to him an image of an exceptional fellow for whom nothing is impossible. If he could always keep moving like this the determination to 'be Boswell and render him as fine a fellow as possible' might commit him to nothing more (nor less) exacting than perpetual energy. His passage through Europe takes him into a series of well-established *mises-en-scène*, many of which furnish ready-made roles to the visitor, like costumes handed out at the door. For the most challenging performances which he arranges for himself at Môtiers, Ferney, and on Corsica, he prepares himself thoroughly in advance. Amid such constant alteration the most protean revolutions in himself can seem natural and resourceful instead of giddy and unstable as they tend to do in more settled circumstances. His vocation is self-realization, in terms not of developing his potential but of discovering the full range of his responsiveness. Openness is all:

As to the future part of it [his life], I can as yet say nothing. I may be thrown into situations which may give me quite a new turn of thinking, make me quite a new man. I have already experienced this in some degree. Since I parted from Mr. Samuel Johnson at Harwich, what a variety of minds have I had![49]

From this perspective the role of 'Mr. Boswell of Auchinleck', which has served at times to banish all other roles as chimerical, appears to be merely one among many in which his talent for being 'all mankind's epitome' has been invested. The danger is, of course, that when he finally reaches the end of the many scenes which have lent him an identity, and comes to rest in his existential self, he will find no one there to meet him.

His return to England, however, early in 1766, he records as an unusually satisfying epoch in the progress of self. After an absence of two and a half years into which he has crammed some pretty remarkable experiences, he comes to measure his stature against the self he left behind, hoping to find a gain of at least a cubit. His journal for the first few days is written in the jotted second-person form of his memoranda, and contains such notes as the following:

Felt by comparison with former days in London how superior you was ... Fine house pleased you, but felt yourself so detached from interest and worldly vanities, was like a Johnson in comparison of former days . . . You was quite master of yourself. You found that, when now enlarged and enlightened by travel, even worth could not make you often bear uncouth Scots manners. . .[50]

He seeks confirmation of the view that he is in a fair way towards the acquisition of a distinct and settled character, one that joins bold originality with refined composure in a creative synthesis. In the notes of a conversation with his friend Temple, whose advice 'to be reserved and grave' and 'to acquire habits of study and self-command' had been registered in the summer of 1763,[51] he reveals a dominant concern: 'You had showed him some leaves of your journal, which he liked much. You said, "Temple, if I was your son, would you be pleased with me?" He replied with real truth, "Entirely pleased." '[52] Johnson has told him, ' "Now you have five and twenty years, and you have employed 'em well." '[53] Boswell is arming himself with quasi-parental expressions of approval in anticipation of a reaction from Lord Auchinleck which may be a good deal less enthusiastic. He has often been the cause of anger and exasperation for his father and now, with his fond mother lately dead, he must return to Edinburgh to prove his enhanced worth to a stern judge.

Brady, in his introduction to the journal volume entitled *Boswell in Search of a Wife*, calls the period 1766–9 Boswell's 'marvellous years',[54] a time in which he is more confidently at one with himself than ever before or after. A recurring note of satisfaction with the way he has turned out sounds in his pages, as in the following complacent extravaganza:

I felt myself quite strong, and exulted when I compared my present mind with my mind some years ago. Formerly my mind was quite a lodging-house for all ideas who chose to put up there, so that it was at the mercy of accident, for I had no fixed mind of my own. Now my mind is a house where, though the street rooms and the upper floors are open to strangers, yet there is always a settled family in the back parlour and sleeping-closet behind it; and this family can judge of the ideas which come to lodge. This family! this landlord, let me say, or this landlady, as the mind and the soul are both she. I shall confuse myself with metaphor.[55]

The very next entry declares, 'The truth is I am now conscious of having attained to a superior character, and so rest satisfied.'[56] As a rising young advocate, an adventurous cosmopolitan, friend of the notable, and author of *Corsica*, he seems to be receiving assurances that he really is becoming Boswell. The years are full of incident, as several continuing concerns and involvements provide him with a satisfying variety of outlets. Reflecting this orientation towards the external world the journal becomes quite sporadic, except when a London jaunt demands to be recorded in detail or when the perturbations in the summer of 1769 over his father's re-marriage and his own choice of Peggy Montgomerie need to make themselves articulate. These latter crises, pregnant with serious consequences, threaten to revive a wildness of mind which he had hoped was safely behind him. In his journal he records, as from a lucid distance, the manifestations of a passion which amazes him:

SUNDAY 16 JULY [1769]. After a wretched, feverish night I awaked in a dreadful state. I have no doubt that evil spirits, enemies to mankind, are permitted to tempt and torment them. 'Damn him. Curse him,' sounded somehow involuntarily in my ears perpetually. I was absolutely mad. I sent for worthy Grange, and was so furious and black-minded and uttered such horrid ideas that he could not help shedding tears, and even went so far as to say that if I talked so he would never see me again. I looked on my father's marrying again as the most ungrateful return to me for my having submitted so much to please him. I thought it an insult on the memory of my valuable mother. I thought it would totally estrange him from his children by her. In short, my wild imagination made it appear as terrible as can be conceived. I rose and took a little broth, and, in order to try if what I liked most could have an effect on me when in such a frame, I went to the chapel in Carrubber's Close, which has always made me fancy myself in heaven. I was really relieved. I thought of M., and loved her fervently. But I was still obstinate. A clergyman from Leith preached on these words, 'I have learned, in whatever state I am, therewith to be content.' He said many good things on contentment, and that the text informed us it was to be *learnt*. I was averse to learn any good.[57]

A few days earlier he has recorded an interview with his father which has left him with a strange mixture of respect and aggrieved hostility. The entry concludes, 'I am truly a composition of many opposite qualities.'[58]

The crisis passes. In the same month, November 1769, Lord Auchinleck remarries and Boswell marries Peggy. Relations between father and son are slowly mended. For several years the journal continues to hibernate in the intervals between the London jaunts which are the great treats of his life, filled with energetic literary socializing. He mentions in March 1772 his by no means newly conceived 'constant plan to write the life of Mr. Johnson',[59] and in the journals of these visits he is openly studying his subject. As he remarks during the visit to Ashbourne in September 1777, 'my journal of every portion of time which I have had the happiness ... to be with him contains valuable materials for his life'.⁶⁰ And of course in the autumn of 1773 the tour to the Hebrides prompts another bout of full-scale journalizing. The resumption of the regular documenting of his ordinary life occurs in June 1774 on the opening day of the Summer Session of the Edinburgh courts. The session is rendered climactic for Boswell by the trial and execution for sheep-stealing of his client John Reid. As for his inner condition, it becomes clear to the reader, and to Boswell himself, that the stable balance of forces in his nature is under stress. Elements are at work in him that threaten his peace, and in the journal he renews that attentiveness to his own interior weather that will enable him to superintend changes in the climate. The tenor of his writing becomes markedly more sober as a lucid seriousness banishes the earlier flamboyance with which he has recorded the signs of his times. Out of the multifarious promise of his younger days there is emerging a man with a great future behind him.

With the passage of time the tendency to indulge in fantastical whims has matured into a susceptibility to Weaknesses of a potentially devastating kind. In returning to plague him at a time when his situation—as a married man with children and a position in society—makes him much less flexible in his response, the evils of his youth take on a more threatening form. James Boswell, Advocate, can't go whoring or catch a clap with the relative insouciance of his younger days. Nor can he greet the recurrence of his old fits of acute depression ('hypochondria') with anything but foreboding. It compels him to realize that a formed character is not somehow self-immunizing against the fevers of youth, but may have to struggle for self-mastery all the length of its days, perhaps in a losing battle. Here he relates a particularly disturbing attack in which he feels himself thrown right back into the swirling waters. (The brother John to whom he refers has been for some years an intermittently violent lunatic.)

TUESDAY 27 FEBRUARY 1776. For some time past my mind has been in a troubled, fretful state. I had a fit of gloomy passion this morning at breakfast, and threw a guinea note in the fire because my wife objected to my subscribing three shillings for a miscellany by a Miss Edwards. I however rescued the note with the tongs before it was consumed, and, though a good part of it was burnt, I got its value from the Royal Bank. This incident shocked me, because it made me dread that I might in some sudden rage do much worse. I attended to business tolerably in the forenoon, and dictated tolerably in the afternoon.

Grange drank tea with us. At night I was in an inanimate, sullen frame, and sat poring over the fire in heavy uneasiness. My dear wife was at pains to console me, and relieved me somewhat; but I had a dismal apprehension of becoming as melancholy as my poor brother John, and the weakness of mind which is thought to occasion that distemper made me miserably vexed from the consideration of being despised. I wondered when I recollected how much of my life since my marriage had been free from hypochondria; and it galled me that at present I was so afflicted with it that I had no just ideas or sensations of any kind. I was anxious to be with Dr. Johnson; but the confused state of my affairs, and my tender concern at being absent from my wife and children, distressed me. I was exceedingly unhappy. I could fix my mind upon no object whatever that could engage it. Futurity was dark, and my soul had no vigour of piety.[61]

As for his sexual proclivities, he apparently succeeds in adapting himself to the role of a contentedly married man for several years before they rise up to threaten a disintegration of his fabric. Even before his marriage, in an entry dated 6 September 1769, intimations of infidelity entered his consciousness:

I recollected my former inconstancy, my vicious profligacy, my feverish gallantry, and I was terrified that I might lose my divine passion for Margaret, in which case I am sure I would suffer more than she. I prayed devoutly to heaven to preserve me from such a misfortune, and became easier.[62]

Now, after some years of marriage, they come to torment him with a vengeance. For months, even years, the allure of sexual variety obsesses him. Typically, he experiences the psychic discordance of sexual unrest much more acutely than people who are unaccustomed to active self-encounter. As in the past when racked by a moral or philosophical dilemma, he seeks an authoritative Ruling which will break the deadlock. But Johnson's views on the subject are unrelenting. When, during his London jaunt in the spring of 1776, Boswell finally lets himself go, he does so without the consolations of philosophy. Here is the conclusion of an evening of heavy drinking:

But when I got into the street, the whoring rage came upon me. I thought I would devote a night to it. I was weary at the same time that I was tumultuous. I went to Charing Cross Bagnio with a wholesome-looking, bouncing wench, stripped, and went to bed with her. But after my desires were satiated by repeated indulgence, I could not rest; so I parted from her after she had honestly delivered to me my watch and ring and handkerchief, which I should not have missed I was so drunk. I took a hackney-coach and was set down in Berkeley Square, and went home cold and disturbed and dreary and vexed, with remorse rising like a black cloud without any distinct form; for in truth my moral principle as to chastity was absolutely eclipsed for a time. I was in the miserable state of those whom the Apostle represents as working all uncleanness with greediness. I thought of my valuable spouse with the highest regard and warmest affection, but had a confused notion that my corporeal connection with whores did not interfere with my love for her. Yet I considered that I might injure my health, which there could be no doubt was an injury to her. This is an exact state of my mind at the time. It shocks me to review it.[63]

Without any of his former bravado he soberly recounts his temporary possession by his demons, the 'eclipse' not only of his 'moral principle as to chastity' but of his very self. It was I , yet it was not I. As he says on 8 December 1776 when Mrs. Boswell insists on reading the journal's many 'explicit instances' of recent whoring and resolves 'never again to consider herself as my *wife*' (though remaining a friend): 'I was awaked from my dream of licentiousness.'[64]

The same condition confronts him repeatedly when he writes down the history of his drinking bouts and the frightful scenes of madness and violence in which they sometimes culminate. Over the winter of 1775–6 the lucid diarist watches as drink and a passion for gambling strengthen their hold. On the morning after a particularly brutish excess, in which he was so 'shockingly affected' as to throw furniture at Mrs. Boswell, he resolves to reform his conduct. He continues:

There is something agreeably delusive in fresh resolution. Reason tells me that I cannot expect to be better restrained now than by former vows; and yet, like a man who has had several blanks in the lottery and fancies that another ticket will certainly be a prize, I flatter myself that I shall have it to say that from the 11 of November 1775 I maintained an uninterrupted moderation in drinking. Indeed the horrid consequences with which my last night's debauch might have been attended may probably awe my mind.[65]

But when a momentum has set in, the prospect of 'horrid consequences' does not lend a kind of easiness to the next abstinence. Boswell can feel himself being carried a growing distance away from that possession of himself which seemed for a while to have been achieved.

Is there anything he can do to arrest or reverse this process? All through the journal he has alternated between the sense of having a power of self-determination, and the sense of floating helplessly on his own tides. Even the grammar in which he articulates psychological experience shifts constantly between the active and passive voices, following the fluctuations of his sense of being the author of his own life. Reporting a conversation on this subject with the second Lady

Auchinleck, whose steadiness of mind temporarily restores Boswell's belief in that quality, he employs an excellent image for this consciousness of dualism:

She said to me, very justly, 'You talk as if men were mere machines, and had not a power of governing their conduct by reason.' Indeed nothing is more dangerous than to lay the bridle on the neck of inclination, and acquiesce in its leading us along without any fixed rule.[66]

But the prospect of having to tug at that bridle all one's life long is certainly pretty demoralizing and perhaps equally dangerous. The ideal state therefore is that in which the inclinations are so entranced by some beneficent power that they keep to the high road of their own accord. Needless to say, he experiences this condition chiefly in the company of Samuel Johnson. He would like to know it also in the relationship with Lord Auchinleck, and sometimes does so:

THURSDAY 26 SEPTEMBER [1776]. Pruned some [*sic*] with my father. Was really in a comfortable frame, and felt more agreeably when under parental awe than when unrestrained. It put a lid on my mind and kept it from boiling vehemently. Being thus kept quiet, I was happier than when agitated with ebullitions.[67]

But a filial relationship with Lord Auchinleck, while exerting plenty of constraint, offers little in the way of gratification. Under his father's sway Boswell feels composed and morally secure, but not valued. Speaking of his leave-taking before his 1778 jaunt to London he says, 'I am depressed in his presence, and cannot get free of the imagination that I am still a boy.'[68] To restore his stature in his own eyes he takes his little daughter Veronica along with him. 'Having a child of my own before me elevates me to the rank of a father and counteracts the depressing imagination to a certain degree. It is like having a little footstool to raise one.'[69] With Johnson such ruses are unnecessary. One reason why the journals of his visits to Johnson are so much more extensive than those of his Edinburgh existence (beyond their material-gathering function), is that the Johnsonian ethos invariably transports him into his ideal experience of himself. Breathing that air, he can be cheerful, confident, rational, pious, affectionate—all without effort and without anxiety. His role has all the satisfactions of sonship with none of its discomforts. He receives constant reassurance of his special value and can lay down his moral burdens under the shade of an over-arching responsibility. The atmosphere of vigorous philosophic morality makes the difficulties under which he labours seem

Katherine Mansfield, c. 1920

W. N. P. Barbellion, c. *1912*

soluble. In Edinburgh he is obliged to be always self-defining, self-sustaining; his values, his moral will, his self-control must be exerted to survive, and the journal is a medium for their exertion. In his relationship with Johnson a role is defined for him and grace imparted to sustain him in it.

... for I really feel myself happier in the company of those of whom I stand in awe than in any other company, except when I have a temporary elevation of mind, and delight in being with my inferiors, or a temporary gay, easy, pleasurable frame, and wish to be with a friend upon an equal footing, or a mistress. To be with those of whom I stand in awe composes the uneasy tumult of my spirits, and gives me the pleasure of contemplating something at least comparatively great. I have often and often experienced this, though I cannot clearly explain or account for it.[70]

A few days later, during the same Ashbourne visit, he shares a pew with his friend at Sunday devotions, and feels 'as serenely and steadily happy as I suppose man can be'.[71] It is a condition of Beatitude.

Manifest in the complex identity-concerns expressed by the diary-persona in Boswell's journals is an unresolved tension between two opposing conceptions of selfhood, of which Ryder and Haydon might be taken as representative. The diaries of Ryder and of Haydon consistently express their fidelity to coherent images of actual self and ideal self. Boswell stands (or falls) between them. He can neither confine himself wholly within the ideal to which Ryder aspires, nor release himself unreservedly into the self-apotheosis enjoyed by Haydon. To a much greater extent than either he is liable to the experience of being suspended between identities. Thus, as J. N. Morris says, when he first came to London 'to be something', 'The great question was, Could he be Boswell? Or, rather, Was there a Boswell to be?'[72] Neither Ryder nor Haydon would experience questions of identity in these terms. The former could not conceive of 'Ryder' as a dramatic role, the name of a *character*; the latter, while he would undoubtedly recognize 'Haydon' as a magnificent part, could never imagine himself not playing it. Boswell hovers between. Once past the high days and holidays of his youth he comes uneasily, as we have seen, to something akin to Ryder's values, struggling in Edinburgh for the state of being in which he dwells when with Johnson, plotting his condition on a vertical scale. At an earlier stage, however, he at times approached that sense of autonomous, privileged multiplicity which, in another generation, was to find the law of its integration in a self-concept to which he had no access—the Romantic notion of the Artist.

7

+++

Forms of Serial Autobiography

HAYDON, KILVERT, BARBELLION,
JACQUIER, NIN

WRITERS on autobiography rightly distinguish their chosen
subject from the diary form of self-delineation. They note
the manifest differences in intention, interpretive standpoint,
significant shape and aesthetic design. Autobiography, says Roy
Pascal, 'is a review of a life from a particular moment in time, while
the diary, however reflective it may be, moves through a series of
moments in time. The diarist notes down what, at that moment,
seems of importance to him; its ultimate, long-range significance
cannot be assessed.'[1] He goes on to observe how the differences are
underlined by the problems involved in an autobiographer's use of
his own diary. The intermixture of the two genres often results in the
collision of alternative modes of authenticity. 'We expect from a
diary all the uncertainties, false starts, momentariness that we find in
them. From the autobiography, however, we expect a coherent
shaping of the past; and if diary entries or letters are quoted, we need
the explanatory, interpretative commentary of the author.'[2] The autobiographer, in other words, should see a wood for the diarist's trees.
In choosing to discuss five major diaries in the light of the term 'serial
autobiography' I do not wish to nullify these formal distinctions. I
intend rather to propose that certain diaries (and not only these five),
by virtue of their authors' conception and practice, and the character
of the written documents—their texture and the shape of their 'authorized' version—are best regarded as a synthesis of the two types. It
must be emphasized at once that I am not concerned to assert that
'serial autobiography' is necessarily the ideal by which all diary-
writing must be judged, or that it is the ideal type of autobiography.

(Both assertions may be tenable but the argument would be unprofit-ably abstract.) The term serves as an organizing conception within which the salient features of diaries of a particular and well-developed type may be related and compared.

In the course of this study I have used the term 'serial autobio-graphy' in a fairly general way to mean any regular narration of a person's life and doings. It is necessary now to stress more particularly the concept of *a* serial autobiography to distinguish the character of certain diaries considered as whole works. To qualify, a diary must first of all cover fairly continuously a good number of the significant years of the writer's life. More is implied by the term, however, than simply a diary kept for a long time. It is also intended to be a more specific category than the notion of the book of the self proposed in Chapter 3. Two sets of factors contribute to the meaning of the term: on the one hand an autobiographical consciousness on the part of the writer; on the other, certain formal characteristics in the resulting book as left by its author. By 'autobiographical consciousness' is meant the sense that one is living a *Life*, that an organic story links one's days together and makes them significant and interesting. This sense may inform the writing of the diary from an early stage, as in Haydon's case, or it may be engendered in the writer's mind comparatively late by a quality discerned in the book itself. This latter case applies to Ivy Jacquier's diary which recognizes itself as an autobiography only towards the end of the period covered by the published book; an autobiographical perspective governs the editorial selection by which she causes her 'story' to appear. Barbellion's 'psychological history of [his] own life'[3] embodies both elements. His writing proceeds from a deliberate autobiographical intention which is redoubled in the course of his own editing. Kilvert makes no claims to a life-story of special significance, but his diary faithfully adheres to the task of advancing little by little his humble narrative. Anaïs Nin, as we have seen, works unceasingly at the task of eliciting the aesthetic forms of her living.

The idea of the book of the self as a personal-historical document introduces into its composition and editing dimensions of critical and aesthetic awareness which have no place in diaries not responsive to the sense of 'my life' as some sort of philosophical category. As an autobiographer a diarist sets a standard for himself—ill-defined, per-haps, and fluctuating—but nonetheless an external conception of the requirements of the genre. He is under an obligation to prosecute actively the task of bringing along a coherent story with significant interest. Instead of an *ad hoc* jotting down of impressions, the writing of the diary entails a continual negotiation between comprehensiveness and digested relevance. And since the notion of autobiography suggests more than a mere narrative of events, the need is felt to find ways of projecting his being as well as his doing. If he were suddenly to die the diary would have the prime responsibility for declaring what he was and what he did, so it had better contain whatever he may want to say by way of explanation and commentary. Thus, from a moving vantage-point, the serial autobiographer constantly mediates between a provisional interpretation of his life's meaning and direction, and the fresh experience which may modify that interpretation. In examining five works under this heading the ensuing chapter proposes such questions as, What kind of 'story' does the diarist consider his life to be? What kind of autobiographical self-concept governs the book, and how does it affect the mode of self-presentation?

From the age of twenty-two until his suicide in 1846 at the age of sixty, Haydon is writing his autobiography. He never pretends that his journal volumes are kept for his private edification or recollection; their acknowledged purpose from the outset is to report himself and his cause aright—to tell his story and to leave to posterity as variegated an imprint as possible of his personality, his spirit, and his genius. In January 1816, on the subject of bardolatry, he writes, 'It is time that all the obscurity about Genius should be dispersed [together with] the belief that such men at once burst into full possession of their knowledge, when it is only that they have acquired it with the same progression tho' with infinitely more rapidity. On this principle it is I write my own life.'[4] The 'principle' varies with the phases of his career, but the explicit avowal of an autobiographical intention persists throughout. Towards the end of his life he actually begins to write a formal autobiography, drawing heavily upon his journals and quoting from them at length. But the work advances only as far as the year 1820 and in his will (leaving his manuscripts to Elizabeth Barrett) he declares, 'My journals will supply the rest. The style, the individuality of Richardson, which I wish not curtailed by an editor.'[5] For over a century the published version of the journals began where the formal memoir left off.[6] Only recently, with the publication of W. B. Pope's splendid edition in 1960, has the original text (which includes some of the richest portions of the journal) become available in print. For better and for worse—for there is no denying that it is a ramshackle monstrosity of a book—it is now possible to view the whole span of this autobiographical epic.

Before proceeding to discuss the character of his book it will be helpful to give a little sketch of Haydon's career. In 1804 he came to London from Plymouth to study at the Royal Academy under Fuseli. For the next fifteen years he worked at a few huge paintings, including 'Dentatus', 'Macbeth', 'The Judgment of Solomon', 'Christ's Entry into Jerusalem', and 'The Raising of Lazarus', some of which won considerable acclaim. He was at loggerheads with the Royal Academy, which he accused of conspiring to thwart his career, and enjoyed the friendship of the literary notables of the day. In 1821 he married a widow, Mary Hyman, whom he loved ardently and who bore him many children. In 1823 he was imprisoned for debt for the first time, and the long decline in his fortunes had definitely begun. Despite some successes, such as George IV's purchase of 'The Mock Election', and a commission to paint the Reform Banquet of 1832, he never regained solvency or critical esteem. During the eighteen-thirties he unavailingly cultivated influential acquaintances, and became briefly infatuated with the Honourable Mrs. Caroline Norton, Lord Melbourne's mistress. To earn money he turned to hack-work— portraits, and an incredible number of paintings entitled 'Napoleon Musing'—while hoping for a chance to redeem himself as England's greatest painter. When his designs for decorations in the new Houses of Parliament were rejected in 1843 and 1844 his career was at an end. Ironically his death earned him belated recognition and a pension for his wife.

The story, as Haydon tells it, is the melodrama which results from the impact upon the world of a Herculean hero. In this lifelong collision of forces nothing humdrum ever takes place. The vehemence and ardour of his language inflate his every encounter with art and life to extravagant proportions. As protagonist he crams into a single self-concept the souls of half a dozen Shakespearian heroes, their strengths and their calamitous weaknesses. The spectacle he presents of passionately wrong-headed magnificence of personality constantly brings to mind a prototype in Lear, Antony, Othello, Coriolanus, Timon; but, unlike Byron whose affectation of Shakespearian poses is more than half ironic, Haydon seems to be fully expressed in them. He does not retain an intelligent self-awareness with which to see through his own self-dramatizations. One feels with him, as with the

Shakespearian character, that he gives away more insights into himself than he keeps. Whereas Boswell constantly surprises one with how much of himself he sees, Haydon is surprising for how much he reveals yet fails to see. Like Lear, with whom he identifies in his last hour with the words, 'Stretch me no longer on this tough world',[7] he hath ever but slenderly known himself.

It is only appropriate, in view of Haydon's compelling sense of the 'plot' of his life story, to look at the diary in terms of its chronological development. More strongly than most diarists he exhibits a vivid feeling for *epochs* in his career. For the first dozen years at least, his imagination is possessed by a vision of the climax of universal acclaim that awaits him, with the result that successive events are registered as milestones on a journey whose destination is already envisaged. Executed in the most glaring colours, without a trace of irony, the diary of these years is truly the portrait of the artist as a passionately ambitious young man. The passage quoted below may be taken as typical of many solemn re-affirmations of his faith in himself and dedication to his calling. The occasion of it (27 September 1817) is the epoch of his moving into new lodgings after nearly ten years in one place. The histrionic tone projects an exaggerated, theatrical perception of himself and of the situation; the language expresses a pained sensitivity to impressions while the culminating declaration of values proclaims nobility of soul. Here is Haydon the Artist:

After a short time I came into my new habitation! I knew nothing of it, it was strange to me. I had no associations with it. All was in the future, a wild abyss, untrod, unknown! There is no pain like the uncertainty of a beginning, nothing that weighs the faculties down so acutely & so oppressively as the disarranged confusion and scattered desolation of furniture, books, and pictures unhung, unsettled, and undusted. For a moment one is suspended. Then one decides with fury, begins with energy, and the cloud disappears as if the sun was rising behind it. I declare solemnly I have no one wish incompatible with the innocence or purity or happiness of any human being, no one wish purely wicked, no one wish to hurt the feelings, disturb the peace, or injure the character of a creature living! I hope humbly to be the greatest painter of my country, to regenerate and to reform its taste. I know I am misunderstood when abused. I have naturally and inherently a love of truth and justice. When I am unmanageable it is not that I am naturally a lover of opposition, but that I see the truth so intensely that I cannot submit tacitly to acquiesce in the prejudices or passions of others. This is not very modest, perhaps, but it is true.[8]

One of the prime functions of language for Haydon is to heighten his romantic imaginings. He employs language not to analyse and clarify ideas but to intensify and inflame his fantasies. For the cultivation of fantasies is a central component of his artist-psyche. With uncritical fervour his imagination intoxicates itself with lurid sensations whose value, beyond the immediate thrill, lies in furnishing him with blazing inspirations. Haydon equates creativity with the capacity to be ravished by the intensity of his own conceptions. Whether elaborating an idea for a painting, indulging a sexual reverie, or projecting himself into the experience of a heroic role-model he invariably has recourse to a melodramatizing purple prose, lavish of imprecise effects. In what follows he is recording the experience of visiting Napoleon's private apartment at Rambouillet in 1814 (during the Elba interlude):

Here I stood, as it were, in the very midst of his soul. Here was his private, secret, sacred closet, painted & arranged by his own orders and for his own particular gratification. This was the stimulant to a Conqueror's appetite. What indecencies are to a debauchee, these mementos are to a tyrant. Here he lay in dim twilight, revelled in associations of dominion, and visions of conquest. Here perhaps he lay & fired his mind to the gigantic enterprise against Russia. He never arose but with his mind filled with bold designs, his blood fevered, his brain in a blaze! I almost trembled to look round & reflect that I stood in the secret sensations of one that made the world shake, that had first been the admiration, then the terror, at last the detestation of the Earth.[9]

'As my object is to trace the process of my mind, it is also with my passions, and really I cannot help saying that no human being can conceive their intensity unless he has felt them to the same degree.'[10] So he says by way of introduction to an account of his phenomenal success with 'lovely Women' and the prodigious ardour of his sexual emotions. Yet to say that he is concerned to 'trace the process' of thought and feeling would not be accurate. Rather he delights in parading their energy. The heroic forcefulness of his mind he exhibits in resounding declamations on such subjects as the principles of High Art, the iniquity of the Royal Academy, the consummate art of the Elgin marbles, and the truth of Christianity. He tends not so much to think analytically as to give vent, in a high rhetorical vein, to Convictions which draw increased strength from the vehemence with which he utters them. As for the 'process' of his passions, he writes to give the reader an impression of their variety and violence, rather than to understand their origins and intricacies. Boswell, as we have seen, is equally capable at times of giving himself up to successive self-dramatizations, but he always returns from them to an experimental and moral lucidity which seeks to understand and to judge. He maintains a remarkable openness to new insights into his own nature, and to the conviction of real personal fault. Haydon's self-encounter on the contrary tends always to reinforce his self-image and to render him increasingly impervious to objective appraisal. He has nothing of Boswell's interest in himself as a specimen of general human nature, nor does he acknowledge ideals of self-development outside himself. It is foreign to the whole tenor of the diary to approach himself questioningly, asking Am I this? Should I be that? The diary proclaims, 'I am'. Consider the following extraordinary self-characterization. It is dated 8 July 1820, the year that he sums up in his customary year-end review and re-dedication as 'the most glorious Year of my life'.[11] His exhibition of 'Christ's Entry' and other works is having a great success; he is at the peak of his career and enjoying the consciousness of having had his commitment to grandiose historical painting resoundingly vindicated:

Perhaps the most delightful moments on Earth, that is the most delightful thing as to calm consciousness, is the chat that takes place with a lovely woman in bed, after having proved vigorously your manhood to her, when you begin to recover from the perspiring stupor of intoxication and rapture. This book is a picture of human life, now full of arguments for religion, now advocating virtue, then drawn from chaste piety, & then melting from a bed of pleasure, idle & active, dissipated & temperate, voluptuous & holy! burning to be a martyr when I read the Gospel! ready to blaze in a battalion when I read Homer! weeping at Rimini and at Othello, laughing & without sixpence, in boisterous spirits when I ought to be sad & melancholy when I have every reason to be happy!—such are the elements of that mysterious, incomprehensible, singular bit of blood, bottom, bone, & genius, B. R. Haydon![12]

Boswell could never have gloried so exultantly in the fertile contradictions of his nature. As was suggested at the end of Chapter 6, it is the Romantic conception of Genius that permits Haydon to celebrate himself in this fashion. Similarly an approach to diary-writing now quite free from the non-conformist earnestness permits him to appreciate 'this book' as 'a picture of human life' on which he congratulates himself. Many years later (in 1844) he observes, 'My Journal seems to have lost all its copiousness and Inspiration',[13] indicating in these two words the qualities for which he prized the book in earlier times.

1820 is also the year in which he falls in love with Mary Hyman. His performance in the role of The Artist Enamoured is characteristically extravagant and entails the delivery of passages of exclamatory rapture, together with some discourse on the purity of connubial desire. He also declares the opening of a new era in his personal history:

The leading Star in the Horizon of my life has hitherto been *ambition*; Love has now lifted its glittering & beautiful head, into the mild Heaven, where without weakening the power, it softens the fierce shine of the other, and seems to guide it with its lovely & gentle light through 'the Heaven's wide pathless way.'[14]

They are married in October 1821 and for a while Haydon's life seems to balance itself on the point between rise and fall. As Benjamin the Married Man he is engagingly uninhibited in his expression of fondness for his wife—unlike many married diarists who appear somewhat embarrassed by the connection. To 'Mary's sweet face' he attributes a softening influence upon his nature. 'The expression of my head is altered; it used to be fierce, determined, & approaching to something brutal about the jaw; it is now looking happy & good-natured.'[15] But even as he works at 'Lazarus' through 1822 and into 1823 the crisis in his economic situation is worsening. At last the blow falls and he finds himself in the King's Bench prison. The response of the diary-persona to this calamity is to resort (predictably) to the tragic posture of the Hero in Adversity. Comparison with Scott's encounter with ruin (see Chapter 5) might suggest itself and would emphasize the gap between Sir Walter's pose of gruff stoicism and the unrestrained theatricality of Haydon's speech-making. To the extent that this kind of rhetoric actually renders the tone of Haydon's consciousness, it indicates the incapacity for realistic engagement with his condition that the diary encourages in him:

After years of the most ardent devotion, after having passed the most rapturous moments of my life in my Painting room, wandering with my beautiful Mary amidst my beautiful casts, talking of my prospects, my happiness, pointing out the forms, & the principles, and the graces of the antique; & then with my hand round her lovely waist, & interspersing my conversation with honied kisses, burst forth in a enthusiastic inspiration of future greatness; after passing days & hours in the solitary hallowed silence of my study, living to myself, & holding converse with Raphael & Michel Angelo, in the midst, too, of the applause of thousands with my last labour before the World, admiring & wondering, to be plucked by the roots from such a home, from the arms of such a woman, & the smile of such an infant, & plunged into a Prison to herd with demireps & gamblers! I who have talents to be an honor to my Sovereign . . . etc.[16]

P.C.—6*

A few days later he declares, 'O God, in thee I trust, for I am convinced I am an instrument for the advance of Historical Painting;'[17] and on 29 June 1823 he hears (not for the first time) a 'voice within saying "Go on".'[18] His appearance in the Bankruptcy Court takes place on 23 July—a scene which he describes as though it were the Last Judgment[19]—and with the liquidation of his assets and settlement with his creditors he is once again at large. But from this time forward the threat of renewed legal action haunts him. To support his growing family he takes up portrait painting and, swallowing his pride, makes a round of conciliatory visits to members of the Academy. Meanwhile the diary self-dramatization expresses increasing humiliation, bitterness, and frustration, and a worsening of the persecution mania which is to blind him to every other interpretation of his lot.

The passage to be quoted next is the climax of a grotesque fantasy of abandoning himself to the wilds and giving full scope to his despair-crazed passions. It should be stressed that such extravagant effusions are rare in the diary and represent only the extremes of melodramatic rant that Haydon is capable of exciting in himself. It is very interesting to compare this outburst with the passage quoted in Chapter 6 (p. 146) in which Boswell reports a bout of fury over his father's plan to re-marry. The comparison illustrates very well the point made several times in this study that the Romantic diarist habitually *enacts* in the presence of the reader states of emotional arousal which his pre-Romantic counterpart only describes. In so doing he endorses these states as valid expressions of his nature rather than as distortions of it. Here, then, is Haydon in a role irresistibly reminiscent of Timon:

. . . and then plunging again into the wild, vent my rage on the trees, the stones, the birds, the animals, & glory with extatic rapture, to meet a *solitary human* being *without defence* on whom I might vent my hatred of human nature! and gratify my tiger feelings tearing out his heart & drinking his blood! and then strip my body, my half clothed & ragged body, & paint it with grinning faces in the blood yet warm and unclotted by the air! Ah, ah, Revenge, Revenge, thou dear, dear, dear passion! Revenge, the great mind's solace! the balm of disappointed Genius! the nectar of a soul parched & dried up by poverty & ruin! Curses, Curses, Curses, endless, withering, Hellish, from that lower Hell where the most Hellish rebels down are deeper thrown—light, blast, scathe those who could dim a brain so brilliant & a heart so tender to such bitter, bitter solace! B. R. Haydon.[20]

(He frequently signs his more declamatory entries, as though to endow them with added impact and finality.)

Through the later eighteen-twenties Haydon's story continues to oscillate between euphoria and desperation, as magnificent inspirations jostle with the prospect of imprisonment. An increasingly prominent theme is his conviction that envy and malice are at work to thwart his career and the growth of historical painting in general. Enemies lurk everywhere, among fellow artists and former students, in the artistic establishment, and among those with the wealth and power to make High Art prosper if they chose. At the end of 1825 for example he declares that, 'The Patrons know I have the power to do what I dare to conceive, and they fear to put means in my hands, because I should become an object of too great distinction! This is the secret.'[21] Change 'Patrons' to 'Gods', and you have a Prometheus speaking. The *meaning* of the autobiographical narrative is undergoing a change; the story of a dauntless young genius triumphing in defiance of the establishment is giving way to the story of a man no longer young, suffering martyrdom for his courage and vision. As he says of some hack-work he is engaged in, 'to think at 42 years of age I am compelled to do this for bread!—pursuing my Art as I have pursued it, with all my heart & all my Soul! for the honor of my Country.'[22] Still he is full of fight. Obsessively he hammers away at stock themes like the ignorance of anatomy among English painters and the failure of the government to promote and encourage artists by commissioning public projects and so forth. And he badgers institutions and leading men with a one-man crusade for the public support of, ultimately, himself.

The early thirties mark a new epoch in his life. The political excitement surrounding the Reform Bill catches his imagination. His hero-worship of the Duke of Wellington is temporarily eclipsed, and he fills the diary with enthusiastic harangue of a loosely Radical cast. While they have no intrinsic worth, Haydon's political utterances display interestingly the veerings of a mind governed by rhetoric and sentiment. In July 1832 he embarks on a huge picture of the Reform Banquet, which requires him to make portrait studies of half of the English governing class. The flatteringly cordial treatment he receives from lords and ministers intoxicates his ego and for many months the reader hears of nothing but the manly good-nature of dear Lord This and the dear Duke of That. With a rather pitiable naïvety he presents himself in the role of urbane companion of the mighty, chatting of great affairs and busily dropping his schemes for public patronage into influential ears. During this time also there takes place his infatuation with Caroline Norton, the course of which is registered by the diary in one of the most transparent pieces of self-deception to be found in the whole genre. The diary form captures here what a retrospective autobiography never could, namely, the progress of a self-justifying mind through a circuit of flagrant rationalizations. It is a case of the diary being much more truthful than the diarist. What makes it the more grotesque to read is the suspicion that the flirtation was largely a figment of Haydon's mind. A couple of specimens must suffice to illustrate the reversal in his attitudes. The first is from June 1834; Mrs. Norton is sitting for the figure of Cassandra and has smitten poor Haydon with her beauty, genius, and charm:

> *June 13.* Stewart Mackenzie sat finally—a delightful person. We talked of dear Mrs. Norton. He said she had *no* passion. This is the cant in the Dandies of High Life, because *she* awes them all, the Beauty. No passion—in those eyes—that mouth. I told him I heard that often, but I fancied that face if once moved would give evidence of passion enough.
>
> I can't bear to hear her talked of so slightingly in that way. I could have given Mackenzie a thump. I felt my vein filling in my forehead. Dear, accomplished, & beautiful Caroline, I love thee as I would have loved Sappho: I love dear Mary as I would have loved Psyche. Till I saw thee, I was never in thought unfaithful— & have no sin but in thought now—yet I can't conceal it—I love her to distraction. She comes to sit next Monday. How shall I get on?[23]

Two years later during the Norton divorce trial in which Lord Melbourne is cited as co-respondent, he is calling her 'as dreadful a whore as ever cursed the World since Messalina', and protesting that, 'On me she failed entirely, but it was a singular evidence of character to watch how she varied her plans of attack, always keeping her ultimate object in view.'[24] For some time to come the diary continues to offer variants of this self-righteous *spiel*, without a hint of acknowledgement that it represents a spectacular turnabout. In the case of his hardly less dramatic disavowal of the Whigs (after the Tories' return to power) he is at least put to some discomfort to explain the appearance of Trimming in his political oscillations. 'It is the Duke's fault; if he had not said, "No Reform was necessary", I should *never* have lost my perceptions as I did. I got exasperated from having seen honest men suffer, for *saying* what the Tories *did*. But I was always in my heart a Duke's Man.'[25] In his last years he resorts to a harrumphing old Toryism and writes letters to *The Times* about the perfidy of France and the 'Namby Pamby impotence' of the Whigs.[26]

To the end of his career Haydon's book continues to resound with battle-cries and desperate prayers, withering tirades, and torrents of self-vindication. His mind goes endlessly over the same ground, rehearsing the old wrongs and declaring an increasingly unrealistic confidence in a glorious retribution to come. The gap widens between the story Haydon is telling and the story we are reading. With his crazy persistence, rebounding from the most devastating blows and all the time asserting the special protection and encouragement of God, he is epic in his own eyes, tragic in the reader's. Especially painful for the reader is the realization of how plainly irrelevant Haydon has become. To all who have to deal with him he is nothing but a daft old nuisance. Yet he persists in fuelling his fantasies of power and significance. Here, from July 1836, is the conclusion of his account of a Parliamentary Committee hearing into the usefulness of the Royal Academy—a proceeding for which Haydon takes unto himself the credit. The three directors referred to had been members of the 1809 hanging committee:

There was I, a living instance, & was not the whole scene a scene of retribution? The very men, the very hangers—Shee, Phillips, & Howard—who 29 years ago,* used me so infamously in hanging Dentatus in the dark—by which all my prospects were blasted for ever—at which Lord Mulgrave so complained—were now at the bar before me like Culprits under examination. How would Sir George have relished this.

Ah, little did they think in the despotism of their power, that I, a poor Student at their mercy, should have had the power to do this—to bring them Face to Face—to have them examined—ransacked—questioned—racked!

Ah, they are deservedly punished!

'Fear thou not, for I am with thee. Be not dismayed, for I am thy God.' How often have I read this; how often have I dwelt on it, in my wants, & never actually despaired.

I do not fear, & I do not despair of rendering my Life ultimately available to my Country's honor. Gratitude & Huzza!

My life has been a romance. God spare me to write it, & the aspiring youth shall hereafter hug it to his heart.[27]

When, in July 1839, he does begin to write his *Life*, it is to the 'aspiring youth' that he addresses it. This character, otherwise referred to as the 'Rising Youth', has a special place in Haydon's autobiographical scenario, the complement of a conception of himself as the Grand Old Rebel delivering his didactic apologia to a rapt audience. Writing his *Life* is essentially an extension of the diary habit, involving only a

* Haydon means 27.

more systematic presentation of material he has been constantly rehashing. The tenor and the interpretive standpoint are already established; the story has been sounding in his head for decades.

Beside Haydon's enormous book, Kilvert's serial autobiography appears as a work on an altogether more modest scale, in a distinctly muted tone. Kilvert's story covers only nine years of his life, from January 1870 to March 1879. Six months from the date of the last surviving entry he is dead, at the age of thirty-eight,* one month married. Even within this short span the diary shows several large gaps, possibly made by the hand of his widow. In particular the manuscript volumes from September 1875 to March 1876, which may be supposed to have told the story of the Ettie affair, no longer exist; and the diary breaks off shortly before Kilvert's meeting with his wife-to-be. Despite these and other losses the book remains a major piece of life-story-telling, attentively and lovingly written, embodying a deeply implanted literary conception of the texture and value of his experience.

By his own admission Kilvert hoped his diary might some day have a reader whom it would 'amuse and interest'.[28] In 1875 he shows parts of it to his friend Mayhew who is reported to be 'much entertained'.[29] What kind of entertainment might he expect his book to supply? It seems evident that in his selection of subject matter, and in his manner of perceiving and handling it, he is making his autobiography a source of just the kinds of satisfaction he himself most enjoys from literature and art. Of his tastes in aesthetic gratification the diary gives ample evidence. In general it may be said that he turns to art for the repeated pleasure of having tears brought to his eyes—by loveliness, romantic pathos, the sweet simplicity of children and humble folk, and stories about the pure in heart. At the London art galleries, especially the annual Royal Academy exhibition to which he likes to make a special visit, he enjoys paintings with direct emotional appeal and moral uplift. Murillo's 'Good Shepherd' strikes him forcefully in a collection of old masters in the winter of 1870.[30] In the 1872 Academy show he is particularly taken by 'the half-length picture of a dark-haired girl, the dark eyes full and large with tears, mournful, beseeching, imploring, and sad with a wistful despairing sadness too

---

* Kilvert probably imagined himself to be 39. He was born on 3 December 1840, but on 3 December, 1872 he announces his thirty-*third* birthday, and persists in this one-year discrepancy.

sad for words.'³¹ The following year a work entitled 'The Turning Point' particularly appeals to him: 'the beautiful face and eyes of the wife looking up to her husband's stern sullen countenance as she leans on his breast, beseeching him, pleading with him, oh so earnestly and imploringly, to give up drinking. It went to my heart.'³² And in 1874 he selects 'Innocence' as his favourite—'the face of a lovely child who has been unjustly blamed and punished for a fault of which she was Innocent, innocent'.³³ He is also attracted by more stirringly Romantic pictures, and describes in detail a 'Paolo and Francesca', and an 'Andromeda'.³⁴ Holman Hunt's 'Shadow of Death', however, strikes him as 'theatrical and detestable' and 'a waste of a good shilling'.³⁵ In poetry he declares his fondness for 'dear old Wordsworth',³⁶ Tennyson ('We were comparing notes, Kathleen and I, about our beloved *In Memoriam* and showing each other our favourite passages and poems'³⁷), and William Barnes, 'the great idyllic Poet of England' whom he visits in April 1874.³⁸ He also engages in a little versifying of his own, mainly nature lyrics and hymns. He sends a selection of them to Ettie at Easter 1876, but is discouraged by his father and Longmans Ltd. as to their publishability. As for prose works, he tells how *Max Kromer, A Story of the Siege of Strasbourg* (By the Author of *Jessica's First Prayer*) leaves him sobbing, choking, and blinded by tears.³⁹ Taken together these indications of Kilvert's aesthetic sensibility point towards the literary ethos of the diary, its predilection for strong pictorial effects of a conventionally 'poetic' kind, and for the blessed charm and pathos of unpretentious lives. In contrast to Sturt, who seeks constructive philosophic insight into the folkways of the rural poor, Kilvert is content with a smile and a tear. He proffers to his reader the fruits of a faith in the morally regenerative power of unabashed sentimentality. Here, for a sample of his lyrical-pious vein, is part of the entry for 27 January 1872:

And down under the poplars out of sight in their lowly hidden place, courting no one's notice, the lovely snowdrops hung their pure white heads and closed their eyes in sleep as the night fell.

So simple, so humble, yet so brave. It comes before the crocus dares. I love the snowdrop, the first of all the flowers, the harbinger of Spring. God's New Year's gift to the earth, the Fair Maid of February, the daughter of the earth and the snow.

And so pure, so spotlessly, stainlessly pure. Who is it that calls the snowdrop the 'pure pale penitent'?

But to me it always seems to be 'the penitent absolved'. Oh that all our sins might thus be washed away and we be presented spotless through the Saviour's atoning blood.[40]

With its sentimental personification, its echoes (probably unconscious) of Shakespeare and Herbert, and its flood of devotional rapture, the passage has the character of a little ode. And, indeed, in his *Collected Verse* recently published by the Kilvert Society, there is to be found the very same cluster of imagery and sentiment, versified:

TO SNOWDROPS
Sweet silent preachers from God's text
That bids man lowly be,
And find his highest ornament
In his humility!
Ye grow,
Your pure heads hanging low,
Earth-bent,
Hiding your faces fair,
Though your bright souls have ne'er been vext
By sinful thought or care.

Preaching ye practise as ye blow,
And with sweet trustful grace,
Vestured in pure humility,
Smile in stern Winter's face.
Pray, pray,
At peep and shut of day,
That we
When Death shall call us hence,
With childlike trust may smiling go,
And lowly penitence.[41]

The function that Dorothy Wordsworth performed in her journal in the generation of William's poetry, Kilvert evidently performed for himself.

As the story of his own life Kilvert's diary has nothing at all comparable to the sense of 'plot' that runs through Haydon's. The autobiographical self-concepts are quite contrasted also. Whereas Haydon represents himself in epic terms, as a *force* acting upon the world, Kilvert appears as an extremely unassertive character, passive and impressionable. Moreover, while cultivating a poetic sensibility he does not project himself in the role of 'the poet' or presume to document the growth of his mind; it is not another portrait of the artist that he writes. He takes his definition of himself from his role as a priest, a loving minister vocationally committed to the Good Shepherd disposition. His life is an Imitation of Christ (as portrayed in Victorian devotional art); gentle Kilvert, meek and mild, whose occupation is to bless everyone and everything with love, and to be loved and blessed in return. Occasionally the feelings aroused in him for his flock quite overwhelm him with their intensity (see Chapter 4, pp. 74–5), at other times he is awed by the effect he apparently has on others:

I had not many minutes to stay and when I rose to go poor Emma clasped my hands in both of hers, gave me a long loving look and turned away with a burst of weeping, in a passion of tears. What is it? What is it? What do they all mean? It is a strange and terrible gift, this power of stealing hearts and exciting such love.[42]

Undoubtedly the power of exciting such love comes largely from the utterly unwitheld nature of his own feelings. He appears to overflow with affection continually; the language of the diary bestows endearments—sweet, lovely, gentle, dear, beloved—on people, places, and things.

Periodically the autobiographical narrative does quicken into a plot and the narrator becomes the main actor in a dramatic situation. The several occasions on which Kilvert falls in love—with Daisy (Fanny) Thomas, 'Kathleen Mavourneen' (Katie Heanley), and Ettie Meredith Brown—provide him with the opportunity to cast his story in the terms of a sentimental novelette or a pathetic poem. Kilvert-in-love is an elaborate literary performance. For example, the occasion of his falling for Kathleen at a wedding on 11 August 1874 has six pages of controlled narrative build-up. Writing apparently on 13 August or later, he describes first his journey to Worthing on the eve of the wedding, and the irony of his having wished he were going to the Isle of Wight, 'little knowing what I was saying, or what was in store for me at Findon', where the wedding was to be held.[43] The entry for 11 August begins, 'Addie Cholmeley's wedding day. This may be one of the happiest and most important days in my life, for today I fell in love at first sight with sweet Kathleen Mavourneen.'[44] He is consciously writing the opening chapter of what he hopes may be the Romance of his Life, and he wants to do it in style. After this opening announcement the narrative proceeds evenly through the events of the morning—the journey to the church, his introduction to the tall dark bridesmaid with whom he has been paired for the day, the service and reception, and the departure of 'our dear little bride .... happy and radiant ... God bless them'.[45] In the afternoon the wedding party goes for a picnic on Chanctonbury Ring. Kilvert and Kathleen walk together; he spreads his coat on the ground for her—'and there we sat and talked and looked into each other's eyes and there I fell in love and lost my heart to the sweetest, noblest, kindest, bravest-hearted girl in England, Kathleen Mavourneen.'[46] By evening he has joined Kathleen's Mutual Improvement Society, and she has given him a flower from one of the bouquets, 'a flower that I will keep till we are married if that should be God's will for us, and in any case until I die'.[47]

No one will claim that this is high narrative art or the imprint of a complex or exceptional sensibility. I have quoted it in some detail only to illustrate how Kilvert's imagination reaches for the most stunningly conventional literary effects to enshrine his precious experiences. Unfortunately (or perhaps fortunately), the relationship with Kathleen seems not to have fulfilled its early promise. After some exchanges of Mutual Improvement Questions and Answers he apparently comes to hold her as a thing ensky'd and sainted, recognizing 'how much nobler and holier her thoughts are than mine'.[48] On New Year's Eve 1874 he prays ardently for her—and hardly ever mentions her again. As if in reaction against Kathleen's chilling piety he is next attracted by Ettie Meredith Brown whose cheeks have 'the dusky bloom and flush of a ripe pomegranate' and whose 'dark wild fine eyes looked with a true gipsy beauty'.[49] (He has always had a Thing about gipsies.) We may never know what took place between them in the autumn of 1875, the diary for this period being lost, but evidently a mutual flame was extinguished by parental hand. When it resumes in March 1876 the diary echoes with impassioned elegies for the 'sweet strange sad story' and the 'wild sad sweet trysts in the snow' of the preceding December.[50] His response to a final letter of farewell reveals again the extent to which Kilvert *realizes* his emotional life in the language of popular romantic fiction:

Ettie, my own only lost love, yet not lost, for we shall meet in heaven. Ettie, oh Ettie, my own dear little girl.

As I walked round the Rectory garden at Monnington this morning thinking of Ettie's last letter and all the wild sweet sorrowful past the great everlasting sigh of the majestic firs, as mournful and soothing as the sighing of the sea, blended with my mood and sympathized with the sadness of my heart. The beautiful weeping birch too wept with me and its graceful drooping tresses softly moving reminded me with a strange sweet thrill of Ettie's hair.[51]

Some weeks later, in a passage too long to quote in full, he records how, when preaching on the words, 'It is expedient for you that I go away, for if I go not away the Comforter will not come unto you' (John 16:7), he uses the episode of his parting from Ettie as the basis for a sermon.[52] The manner in which the story is told—of how a 'broken-hearted man' feeling still 'the last long lingering pressure of the hand and the last long clinging embrace and passionate kiss' wandered desolate into Salisbury Cathedral in the winter twilight and was comforted by the words of the gospel—suggests exactly the kind of autobiographical novel that would compose itself in Kilvert's imagination, if he were inclined that way.

Barbellion, as has already been demonstrated, shows a quite patent inclination that way. The difference between the *Journal of a Disappointed Man* and an autobiographical novel is essentially that the early part of the *Journal* consists of deposits made before the idea of a publishable book had been conceived. A 'real' novel in diary form would have to consist either of entries that an earlier stage of the author's consciousness (so far as he can recreate it) *might have* written; or of entries composed from the author's contemporary consciousness but responsive to the requirements of an aesthetic design before those of *ad hoc* authenticity. Barbellion's mode of expression tends increasingly towards this latter option. With the discovery of terminal disease in November 1915 his 'scenario' is completed; henceforth he documents his living in the light of a more or less definitely realized ending. The meaning and quality of his life-story are fatally established, together with the role of the author–protagonist. His task is to sustain for a period of months or years a last-act soliloquy befitting his condition, and to extract a copy-text of Acts I to IV from the improvisations accumulated over several years. As he says in December 1916,

The reason why I do not spend my days in despair and my nights in hopeless weeping simply is that I am in love with my own ruin. I therefore deserve no sympathy, and probably shan't get it: my own profound self-compassion is enough. I am so abominably self-conscious that no smallest detail in this tragedy eludes me. Day after day I sit in the theatre of my own life and watch the drama of my own history proceeding to its close. Pray God the curtain falls at the right moment lest the play drag on into some long and tedious anticlimax.[53]

It is to obviate this last indignity that he takes the step of committing literary suicide.

An ironic circumstance that Barbellion/Cummings discovers only later is that while he was fashioning with so much anxious ambition his portrait of the tragically blighted artist, James Joyce was completing and publishing the work that has totally eclipsed it. The comparison is cruel but unavoidable; Barbellion makes it himself in *A Last Diary*, calling Joyce's *Portrait of the Artist as a Young Man*, 'Just the book I intended to write'.[54] All too eagerly he covets the place in autobiographical literature won for Stephen Daedalus, but lacks the imagination, the discipline, and the nerve to bring it off. Earlier chapters have indicated the hopes Barbellion entertained for his book's success— as a compensation for the sympathy and recognition denied him in life, and as a self-contained literary work. To take the latter ambition: in giving the book a conclusion and publishing it, what kind of a literary achievement does he take it to be? Two qualities particularly impress him: one is the challenging subtlety and *difficulty* of the personality that has displayed itself with such heroic truthfulness; the other, the bitterly tragic nature of the story, its pathos and its horror.

To some extent these two perspectives conflict with one another, and in so doing embody an ambivalence in Barbellion's self-concept. The ambivalence is apparent throughout much of the *Journal* and Barbellion himself is aware of it. The following passage, entitled 'A Potted Novel', appears towards the end of the book and outlines a literary organization to which the facts of his life would lend themselves. (The fragments of direct speech are quoted from the 1912–14 pages of the diary.)

1) He was an imaginative youth, and she a tragedy queen. So he fell in love with her because she was melancholy and her past tragic. 'She is *capable* of tragedy, too,' he said, which was a high encomium.

But he was also an ambitious youth and all for dalliance in love. 'Marriage,' said he sententiously, 'is an economic trap.' And then, a little wistfully: 'If she were a bit more melancholy and a bit more beautiful she would be quite irresistible.'

2) But he was a miserable youth, too, and in the anguish of loneliness and lovelessness a home tempted him sorely. Still, he dallied. *She* waited. Ill-health after all made marriage impossible.

3) Yet love and misery drove him towards it. So one day he closed his eyes and offered himself up with sacrificial hands ... 'Too late,' she said. 'Once perhaps ... but now ...' His eyes opened again, and in a second Love entered his Temple once more and finally ejected the money changers.

4) So they married after all, and he was under the impression that she had made a good match. He had ill-health perhaps, yet who could doubt his ultimate fame?

Then the War came, and he had the hardihood to open a sealed letter from
his Doctor to the M.O. examining recruits ... Stars and staggers!! So it
was she who was the victim in marriage! That harassing question: Did she
know? What an ass he had been all through, what superlative egoism and
superlative conceit!
5) Then a baby came. He broke under the strain and daily the symptoms grew
more obvious. Did she know? ... The question dazed him.

Well, she *did* know, and had married him for love, nevertheless, against every
friendly counsel, the Doctor's included.
6) And now the invalid's gratitude is almost cringeing, his admiration boundless and his love for always. It is the perfect *rapprochement* between two souls,
one that was honeycombed with self-love and lost in the labyrinthine ways of
his own motives and the other straight, direct, almost imperious in love and
altogether adorable.⁵⁵

It is a distinctly ambiguous state of self-consciousness that prompts an
exercise of this kind. First of all the reduction of his emotional career
to a glib dust-jacket formula constitutes an act of self-mockery in
itself. And then what is one to make of the peculiar tone of the summary? From his stance of narrative detachment, is he rendering his
life (and the journal up to this point) as an ironic comedy or as an
affecting love-story? In a subtle way the self-parody with which he
outlines the early 'chapters' seems to pervade the ostensible sublimity of
the conclusion. As though to redeem his ego from the humiliating
role of cringingly grateful invalid, Barbellion slightly undercuts the
concluding tableau.

The above-quoted version of his story and of the figure he cuts in it
comes from a stage at which the autobiographical intention has developed to a highly conscious state. His self-encounter has not always
been so tortuous. Going back to the early imprints that Barbellion has
chosen to compose his 'detailed, intimate psychological history'⁵⁶
one finds the expression of relatively uncomplicated psychic
states. The first of three editorial divisions of the book, entitled 'At
Home' and going to the end of 1911, comprises a kind of overture to
the main body of the diary. It covers the period in which he worked on
a local newspaper while seeking admission to a university or to the
British Museum of Natural History, and ends with his departure to the
latter institution. The entries for this epoch reveal the Promising
Youth in a variety of lights—enthusiastic over *flora* and *fauna*, wittily
observant of character, acute in his perceptions of himself, and ardently
ambitious, though not without premonitions of perilous health. They

foreshadow also the fluctuations of self-love and self-hatred which
appear prominently later on, as one day's delight with his performance becomes the next day's disgust at his insincerity. In the main,
however, this period is presented as a treacherously bright morning
in which the omens are apparent only in retrospect. Once, in an entry
dated September 1911, the autobiographer with a taste for irony reveals
himself behind the innocent diarist. *A propos* of his father's funeral
Barbellion remarks, '*It is not death but the dreadful possibilities of life
which are so depressing.*'[57] A footnote observes, 'Italics added 1917.'

Taking the story as far as September 1915, Part II ('In London')
records three years of mostly wretchedness from which he is rescued
by marriage to 'E.', only to be transported into an altogether more
exquisite tragedy. Leading a rather solitary life in West Kensington
digs, he spends a great deal of time staring at himself in the mirror,
figuratively speaking. And even literally:

> Then I got up, lit the gas and looking at myself in the mirror, found it was
> really true,—I was a mean creature, wholly absorbed in self.
>   As an act of contrition, I ought to have gone out into the garden and eaten
> worms. But the mirror brought back my self-consciousness and I began to crawl
> back into my recently discarded skin—I began to be less loathesome to myself.
> For as soon as I felt interested or amused or curious over the fact that I had
> been really loathesome to myself I began to regain my equilibrium. *Now* I
> and myself are on comparatively easy terms with one another.[58]

The diary of this period registers a self-preoccupation which intensifies
his sense of the inauthenticity of his existence—as though he has become entangled in a piece of third-rate art. He very frequently renders
situations and encounters in the form of a theatrical script, complete
with sarcastic stage directions. The effect of this device is to emphasize the artificiality of his role-playing. Often he characterizes himself
as the typical 'clever young man', a role which he alternately admires
and despises. When disposed to admire it he regales the reader with
accounts of the agile whimsy and smart repartee with which he and his
friend R. amuse one another. See how well I play these elegant games,
he declares; a veritable Algernon Moncrieff and not even an Oxonian!
(Sad to say, many of the brilliant sallies at which R. is reported to have
bellowed with laughter strike the reader as embarrassingly jejune.)
Sometimes too the clever young man performs directly for the reader's
benefit, affecting an air of sophisticated banter. The book, after all, is
dedicated to preserving the special quality that was Barbellion and, for
better or for worse, this is a mode in which he rather fancies himself:

I tried my best, I've sought every loophole of escape, but I am quite unable to avoid the melancholy fact that her thumbs are—lamentable. I am genuinely upset about it for I like her. No one more than I would be more delighted if they were otherwise . . . Poor dear! how I love her! That's why I'm so concerned about her thumbs.[59]

The obverse of this satisfaction with his good lines and accomplished poses is a frustrated self-contempt provoked by the reflection of his phoniness and pretension. Self-consciousness corrupts the natural spontaneity of his feelings and behaviour, especially with E. whom he courts on and off from 1912. Longing, as he says, for a romantic '*bouleversement*'[60] (something which came so easily to Kilvert), he experiences instead the intermittent stoppage of emotion and the endless talking in the head. The diary both describes the manifestations of his self-consciousness in human intercourse, and continues to exacerbate it with tortuous self-dissection. Here in November 1914, for example, shortly after E. has rejected his first proposal of marriage with the 'Once perhaps . . . but now . . .' formula quoted in the 'Potted Novel', he prepares to make his visit:

Before going over to-night bought *London Opinion* deliberately in order to find a joke or better still some cynicism about women to fire off at her. Rehearsed one joke, one witticism from Oscar Wilde, and one personal anecdote (the latter for the most part false), none of which came off, tho' I succeeded in carrying off a nonchalant or even jaunty bearing.[61]

He then records a couple of cheap *mots* to which she apparently responded coolly, and concludes. 'Is it a wonder she does not love me?' After a row of dots he falls to meditation; for Barbellion even introspection is a public performance, to be conducted with a certain mordant elegance:

I wonder why I paint myself in such horrid colours—why have I this morbid pleasure in pretending to those I love that I am a beast and a cynic? I suffer, I suppose, from a lacerated self-esteem, from a painful loneliness, from the consciousness of how ridiculous I have made myself, and that most people if they knew would regard me with loathing and disgust.

I am very unhappy. I am unhappy because she does not care for me, and I am chiefly unhappy because I do not care for her.[62]

Only a few weeks later, however, she consents to marry him.

The journal immediately begins to bustle with energy, prompted in part by the restoration of faith in himself and interest in life, in part by the declared intention to publish a volume composed of

journal entries. Since his 'story' has not yet acquired its particularly
literary character, the published book would supposedly consist of
'occasional pieces', the gleanings of his teeming brain and flowers of his
spirit. Blithely he delivers himself of dozens of well-turned little
essays to startle and amuse, like a magazine columnist feeding a regular
public. A recurring subject is what he calls 'the Gothic architecture of
my own fantastic soul',[63] but he engages not so much in introspection
now as in the complacent parade of what he takes to be his fascinating
originality. And here is the true pathos of the book, the cruellest
irony of all—he really is not very interesting. Poor Barbellion places
so much faith in the arresting impact of his story when it shall be
known. He even flatters himself in the perverse belief that his book will
disgust and offend the *hypocrite lecteur* with its revelations of a rancid
psyche:

> I toss these pages in the faces of timid, furtive, respectable people and say:
> 'There! that's me! You may like it or lump it, but it's true. And I challenge
> you to follow suit, to flash the searchlight of your self-consciousness into every
> remotest corner of your life and invite everybody's inspection. Be candid, be
> honest, break down the partitions of your cubicle, come out of your burrow,
> little worm.' As we are all such worms we should at least be honest worms.[64]

What a dismal irony that he should be merely ignored!

The third part of the *Journal* ('Marriage') corresponds to sections
4, 5 and 6 of the 'Potted Novel'. It would be presumptuous in a
healthy person to tell a man with arterial sclerosis how to conduct
himself while dying. But in so far as the Disappointed Man's last two
years are a literary arrangement, a work of autobiographical art seeking
recognition on these terms, they have to be declared an artistic mis-
calculation. Like the final movement of Tchaikovsky's 'Pathetique'
Symphony (which Barbellion admires) they seem to be drawn out to
lingering sufferance. 'No smallest detail in this tragedy eludes me',[65]
and he makes sure that it won't elude the reader either. It is all very well
for him to say that 'This continuous pre-occupation with self sickens
me ... It is inconceivable that I should be here steadily writing up
my ego day by day in the middle of this disastrous war ...';[66] he keeps
on, nonetheless, ringing the changes on the themes of desolation,
bitterness, and anguish. Tragic ironies are underscored with gratuitous
footnotes, as for example the 'So it proved. See September 26 *et seq.*'
appended to a May 1916 remark that his state of happiness is 'too good
to last'.[67] And an entry like the following (quoted as it stands) seems

to perform a purely literary function: '*December 4* [1916] The Baby touch is the most harrowing of all. If we were childless we should be merely unfortunate, but an infant . . .'[68]

As for his own role, it need hardly be said that he takes it seriously. 'If I were the cheap hero of a ladies' novel,' he observes, speaking of the gratitude he feels towards E., 'I should immolate my journals as a token, and you would have a pretty picture of a pale young man watching his days go up in smoke by the drawing-room fire.'[69] Would he regard the 'Potted Novel' as fit only for ladies? one wonders. If so, then what distinguishes him from its 'cheap hero' must be his capacity to write it as well as to enact it, in other words, to retain a complex consciousness of his situation. (Immortality in a ladies' novel would surely be the utmost of Kilvert's hopes.) Among the prototypes with whom Barbellion tends to identify, Marie Bashkirtseff has been mentioned earlier; two others are Gregers Werle (in *The Wild Duck*) and John Keats. The former provides an interestingly ambiguous self-image. At one time Barbellion recognizes in Ibsen's character his own 'passion for life to be lived on a foundation of truth in every inter-course',[70] while at another he notes, 'There is a good deal of that ass, Gregers Werle, in my nature.'[71] Considering, however, that he con-ceals from E. for a whole year the fatal nature of his disease (which, as it turns out, she knew before he did), he cannot take the identifi-cation very seriously. The ghost of Keats, on the other hand, has haunted the *Journal* from its beginning. This entry for 1 March 1907 (when he was seventeen) is so stunningly prophetic that one suspects the hand of the artist:

As long as he has good health, a man need never despair. Without good health, I *might* keep a long while in the race, yet as the goal of my ambition grew more and more unattainable I should surely remember the words of Keats and give up: 'There is no fiercer Hell than the failure of a great ambition.'[72]

For several years Barbellion is to be seen in one or another of the 'Nightingale Ode' poses, until at last he finds himself pale, spectre-thin, and dying. In his last years it is Keats the letter-writer, Keats dying in Italy, that he identifies with. ' "My dear Brown, what am I to do?" (I like to dramatize myself like that—it is an anodyne.)'[73] A footnote helpfully locates the quotation as being 'from a letter written by the dying Keats'. Beyond the explicit quotations and ref-erences Barbellion seems to articulate similar attitudes in similar lan-guage to those of the *Letters*. For example, his June 1916 remark that 'my

life has become entirely posthumous'[74] seems to echo another of Keats's
letters to Brown (30 November 1820): 'I have an habitual feeling of my
real life having past, and that I am leading a posthumous existence.'[75]

In its final pages Cummings's book gathers itself for its most artistic
effects. Obviously the closer he comes to the death of 'Barbellion',
the more the entries will tend to be imaginative compositions for a
surrogate, rather than first-hand responses to the writer's situation.
The selection of entries, too, must be especially responsive to aesthetic
considerations, if the book is to have a shapely and satisfying conclusion.
The last dozen or so entries, dated September and October 1917,
constitute a final bid for tragic poignancy. On 1 September he addresses his wife: 'Your love, darling, impregnates my heart, touches it
into calm, strongly beating life so that when I am with you, I forget
I am a dying man.'[76] And he proceeds to speak of the great need for
love which has been thwarted in him and turned to bitterness. On
3 September he describes at length how he dragged his paralysed limbs
around the cottage in search of a bottle of laudanum. An entry entitled
'*Liebestod*' (5 September) concludes with the thought 'that never, never,
never again should I walk thro' the path-fields to the uplands'.[77] And so
he goes on, alternating bleak statements of misery with obliquely
pathetic observations of a lark singing. At last, on 12 October, he
breaks into his final speech:

You would pity me would you? I am lonely, penniless, paralysed, and just
turned twenty-eight. But I snap my fingers in your face and with equal ar-
rogance I pity you. I pity you your smooth-running good luck and the
stagnant serenity of your mind. I prefer my own torment. I am dying, but
you are already a corpse. You have never really lived. Your body has never
been flayed into tingling life by hopeless desire to love, to know, to act, to
achieve. I do not envy you your absorption in the petty cares of a commonplace existence . . .

I am only twenty-eight, but I have telescoped into those few years a tolerably
long life: I have loved and married, and have a family; I have wept and enjoyed; struggled and overcome, and when the hour comes I shall be content to
die.[78]

Two more entries follow. Having sounded his last harmonious
cadence he jars its echo with two single discordant notes, 'Miserable,'
and 'Self-disgust.'[79]

In September 1920 Ivy Jacquier is engaged to be married to a
kindly, taciturn Scot (whom the diary calls 'A.'). She writes: 'In

Evian I started compiling my diary from 1907. It would be of interest in the whole: each part in relation to the other. I feel I may want such things. It is not right to give up what one was. In St. Germain it seemed an added volupté to sacrifice one's own individuality the better to embrace another's. But it is not honest to anyone.'[80] Marriage to A. and life in provincial England will turn her away definitively from all that she has been and imagined herself to be. She is now thirty years old. Her development, of which the diary has received an imprint since she was seventeen, has contained no intimation that this would be its direction. Of mixed French–English parentage, born and brought up in Lyon, educated in England, Dresden, and Paris, and from her teens a devotee of Marie Bashkirtseff, she has hitherto experienced her life as the becoming of a cosmopolitan artist. Now that it has turned out to be the becoming of an English wife she feels a severing of those continuities which she has been used to recognizing as her Self. She can see the past thirteen years of the diary as something apart from her, not a closed book exactly, but a finished bloc of chapters. Three years later, under the influence of considerations noted in Chapters 3 and 4 of this study, she begins to contemplate publication. Actually, it is not until 1960 that the book is published, but 1923 witnesses the essential autobiographical processes of encountering and making accessible her past selves—processes which themselves fertilize a fresh crop of diary imprints. Reviewing her life from this vantage point she perceives a quality and a significant shape which her editing tactfully elicits to make a most attractive and satisfying serial autobiography. 'It is only a small life, if occasionally vivid,' she remarks;[81] 'the sole interest lies in the development'[82] and 'One never is, one has been or is becoming.'[83]

Still another autobiographical perspective is incorporated into the texture of the book when, at the age of sixty, she writes a series of introductory 'Explanations' for different epochs of the diary, identifying the main characters and telling something of their background and what became of them. The effect of this is to surround the entries from her youthful days with the ambiance of time remembered. In reading the testament of the young Ivy Jacquier one is attuned to the consciousness of Ivy Jacquier grown older and wondering at the sheer actuality of her life. An intensely Proustian valuation of the past impels her, in contrast, say, to Barbellion who wants to *exploit* his past rather than to distil and re-possess it. Neither in the bias of her editing nor in retrospective comment from 1923 and 1950 does she brandish or patronize her earlier selves; nor does she point out dramatic ironies in her 'story'. She does, however, maintain a belief (quoted in Chapter 4, p. 91) that for a time she approached a degree of immediate self-realization which subsequently faded and dispersed. Why publish a diary? she asks herself in the 'Explanation for 1907', which also introduces the book as a whole. Because, she replies,

> I realise anew the impossibility of being of one's day, contemporary, except in brief ecstatic moments, or in moments of emotion. Now is timeless.
> In those moments, which are only to be caught by looking backward—when they become more real than reality, being wholly of the spirit—one gets the sense of continuity and of fulfilling a universal law.
> It is for such instants that one lives, and it is of such instances that art is made.[84]

And she goes on to express her sense that the pattern revealed in her life as it unfolded is in many ways an archetypal one—typical of her generation and typical perhaps of a pattern discernible in the experience of women generally. In this possibility lies 'the reason why I think this book might be justified'.[85]

The aspect of her life that in retrospect fills her with wonderment is the state of being registered by the diary between 1907 and 1914. Those are indeed her 'marvellous years', years which not only appear to have been apparelled in a privileged radiance when recalled from fifteen years later, but which seem, from the imprint they made, to have been actually experienced 'on the heights'. At the end of 1916 she reads Pater's *Renaissance* and copies into her diary the famous phrases about the numbered pulses of a variegated, dramatic life, and burning with a gemlike flame.[86] But what seems like the impact of an influence is really, as so often, a recognition in its classic formulation of the law by which she has already lived. Indeed, by 1916 the days of maintaining that ecstasy which is success in life are over, and she has in effect discovered in Pater's words their epitaph. Until the coming of the war, however, Ivy Jacquier was communicating to her diary the resonances of a pitch of intense arousal. The quotation of single entries cannot really convey the character of these years. Their magnetism comes not from any concentrated vividness of language or insight, but from the current of energy that breaks into snatches of abrupt notes and impulsive declarations. As she says of the 'manifesto' in which (at eighteen) she expresses her 'personal conception of art', it is very 'jeune fille'[87]—but that is its special quality. She acts out the role of the *jeune fille passionnée* to its utmost, thrilling to romantic literature (Maeterlinck, D'Annunzio, Meredith . . .), devastated by German opera and later by the Diaghilev Ballet, dedicated to the growth of her art and continually *penetrée* by the arrows of Life. (She also resorts to French quite frequently.) A feeling of vital preparation possesses her; every day is pregnant with crucially formative experiences. Very soon now her life is going to begin, the life in which she will be *striking*, have lovers, live alone in foreign cities, and read all night in sleeping-cars of continental expresses. It would be easy enough to dismiss the diary of this period as little more than the self-dramatizings of an over-literary imagination—but what a way of experiencing the state of being young!

In Dresden in 1908 she comes under the spell of an older girl, Gretchen, the daughter of the family with whom she is living. The relationship is a climactic one with something of the character of an initiation into new complexities, deeper waters. The following three entries (quoted in their entirety with no intervening entries omitted) will serve to illustrate both the impact of Gretchen and the style of her diary's dramatization at this period:

Oct. 15. I seem outside myself; drawn out; not in my own possession. Gretchen and I go to Meissen together where I have continually imagined her. I see her dressed in blue brocade in the castle. I cannot bear the warm tea shop and we come out and have tea in the silent wrecked tragic arbour of a deserted restaurant. We wander into a church where the organist is practising. Gretchen seems to draw my soul out of my body.

Oct. 16. A wonderful day, as all these days are wonderful, leading I know not where—if not to the full realisation of my character through another. I grow older and more 'beautiful' in the Maeterlinck sense of the word, by this feeling that possesses me. I am happy. When shall I again have such a week so nearly perfect? The light of a lamp and the coal fire in the salon and Gretchen playing Beethoven. The human voice grows soft and caressing. I can feel myself changing, growing, and it is almost physically painful, as though I were being stretched —stretched hourly—beyond my height and size and age.

Oct. 20. I play with feeling. Never having suffered I am on a voyage of discovery and all is infinitely vital. I can write this calmly now the quarrel is past. One is like a violin. Only very few can be happy as I was, listening to 'Lohengrin' tonight. I have left England and childhood far behind. If there is suffering in this friendship I accept it. I feel as in a dream. The dream ripens, develops me.[88]

Gretchen is her *animatrice* or, as the 'Explanation for 1909' puts it, 'Reynaldo Hahn to my Proust where music was concerned and Lord Henry to my Dorian Gray'.[89] Under Gretchen's tutelage she loses her religious faith and redoubles her dedication to art. Despairs as well as raptures are accepted as the price of growth into the person who will be worthy of the artistic vocation and Gretchen's love. Looking back in 1923 she writes, 'Now as I truly realize the place Gretchen took up in my life I resent it. One resents domination as nothing else. And yet it was not for the bad. Certainly not for the art for which G. was a spur and a flame.'[90]

From 1910 onwards her life is centred in Paris and Lyon. For four more years—the latter two very sparsely covered, at least as published—she continues to register the vibrations of an ardent nature to music, the theatre, fiction, people, and her own imaginings. Lyon and her home stifle her; Paris and her friends intoxicate. Occasionally she notes down a plan for a novel or a play. Images projected from the diarist's fantasy-life in the form of artistic conceptions naturally have a special interest in this consideration of the self-as-literature. Here are some samples from early in 1911: 'A girl, with her new energy, giving herself to renew an artist—whose life is too intense to be possibly long. The sacrifice would be approved of, providing the artist's genius justified it.' 'A woman submitting herself to the experiments of a young surgeon—her lover—to keep his love and to feel her own to the full sensual measure—which *must* be pain.' 'An intense man loves a woman as intellectually intense as himself. She has brain fever, can recover, but will be mad. He kills her.'[91] A sophisticated Lyonnais named Marcel Schulz, somewhat older than herself, is the original of the man to whom Ivy Jacquier sacrifices herself so splendidly in these fantasies. He utters memorable and dramatic sayings, lectures on Ninon de Lenclos, and 'loves those who live for an ideal'.[92] He is the subject of the following passage, from an entry dated 12 March 1911. With a minimum of transposition into the third person the passage might come straight from one of the 'novels' outlined above—the scene dramatically rendered, a romantic atmosphere evoked in the repeated mention of the Rhône, the quality of the encounter expressed in the psycho-sensual communion of the dance. She has told him that her family find her paintings ugly:

He said: 'd'autres, les, trouveront, belles' very slowly. Today I am eager to live my art. He spoke of the charm of the experienced man for the woman, and the strange antipathy women have for the man who has never lived his life. Also of the impossibility of living one's life and that of one's milieu. The Rhône was purple beneath the windows in the night. The lights went out on the quay. We had supper together: ham, and fish-in-jelly, into which my powder puff fell. In the middle, the orchestra played 'Mon Coeur s'ouvre à ta Voix' from 'Samson et Dalila', and we leapt up and danced alone to it, in a far room on a brown silky carpet, moving with absolute truth to the music, which is impassioned, joyful, youthful and warning. In the dance I learn something which is for my painting. Until three we go on. The quays are silent, the Rhône fathomlessly reflecting lights.[93]

But in 1914 the charmed life is suddenly abolished. Her state of ex-alted imagination has depended so heavily on the waking dream of the European *beau monde*, that she experiences acutely on an individual level the shock of its dispersal. For a short while she participates in the romantic glamorization of the war. On 17 August 1914 she announces, 'J'ai interrompu le livre pour commencer un journal des faits. Devant la guerre la vie personnelle s'efface.'[94] Clearly she expects some kind of self-transcendence in a more glorious dream. She tells of 'Old Gen-eral D'Aubigny' who dines with her family and is 'aflame for France', and of her own realization of a passionate loyalty to that country; she becomes a nurse 'in order to grow, egotistically', and expresses the fear that she will not be 'assez changée par cette guerre' compared with those who will be changed utterly by its terrible beauty.[95] She need have had no fear on this score:

Formerly I had not realized death, loss, vice. Now they seem to be so near. Like poverty. Was it that I did not see them, or is it the war that banishes beautiful things like joy and even beauty in women, jewels, clothes, and in-souciance? Nothing protects one now. One cannot shut doors any more. It is like a veil that has fallen, one is abandoned, and amid crouching sordidity. It is the war. The war has killed youth.[96]

The war lengthens, people close to her are killed; 'the voids are begin-ning in life'.[97] The sublime selfishness of the pre-war days is no longer possible. Her writing grows noticeably more reflective as the moods which send her to the diary become soberly complex, widening to include emotions of loss, regret, weariness, anxiety. She continues to express a passionate appreciation of beautiful things and a belief in the primacy of the emotional response; but as experience comes to include more difficulty and pain, so the openness to it that Pater advocates demands increasingly the exertion of active moral courage.

Moreover the dissolution of the pre-war fantasy has left her in the throes of a crisis of self-definition. As her mid-twenties pass she encounters that clash of mutually exclusive life-options so central in the lives of imaginative women, and virtually unknown to men.

Marriage seems inevitable yet in many ways intolerable, entailing the subordination of her independence and creativity. She who longs 'to grow by everything and feel [herself] evolving'[98] has difficulty envisaging marriage as a context in which to grow. In August 1918 she copies this from Meredith's *Diana of the Crossways*, a book she has come back to with satisfaction: ' "Solitariness is a common human fate, and the one chance for growth, like space for timber".'[99] Yet the prospect of a solitary life is not an inviting one either. The options are so confining, but to abdicate choice and remain at home in Lyon is clearly no solution. Should she blame herself for the restlessness and discontent to which she is subject? Are they a manifestation of the dual temperament to which she was born and which her multi-cultural education intensified? Certainly she has come to regard England and France as poles in her own nature, a commitment to either one requiring the suppression of much that is vital to her. Two entries from February 1919 convey something of the spirit of unrest that torments her. During this time some Americans from a nearby army camp, and in particular an engineer from San Francisco, have been providing an innocuous, if somewhat superficial diversion:

Feb. 2. The Americans to tea this snowy Sunday afternoon. The San Franciscan so human and the comradeship he holds out in a measure allaying the desperation I feel. For I am moody, nervy, kicking against the convention, the protectiveness (he says imprisonment) of our life here, some day soon something will have to come of it. I shall have to do, to be, by myself. If marriage as a liberation fails me, then I shall have to stand on my own feet. Ye Gods . . . I feel frantic.

Feb. 5. Yesterday snowballing with the group, then a long good tired night, sleep with one's body tingling with health. I doubt if I shall long write to my engineer. Why? Missishness with me? That thing I am out to cure in myself? Fastidiousness? Evening—drawing. If I made progress, if I left something behind me however small but delicately lasting in the eyes of three or four people, I could rest at night. I should feel I had participated, feebly perhaps, but participated in life.[100]

'Fastidiousness' means resisting the betrayal of those uncompromising claims on life with which she set out. 'When the fulfilment of passion comes in life it must be the complete thing of brain, and soul, and body. Will this thing be denied me always? I prefer to suffer and not desecrate such passion as I am capable of.'[101]

The last phase of the book, from 1919 to 1926, is the diary of a marriage—a marriage entered upon with trepidation and experienced

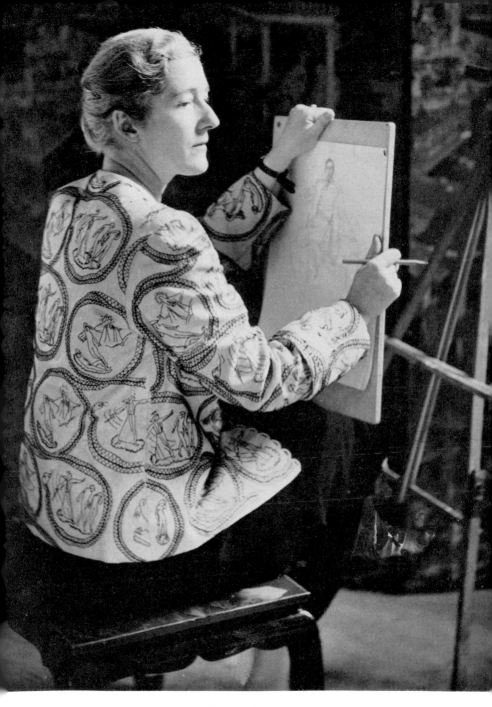

Ivy Jacquier in 1938
She is wearing a coat designed and embroidered by herself

Anaïs Nin

with insistent consciousness. 'Often lately . . . I turn my happiness in my hand, and A., and look at them both, curiously, almost superstitiously. But I *will* be conscious and state what I find!'[102] Increasingly the book reveals the autobiographical design which has informed her editing. She comes to view her career as a kind of test-case, an exploration of the possibilities for self-realization in the life of a woman. While not being a polemically feminist book—she is open to recurring doubts about the worth of the feminine mentality *vis à vis* the masculine—it bases itself in the specifically feminine experience. She is committed to taking note honestly of the fluctuations of feeling and making them expose themselves. Of marriage she writes (in September 1920):

Why risk it for the sake of experience! Why indeed?—when two lonelinesses together are worse than one's own unshared. Because of other people's phrases about 'Fulfilment, Perfection, Completion'? Because once and for all one must know? Because life was sterile, because one must exchange sufferings and accept fate in another way, a new way? Because marriage is expression; and because along the paths of celibacy one has come to the full stop? Because, lurking perhaps timidly, is the idea one might repay devotion and because, perhaps, one's dreams may justify themselves. I force sense into myself. Patience. And draw no sweeping conclusions. And now again the beauty of risk, and enterprise, takes me . . . but only at a whisper. Moods . . . Moods . . . [103]

She is married on 7 May 1921 and early in the following year has a baby girl, Sally. No other diary is so directly *about* the condition of being married. As though to make trial of the myth that marriage is a woman's highest fulfilment she interrogates herself to learn whether it is really enough. As her part of the bargain she invests herself unreservedly in the relationship and prepares to receive its lessons. As it turns out the texture of her happiness is not simple. On balance the diary's testimony is positive, but the imprint does not conceal disappointments and regrets, including the trade-off between passion and a soberer contentment. A mature sensibility engages with the actual and turns it to account:

Discovery: that love is not all in life even for women . . . If we faced love as men do we would be happier. As episodes, accesses. Life is not meant for love alone. We are hipped by the old saws of women about life turning on love etc., etc. Je veux surmonter ma fémininité. Love is not the whole of life. One ought to use men as they use us, as a means of experience to more knowledge. (Not more men because one is fairly monogamous.) To realise what A.'s given me for instance. A fuller life, more established, more rounded, ... and then be self-supporting, a person, not a wife. Love like my creative powers comes and goes. I think often I shall never paint again—and it comes back.[104]

She seeks an equilibrium that takes account of those claims of her nature that must be reconciled.

An important element of Ivy Jacquier's life has always been the moral and creative sway of certain exceptional women, notably Gretchen and Kate Hardy (the latter an American in her fifties, living in Paris, whom the diarist first met in 1910). The last pages of the book are dominated by the figure of Mrs. Wilson, the wife of a Canon Wilson of Worcester. In 1922 Mrs. Wilson is sixty-five and a woman whose vitality and balance declare that she has dealt creatively with the second half of life. Neither simple nor resigned, she has a wisdom of which Ivy Jacquier feels the need, as she herself endeavours to live coherently by values authentically arrived at. Especially for the sake of her daughter she desires to continue growing in spirit and intelligence. Mrs. Wilson, she says, is a recurrent inspiration, 'an "animatrice" ', 'a trumpet call to my spirit',[105] an embodied goal of self-development. With the fact of Mrs. Wilson she seeks to arm herself against the incursions of futility and fear: 'We cultivate more power, more knowledge, more charm. How sad—for so soon our vitality lowers and we ape our best days. Yet Mrs. Wilson says, "Do look forward to old age, I beg of you." I cannot believe it.'[106]

With the year 1926 the serial autobiography comes to an unobtrusively artistic close. She is thirty-six. In an entry dated 8 January 1907—the second entry in the book—she had written, 'When I am calmer and better balanced I shall like things in a better way, in a calmer, better balanced way. That is why I think I should like to be 36 years old—it is the uncertainty I hate.'[107] 1926 is also the year of Mrs. Wilson's death, and four of the year's seven pages are taken up by two entries relating to her. The first is a long letter from Mrs. Wilson herself, a direct imprint of the qualities of humane intelligence and courage in the face of death which the diarist reveres. The second consists of a eulogy written, as Ivy Jacquier says, 'self-consciously, not diary-fashion, yet impulsively'.[108] Her tribute to the dead woman's greatness—'mankind at its best'[109]—constitutes her profession of faith in an ideal of Culture (in the largest sense), the achievement of which would justify existence. She concludes the entry, 'I am beset ever by the fear of infidelity of memory; therefore I write of her, to register

that which she gave me once and for all.'[110] Some half-a-dozen more
brief entries return attention to the life which goes on, and the book ends.

A central concern of this study has been with the manner in which
Life imitates Art. It has dealt with diarists who in various ways have
projected themselves and their experience *imaginatively*; who, through
styles of language and identification with literary roles, have cultivated
transformations of themselves. Some have been relatively unaware of
the process and would have believed that they were expressing themselves 'naturally'; others have consciously sought to draw towards
literary models, but for ulterior motives of self-development or self-
promotion. Anaïs Nin differs from both types. Her diary is the instrument of a deliberate and general endeavour to transform reality
through the exercise of imagination—not to escape or distort it, but
to fulfil it; to realize reality at a level attainable only by imaginative
penetration into it. A good deal has already been said about Anaïs Nin
earlier in this investigation. To conclude this chapter, and the study
as a whole, consideration will be given briefly to one cardinal feature
of her writing, a feature summed up in the following claim: 'My self
is like the self of Proust. It is an instrument to connect life and the
myth.'[111]

Anaïs Nin is really the only diarist fully to recognize and exploit the
tendency of serial autobiography to intensify whatever perceptions of
the self's relation to the world are registered by it. As has been shown
(in Chapters 3 and 4) it was some time before she could be liberated
from misgivings about the role of the diary in her life and could come
to affirm its life-enhancing power. In February 1940 she writes:

When Gonzalo discusses his talks with Antonin Artaud, the period of working
for his theater, the long walks through Paris after the evenings of rehearsals,
when they were staging *Beatrice Cenci*, and he described Artaud in a fever of
ideas and projects; or when Henry described his nights with June and Jean in
the cellar room on Henry Street, I always listened with a kind of jealousy and
envy, as if I had never known, or would ever know such nights. This was
because their way of telling their experiences heightened them so much that
they seemed to bear no resemblance to any experience in my own life. . . . It
was not until I achieved the same power of dramatization of my own life that
I could begin to live it with a sense of the extraordinary. It was this that made
me so restless, the disparity between the imagined and the actual.[112]

To live with a sense of the extraordinary is her constant quest, drawing
her towards the forms of thought which promise to extend the

imaginative dimensions of experience. Psychoanalysis, astrology, the study of myth and dream, surrealism, and what she calls 'the madness of the poets' all feed the imagination with structures of symbolic meaning, suggesting levels of 'correspondance' beneath the separate appearances of things. To be attuned to such modes of interpretation is to remain open to the marvellous, to endow life with the properties of dream. It is essential, however, that the flow of suggestion be free and unforced, and she several times expresses disappointment with the surrealists and with Joyce for, as she says, 'imitating' the life of the unconscious rather than making it directly articulate.

Surrealism reached an impasse by listing unfinished, incomplete dreams considered by themselves. But the dream passes again into reality, affects reality, and from the acts stems the dream, and it continues to make an interlocking chain which contains the mysterious pattern we must unravel. We cannot merely contemplate or register it. It is an interdependence which produces the highest form of life, an expanded consciousness.[113]

Similarly she rejects the tendency of psychoanalysis to systematize, to become doctrinaire, and to set up a sterile conception of psychic health.

To experience waking life as though it were a dream does not mean drifting into vague reverie; quite the contrary. In the dream-experience situations, encounters, phenomena are apprehended with a praeternatural clarity and immediacy, and contain intimations of mysterious significance. Recounting a dream one must guard against obliterating its singularity by the imposition of debased and inert language or of commonplace structures of interpretation. Only the creative-exploratory testing of words against the experience will succeed in rendering it faithfully and in keeping the mind responsive to fresh impressions. In effect, Anaïs Nin's diary is the narration of a years-long dream. The techniques of her writing are exactly those best suited to the description of dream-experience: very often she writes in the present tense, as though to render impressions which are immediately present to her mind's eye; abrupt transitions convey the dreamlike effect in which one scene becomes another without intermediate progression; she seeks to impart the vivid 'feel' of the dream situation, the air of symbolic redolence. In the following passage, from June 1933, she is describing the occasion of a visit to Artaud:

I have come dressed in black, red, and steel, like a warrior, to defend myself against possession. His room is bare like a monk's cell. A bed, a desk, a chair.

I look at the photographs of his amazing face, an actor's changeful face, bitter, dark, or sometimes radiant with a spiritual ecstasy. He is of the Middle Ages, so intense, so grave. He is Savonarola burning pagan books, burning pleasures. His humor is almost satanic, no clear joy, just a diabolical mirth. His presence is powerful; he is all tautness and white flames. In his movements there is a setness, an intensity, a fierceness, a fever which breaks out in perspiration over his face.

He shows me his manuscripts, talks about his plans, he talks darkly, he woos me, kneeling before me. I repeat all I have said before. Everything is whirling around us. He rises, his face twisted, set, stony.[114]

To revive and re-enter the scene through the medium of this kind of prose is to give rein to total subjectivity. Not what 'really' took place, but what really *seemed* to be taking place is the important thing to lay hold of. The 'meaning' of an experience, its contribution to the evolution of the self, will be elicited not by setting aside the subjective response but by compelling it to express itself in images which will be the clues to its symbolic dimensions. Of the poet Robert Duncan, with whom she has been exchanging diaries for a time, she writes: 'Robert's diary could flow into this one and become a part of it because the quest is similar. We seek ultimate awareness by way of the symbolical meaning of our acts and dreams.'[115] This is not to suggest that the diary reads like a work of occult mysticism; it is more like a symphonic prose-poem, the intricate unceasing elaboration of a legend. The transmutation of prose into poetry embodies for her the task of imagination in the face of reality. When she goes to live in America at the outbreak of war the task becomes doubly demanding as the whole culture, the tenor of human intercourse, resists such a process.

In America, poetry is being retranslated into prose. All effort to make the transmutation required of poetry, which is an alchemy of ordinary natural events into heightened myth, is taboo. Yet the very role of the poet is to exalt whatever he touches, it is to take ordinary reality and give it a fiery incandescence which reveals its meaning.[116]

A primary effect of this 'alchemy' is the magnification of real individuals into legendary figures. Her world, as the diary captures it, seems to be peopled by superbly larger-than-life characters, each one the protagonist of a drama. Two aspects of her power to effect this transfiguration may be distinguished. First, in her actual relationships she undoubtedly stimulates people to enact their most creative self-dramatizations. Her concentrated responsiveness to each relationship draws from the other party to it a uniqueness he or she may never have experienced before. She writes:

How each friend represents a world in us, a world possibly not born until they arrive, and it is only by this meeting that a new world is born. With Gonzalo I rediscovered my Spanish world, my Spanish blood, warmth and personal involvement, direct passionate response to experience, fire, fanaticism, fervor, faith, the power to act *whole*, wholeness, caring.[117]

As she seeks to realize herself anew in each encounter, at the same time she evokes the self-realization of the other. Meditating on the relationship between Luise Rainer and Clifford Odets, and the impossibility of perceiving the lover's image of the beloved, she continues, 'Because love not only can detect a potential, an unborn personality, a buried one, a disguised one, but also bring it into reality.'[118] In at least this sense Anaïs Nin approaches everyone with love. The second aspect of her 'creation' of characters is the manner in which she renders them in the diary. In the case of people with whom she is intimately involved she returns again and again to the search for the imagery, the identification, the symbolism that will express her realization of them. As portraits they are complex, many-sided composites. She actively pursues the contradictions, dualities in their natures, seeking to apprehend them as essentially nondefinable, not larger than life she might say, but *as large*. Here is a fragment of her rendering of Gonzalo, the Peruvian revolutionary. When she first meets him, early in 1936, he has descended to the level of a Montparnasse bum, living in utter poverty with his wife Helba, once a Latin-American dancer, now wrapt in deafness and disease. Anaïs inspires him with a revival of pride and revolutionary fervour which he invests in the Spanish Republican cause.

There is in him an anarchist, a naïve child who trusts and forgives, a Bohemian who does not care a damn, a fanatic who is ready to kill for Marxism, a drunkard who forgets all his responsibilities at a bar, a religious mystic who falls into a trance at Notre Dame, an Indian with his secrets from all white men, his melancholy and inertia, a violent Moor, a Catholic nursemaid to Helba, an Indian slave, an Indian rebel. He has a lashing Voltairian tongue when he is angry, he has sudden miraculous generosities, nobilities, he will give his life for a friend, for the weak, yet his own life is filled with mishaps, and at times great storms of bitter anger which take the form of long tongue-lashing monologues.[119]

'The Inca Don Quixote,' she calls him, 'the dark Indian . . . cursed with a soul.'[120] The diary devotes many pages to the stories he tells of his early life in Peru, elaborating his legend. Characteristically she lets him stand for one of the theses of the psychic dialectic of her own evolution. Many of her relationships are rendered as dramatic enactments of aspects of dualities in herself, and for a time Gonzalo and Henry Miller are perceived as opposing principles. The one insists on her obligation as an artist and as human being to engage in political commitment; the other asserts the absolute selfishness of the artist. Gonzalo demands that she should subordinate her private world to the claims of the revolutionary struggle in Spain and harness her consciousness to Marxism. He persuades her to burn all her books. 'It seemed like a barbaric ritual, burn the books which taught me to dream. Gonzalo's eyes were burning with a fierce pride. The greatest sacrifice I could offer to his faith: if I stopped dreaming and being merely the nurse to the wounded, I could help to transform the world.'[121] She is convinced by the sincerity of his faith, his own readiness to sacrifice, yet cannot believe steadily in the value of revolutionary action:

And I asked myself if the artist who creates a world of beauty to sustain and transcend and transmute suffering is wiser than those who believe a revolution will remove the causes of suffering. The question remains unanswered. Was art, like religion, a mere palliative, a drug, an opium? Some of the artists I knew were destroyed by the same poverty which destroys the people. Artaud is insane in Sainte-Anne.[122]

Moreover she sees with increasing clarity the chaotic irresponsibility of the man whose energy can be diverted so easily into evasive indulgences. She had wanted to realize in Gonzalo a revolutionary leader whose personal greatness of character would overpower her imagination, and she finds instead a helpless child, psychologically and materially dependent on her. She writes in January 1939:

Gonzalo has not led me out of my world into a better one. I thought my father would lead me into a vaster world of experience, but he could not do it because he was bound in guilt, and this guilt took the form of idealizing his actions, and camouflaging them. Henry was never a leader, he was always letting things happen. Somehow or other, the man who could take me out of my own world never crossed my path, or if he did he disguised himself in my presence.[123]

Gonzalo, Henry, her father; she might also add Allendy and Otto Rank to the gallery of characters out of whom she has sought to create the hero and teacher in whom faith might be possible. In this endeavour the roles of the artist and of the woman are fused. Repeatedly she has attempted to make the effort of faith and imagination that will bring into being the mythic figure, the one whose existence will reciprocally transfigure her own life. And not only the male figures; on June Miller too she exercised her mythopoeic imagination in an effort to seize upon the incarnation of a goddess:

All the poetry written, all the erotic imaginings, all the obsessions, illusions, nightmares, manias, what are they if there is no June, the warm being walking and touching us? Sterile, all our cries, all our staggering words, all the heat and fervor of storytelling, sterile our creations, if there were no June passing through like the supreme materialization of them all, with a demonic indifference to human order, human limitations and restrictions.[124]

Much later she comes to identify June and Gonzalo as belonging among 'the uncreative ones', the bearers of chaos.[125] As she plumbs the anarchic disorder of Gonzalo's life she writes, 'At times I think I am Henry describing June and I am writing my own *Capricorn*. But Henry was blind while it happened while I am not blind.'[126]

One of the deep rhythms of her serial autobiography is the ebb and flow of that energy with which she seeks to actualize the life-enhancing myths. After each failure she seems to withdraw, to repossess herself in preparation for the next voyage. As rendered by the diary her search for a viable orientation to life has the character of an archetypal quest; as she says 'Any experience carried out deeply to its ultimate leads you beyond yourself into a larger relation to the experience of others.'[127] Thus she encounters *herself* on a mythic plane, exploring the connection between individual and universal experience. It is in reply to Lawrence Durrell and Henry that she makes the claim quoted earlier and here placed in its context:

They suddenly attacked my personal relation to all things, by personification of ideas. To make history or psychology alive I personify it. Also everything depends on the nature of the personal relationship. My self is like the self of Proust. It is an instrument to connect life and the myth. I quoted Spengler, who said that all historical patterns are reproduced in individual man, entire historical evolutions are reproduced in one man in one lifetime.[128]

Her life dramatizes a universal quest for transcendence of the dualities that hold life down. More particularly, however, it is the psychic evolution of woman that she seeks to reproduce in her individual life. In her imaginative re-entry into episodes like the encounter with her father and the birth of the dead baby she pursues the elemental quality of the experience. Rank helps her to understand the former in terms of Father and Daughter myths; the story of the latter she describes as 'woman facing nature'.[129] A recurring theme is the psychic conflict between femininity and artistic creation. She finds in herself that the role of the artist runs counter to the role of the woman (as she has learned it), breeding a guilt which drives her to masochistic degrees of self-sacrifice. To atone for her usurpation of a masculine prerogative she martyrs herself in the role of mother to any number of dependent males. Later in 1942, at the crisis of a period during which she has been making enormous expenditures of herself to sustain those around her, she turns again to psychoanalysis. The analyst is a woman, Martha Jaeger, and Anaïs writes: 'It is strange how I turned to the woman and the mother for understanding. I have had all my relationships with men, of all kinds. Now my drama is that of the woman in relation to herself—her conflict between selfishness and individuality . . .'[130] As they attack together a problem in the psychology of women which Rank had confessed himself unable to understand, she expresses the sense of undertaking an exploration on behalf of many others:

> I represent, for other women too, the one who wanted to create with, by, and through her femininity.
> I am a good subject because I have lived out everything, and because contrary to most creative women of our time I have not imitated man, or become man . . .
> The evolution of woman. I am living it and suffering it for all women. I have loved as woman loves.[131]

The third volume of the diary ends in a mood of harmony and re-affirmation. 'Analysis has to do with flow,' she writes; 'I am flowing again.'[132] During 1943 she spends much time in the society of a group of Haitians. After the debilitations of the New York literary cliques and the constant depression of the war, their joyousness and tropical vitality are a refreshment to her. 'I took the Haitians into my devastated life and into my diary as one places fragrant flowers in a book, my life blossoming anew because of them.'[133] She speaks of a sense of 'integration . . . like watching dispersed mercury magnetically gather itself into one unit.'[134] Identifying 'romanticism' with neurosis, as 'a quest for passion and intensity merely as a cure for anxiety,'[135] she refocuses her attention from the remote to the close-at-hand. Her first two volumes ended with a setting out. In 1934 she was leaving Paris to join Rank in New York, full of the exhilaration of a new psychic freedom:

> I may not become a saint, but I am very full and very rich. I cannot install myself anywhere yet; I must climb dizzier heights. But I still love the relative,

P.C.—7*

not the absolute: the cabbage and the warmth of a fire, Bach on the phono-
graph, and laughter, and talk in the cafés, and a trunk packed for departure,
with copies of *Tropic of Cancer*, and Rank's last SOS and the telephone ringing
all day, good-bye, good-bye, good-bye . . .[136]

Five years later another volume ends with another departure, a flight
from war: 'We all knew we were parting from a pattern of life we
would never see again, from friends we might never see again. I knew
it was the end of our romantic life.'[137] The conclusion of Volume 3
is a spiritual homecoming, a sojourn in Ithaca:

Having gathered together the fevers, the conquests, the passions, having
pulled in the sails of my ever-restless, ever-wandering ships of dreams . . .
having garnered, collected, called back from the Tibetan desert my ever-roaming
soul, having rescued my spirit from the webs of the past, from the stranglehold
of responsibility for the lives of others, having cured myself of the drugs of
romanticism, surrendered the impossible dreams and called back an exhausted
Don Quixote, I close the window, and the door, and open the diary once
more.[138]

★   ★   ★

Briefly to conclude this chapter and the study as a whole: it has been
the aim of the foregoing chapter to elaborate, in the case of five diaries
particularly susceptible to such an approach, the conception of the
'serial autobiography'—a literary character which, this book has
argued, expresses diary-writing in its most developed form. In the
light of this conception a diary will reveal the nature and degree of its
responsiveness to literary models for the organization of experience
and the dramatization of the personal role. It will also define a place
for itself in the genre, in terms both of its historical significance in
an evolving convention, and of its distinction, its stature, and its
interest as—to end appropriately on a key-note—a 'book of the self'.

Notes

✟✟✟

(Bibliographical details of books mentioned in the text, but not directly quoted, are to be found in the Bibliography. Direct quotations from and specific references to works listed in the Bibliography are identified in the following notes in the simplest form consistent with clarity. When two or more publishers of a work are listed in the Bibliography, but the pagination is the same for each, the notes do not indicate the edition specifically quoted.)

CHAPTER ONE Introduction

1. Ponsonby, *English Diaries*, 5.
2. Spalding, *Self Harvest*, 46.
3. Ponsonby, *English Diaries*, 34–5.
4. Ibid., 9.
5. D. Wordsworth, *Journals*, 121.

CHAPTER TWO Historical Perspectives

1. Spalding, *Self Harvest*, 66–7.
2. Pepys, *Diary*, ed. Latham and Matthews, II, 64–5. (N.B. At the time of writing, publication of the Latham-Matthews edition of Pepys's *Diary* has proceeded as far as Volume VII, which runs to the end of the year 1666. Since this is the definitive edition it seems perverse not to use as much of it as is currently available. For the period 1667–9, the Wheatley edition is used. See Bibliography for details of the two editions. Subsequent footnotes will identify quotations from Pepys as follows: Pepys, LM, II, 66; or Pepys, W, IV, 66.)
3. Bacon, *Essays*, 'Of Travel'.
4. E. S. de Beer's introduction to *The Diary of John Evelyn* provides a thorough account of the compilation and composition of this book, Vol. I, 44–114.
5. Ward, 'Diary', in *Two Elizabethan Puritan Diaries*, ed. Knappen, 104.
6. Rogers, 'Diary', ibid., 84 (Editorial insertions by Knappen).
7. Hoby, *Diary*, 67.
8. See Evelyn, *Diary*, I, 75–7 (Introduction), for discussion and facsimiles.
9. Dee, *Diary*, 23.
10. Eyre, 'Diary', in *Yorkshire Diaries*, ed. Morehouse, 81.
11. Ben Jonson, *Volpone*, ed. P. Brockbank (New Mermaid Series, London: Benn, 1968); IV, i, 135–44.
12. Slingsby, *Diary*, 54–5; Montaigne, *Essays* (Florio translation), Book I, Ch. 34, 'Of a Defect in our Policies'.
13. Boswell, *Ominous Years*, 265.
14. Kay, *Diary*, 24.

15. Jones, *Diary*, 4.
16. Ibid., 55–6.
17. Johnson, *Diaries, Prayers, and Annals*, 155.
18. Mary Cowper, *Diary*, 1.
19. H. L. Thrale, *Thraliana*, 482.
20. Fielding, 'Journal of a Voyage to Lisbon', *Works*, VIII, 83.
21. Byrd, *London Diary*, 136.
22. Sterne, *Journal to Eliza*, 137.
23. H. L. Thrale, *Thraliana*, 583.
24. Pepys, LM, I, xcvii–cvi.
25. Scott, *Journal*, I, 1.
26. See Girard, *Le Journal Intime*.
27. Quentin Bell's edition of the complete Virginia Woolf Diaries is expected to appear in the mid-1970s.

CHAPTER THREE The Diary as Literature

1. Ponsonby, *British Diarists*, Chapter IX. His choice of the nine best diarists lists Pepys, Woodforde, Fanny Burney, Jones, Haydon, Dorothy Wordsworth, Scott, Caroline Fox, and Barbellion.
2. Ponsonby, *English Diaries*, 1.
3. O'Brien, *English Diaries and Journals*, 7–8.
4. Ibid., 8.
5. Ibid., 9.
6. Ponsonby, *English Diaries*, 1.
7. Matthews, 'The Diary as Literature', in the Latham-Matthews edition of Pepys's *Diary*, I, xcvii–cxiii.
8. Matthews, *Bibliography*, x.
9. Ponsonby, *English Diaries*, 82.
10. Ibid., 35.
11. Pepys, LM, I, ciii.
12. Ponsonby, *English Diaries*, 82.
13. Pepys, LM, II, 73.
14. Pepys, W, VIII, 313.
15. Pepys, LM, I, xlv.
16. Webb, *Diaries*, I, 80.
17. Jacquier, *Diary*, 199.
18. Boswell, *London Journal*, 205–6.
19. Ibid., 269.
20. Boswell, *Holland*, 114.
21. Boswell, *In Search of a Wife*, 238.
22. Boswell, *London Journal*, 84–161; *Germany and Switzerland*, 212–13.
23. Haydon, *Diary*, V, 263–4.
24. Ibid., II, 265.
25. Ibid., II, 363.
26. Ibid., III, 195.
27. Ibid., V, 553.
28. Barbellion, *Last Diary*, viii.
29. Barbellion, *Journal of a Disappointed Man*, 68.

30. Ibid., 158.
31. Ibid, 280.
32. Scott, *Journal*, I, 124.
33. Nin, *Diary*, 11, 244.
34. Ibid., I, 333–4.
35. Ibid., II, 110.
36. Ibid., II, 202.
37. Ibid., II, 115.
38. Woolf, *A Writer's Diary* (Hogarth Press), 13–14.
39. Nin, *Diary*, III, 173.
40. Kilvert, *Diary*, II, 210–11.
41. Ibid., II, 83.
42. Burney, *Early Diary*, I, 189.
43. Ibid., I, 282.
44. Burney, *Evelina*, 255.
45. Brown, *Symonds: A Biography*, 81–2.
46. Ibid., 120.
47. Barbellion, *Journal of a Disappointed Man*, 287.
48. Ibid., 210.
49. Quennell, ed., *Byron: A Self-Portrait*, I, 234.
50. Boswell, *In Search of a Wife*, 258.
51. Bennett, *Journals*, I, 155.
52. D. Wordsworth, *Journals*, 122–3.
53. E. Barrett, *Diary*, 45–6.
54. A. James, *Diary*, 64.
55. Ibid., 158.

CHAPTER FOUR Motive and Manner

1. Boswell, *Ominous Years*, 220.
2. Franz Kafka, *The Diaries of Franz Kafka, 1910–13*, tr. J. Kresh, ed. Max Brod (London: Penguin Modern Classics, 1972), 35.
3. Ryder, *Diary*, 29.
4. Ibid., 196.
5. Ibid., 250.
6. Windham, *Diary*, 161.
7. Ibid., 130–1.
8. Ibid., 131.
9. Boswell, *Ominous Years*, 265.
10. Pepys, W, VIII, 152.
11. Slingsby, *Diary*, 54.
12. Slingsby, *Original Memoirs*.
13. Scott, *Journal*, I, 1.
14. Ibid., I, 132.
15. Kilvert, *Diary*, III, 107.
16. Ibid., II, 17–18.
17. Sturt, *Journals*, 116.
18. Ibid., 148.
19. Ibid., 150.

20. *Memoirs of a Surrey Labourer, The Bettesworth Book.*
21. Sturt, *Journals*, 266–7.
22. Boswell, *London Journal*, 39–40.
23. Pottle, introduction to *London Journal*, 10–16.
24. Boswell, *London Journal*, 255–6.
25. Ibid., 257–8.
26. Boswell, *In Search of a Wife*, 134.
27. Boswell, *Germany and Switzerland*, 56.
28. Boswell, *London Journal*, 337–8.
29. Boswell, *Ominous Years*, 174–5.
30. Boswell, *London Journal*, 305.
31. Boswell, *For the Defence*, 182.
32. Boswell, *Ominous Years*, 66.
33. Ibid., 214.
34. Haydon, *Diary*, V, 457.
35. Neville, *Diary*, 221–2.
36. Ibid., 85–6.
37. Ibid., 113.
38. Ibid., 45.
39. Ibid., 149.
40. Ibid., 160.
41. Ibid., 161.
42. Ibid., 166.
43. Ibid., 181–2.
44. Barbellion, *Journal of a Disappointed Man*, 168–9.
45. Ibid., 170.
46. Ibid., 179.
47. Ibid., 134.
48. Ibid., 136.
49. Ibid., 137.
50. Ibid., 255.
51. Burney, *Early Diary*, I, 52.
52. Ibid., I, 5.
53. Ibid., I, 314.
54. D. Wordsworth, *Journals*, 15–16.
55. Ibid., 139.
56. E. Barrett, *Diary*, i.
57. Ibid., 19.
58. A. James, *Diary*, 25.
59. Jacquier, *Diary*, 151.
60. Ibid, 204.
61. Boswell, *Germany and Switzerland*, 56.
62. Nin, *Diary*, I, 155.
63. Ibid., I, 307.
64. Ibid., I, 202.
65. Ibid., I, 277.
66. Ibid., I, 307.
67. Ibid., II, 205.

CHAPTER FIVE Style, Tone, and Self-Projection

1. Jones, *Diary*, 113.
2. Pepys, LM, I, civ.
3. Ibid., III, 174–9.
4. Ibid., III, 86.
5. Pepys, W, VII, 326–7.
6. Ibid., VII, 329.
7. Boswell, *London Journal*, 279.
8. Pepys, LM, III, 64.
9. Ibid., VI, 46–7.
10. Pepys, W, VIII, 144.
11. Pepys, LM, III, 205.
12. Kay, *Diary*, 49.
13. Ibid., 112.
14. Ibid., 145.
15. Ibid., 157.
16. Ibid., 157.
17. Ibid., 158.
18. Ibid., 159.
19. Ibid., 160.
20. Jones, *Diary*, 113.
21. Ibid., 147.
22. Ibid., 221.
23. Ibid., 206.
24. Ibid., 274.
25. Ibid., 175–6, 179.
26. Ibid., 198.
27. Ibid., 230.
28. Ibid., 158, 180, and 213–15 respectively.
29. Ibid., 114–26.
30. Ibid., 210.
31. Ibid., 208, 249–50.
32. Ibid., 211.
33. Ibid., 180.
34. Ibid., 94.
35. Ibid., 175.
36. Scott, *Journal*, I, 279.
37. Ibid., I, 256.
38. Ibid, I, 49.
39. Moore, *Memoirs*, IV, 331–43 and V, 3–5.
40. Scott, *Journal*, I, 6.
41. Ibid., I, 7.
42. Ibid., I, 11.
43. Pepys, LM, II, 9.
44. Scott, *Journal*, II, 103.
45. Ibid., I, 46.
46. Ibid., I, 49–50.
47. Ibid., I, 171.

48. Ibid., I, 173.
49. Ibid., I, 172.
50. Ibid., I, 290.
51. Quennell, ed., *Byron: A Self Portrait*, I, 290.
52. Ibid., I, 220–1.
53. Ibid., I, 226.
54. *Byron and Shakespeare* and 'Byron's Dramatic Prose' in *Poets of Action*, (Methuen), 266–93.
55. Quennell, ed., *Byron: A Self Portrait*, I, 247.
56. Ibid., I, 226.
57. Ibid., I, 244.
58. Ibid., I, 250–1.
59. Ibid., I, 252.
60. Ibid., I, 232.
61. Ibid., I, 256–7.
62. G. Wilson Knight, *Poets of Action* (Methuen), 287.
63. Alice James, *Diary*, 45.
64. Ibid., 87.
65. Ibid., 218.
66. Ibid., 73.
67. Ibid., 121.
68. Ibid., 76.
69. Barbellion, *Journal of a Disappointed Man*, 136.
70. Alice James, *Diary*, 206–7.
71. Ibid., 218
72. Ibid., 135.
73. Ibid., 78–9.
74. Ibid., 79.
75. Ibid., 125.
76. Katherine Mansfield, *Journal*, 3.
77. Ibid., 37.
78. Ibid., 96.
79. Ibid., 70.
80. Ibid., 80.
81. Ibid., 96.
82. Ibid., 97.
83. Ibid., 94.
84. Ibid., 186.
85. Ibid., 296–7.
86. Ibid., 199.

CHAPTER SIX Ego and Ideal

1. Sturt, *Journals*, I, 156.
2. Barbellion, *Journal of a Disappointed Man*, 185.
3. Ibid., 180, 238, 212.
4. K. Mansfield, *Journal*, 205.
5. Nin, *Diary*, I, 47.
6. Ryder, *Diary*, 358–9.

7. Ibid., 90.
8. Ibid., 51, 242.
9. Ibid., 90.
10. Ibid., 357, 346.
11. Ibid., 195, 272, 274.
12. Ibid., 228.
13. Ibid., 309.
14. Ibid., 200.
15. Ibid., 204.
16. Locke, *Essay*, I, 216.
17. Ibid., I, 218.
18. Ibid., I, 221.
19. Ibid., I, 211.
20. Ryder, *Diary*, 219.
21. Ibid., 63, 117.
22. Ibid., 91.
23. Ibid., 207, 122–3, 76.
24. Ibid., 185.
25. Ibid., 263.
26. Ibid., 294.
27. Ibid., 335.
28. Ibid., 348.
29. Ibid., 342–3.
30. Ibid., 272–3.
31. Ibid., 121.
32. Ibid., 214–15.
33. Ibid., 91.
34. Ibid., 359.
35. Ibid., 359.
36. Quennell, ed., *Byron: A Self Portrait*, I, 219–20.
37. Windham, *Diary*, 96.
38. Ibid., 110.
39. Ibid., 44.
40. Ibid., 77.
41. Ibid., 284.
42. Ibid., 284.
43. Ibid., 286.
44. Boswell, *In Search of a Wife*, 343.
45. Boswell, *London Journal*, 39.
46. Boswell, *Holland*, 375–8.
47. Ibid., 377.
48. Boswell, *Germany and Switzerland*, 28–9.
49. Ibid., 143.
50. Boswell, *Italy, Corsica, France*, 299–300.
51. Boswell, *London Journal*, 269, 288.
52. Boswell, *Italy, Corsica, France*, 303.
53. Ibid., 297.
54. Boswell, *In Search of a Wife*, xi.

55. Ibid., 147.
56. Ibid., 148.
57. Ibid., 245–6.
58. Ibid., 241.
59. Boswell, *For the Defence*, 86.
60. Boswell, *In Extremes*, 178–9.
61. Boswell, *Ominous Years*, 239–40.
62. Boswell, *In Search of a Wife*, 299.
63. Boswell, *Ominous Years*, 306.
64. Boswell, *In Extremes*, 64–5.
65. Boswell, *Ominous Years*, 178.
66. Boswell, *In Extremes*, 42.
67. Ibid., 34.
68. Ibid., 217.
69. Ibid., 217.
70. Ibid., 168.
71. Ibid., 173.
72. Morris, *Versions of the Self*, 208.

CHAPTER SEVEN Forms of Serial Autobiography

1. Pascal, *Design and Truth in Autobiography*, 3.
2. Ibid., 5.
3. Barbellion, *Journal of a Disappointed Man*, 68.
4. Haydon, *Diary*, II, 4.
5. Ibid., V, 556.
6. Published by Tom Taylor in 1843 as *Life of Benjamin R. Haydon* (see Bibliography).
7. Haydon, *Diary*, V, 553.
8. Ibid., II, 131–2.
9. Ibid., I, 369.
10. Ibid., II, 10.
11. Ibid., II, 298.
12. Ibid., II, 273.
13. Ibid., V, 397.
14. Ibid., II, 285–6.
15. Ibid., II, 358.
16. Ibid., II, 412–13.
17. Ibid., II, 417.
18. Ibid., II, 419.
19. Ibid., II, 420–1.
20. Ibid., II, 475.
21. Ibid., III, 74.
22. Ibid., III, 268.
23. Ibid., IV, 200–1.
24. Ibid., IV, 347.
25. Ibid., IV, 557–8.
26. Ibid., IV, 601.

27. Ibid., IV, 362.
28. Kilvert, *Diary*, III, 107.
29. Ibid., III, 213.
30. Ibid., I, 23.
31. Ibid., II, 201–2.
32. Ibid., II, 350.
33. Ibid., III, 43.
34. Ibid., II, 109–10, 350.
35. Ibid., III, 45.
36. Ibid., I, 133.
37. Ibid., III, 88.
38. Ibid., II, 437.
39. Ibid., II, 194.
40. Ibid., II, 129.
41. Kilvert, *Collected Verse*, 24–5.
42. Kilvert, *Diary*, II, 338.
43. Ibid., III, 61.
44. Ibid., III, 63.
45. Ibid., III, 65–6.
46. Ibid., III, 66.
47. Ibid., III, 67.
48. Ibid., III, 94.
49. Ibid., III, 229.
50. Ibid., III, 246.
51. Ibid., III, 261.
52. Ibid., III, 298–9.
53. Barbellion, *Journal of a Disappointed Man*, 265–6.
54. Barbellion, *A Last Diary*, 92.
55. Barbellion, *Journal of a Disappointed Man*, 284–5.
56. Ibid., 68.
57. Ibid., 51.
58. Ibid., 77.
59. Ibid., 96.
60. Ibid., 100.
61. Ibid., 152.
62. Ibid., 152.
63. Ibid., 180.
64. Ibid., 238.
65. Ibid., 265.
66. Ibid., 267.
67. Ibid., 236.
68. Ibid., 259.
69. Ibid., 238.
70. Ibid., 211.
71. Ibid., 298.
72. Ibid., 10.
73. Ibid., 255.
74. Ibid., 238.

75. John Keats, *The Letters of John Keats*, ed. H. E. Rollins (Cambridge: Harvard U.P., 1958), II, 359.
76. Barbellion, *Journal of a Disappointed Man*, 299.
77. Ibid., 302.
78. Ibid., 304–5.
79. Ibid., 305.
80. Jacquier, *Diary*, 172
81. Ibid., 200.
82. Ibid., 199.
83. Ibid., 204.
84. Ibid., 16–17.
85. Ibid., 17.
86. Ibid., 141.
87. Ibid., 44.
88. Ibid., 56.
89. Ibid., 61.
90. Ibid., 199.
91. Ibid., 102–3.
92. Ibid., 103.
93. Ibid., 103.
94. Ibid., 125.
95. Ibid., 126.
96. Ibid., 143.
97. Ibid., 137.
98. Ibid., 151.
99. Ibid., 157.
100. Ibid., 163.
101. Ibid., 167.
102. Ibid., 197.
103. Ibid., 173.
104. Ibid., 192.
105. Ibid., 198, 205.
106. Ibid., 206.
107. Ibid., 19.
108. Ibid., 216.
109. Ibid., 218.
110. Ibid., 218.
111. Nin, *Diary*, II, 232.
112. Ibid., III, 19–20.
113. Ibid., III, 251.
114. Ibid., I, 230–1.
115. Ibid., III, 76.
116. Ibid., III, 175.
117. Ibid., II, 193.
118. Ibid., III, 140.
119. Ibid., II, 210.
120. Ibid., II, 210, 154.
121. Ibid., II, 311–12.

122. Ibid., II, 346.
123. Ibid., II, 322.
124. Ibid., I, 49.
125. Ibid., II, 251.
126. Ibid., II, 328.
127. Ibid., III, 299.
128. Ibid., II, 231–2.
129. Ibid., II, 167.
130. Ibid., III, 241.
131. Ibid., III, 264.
132. Ibid., III, 264.
133. Ibid., III, 281–2.
134. Ibid., III, 296.
135. Ibid., III, 293.
136. Ibid., I, 360.
137. Ibid., II, 349.
138. Ibid., III, 313.

Select Bibliography

Primary Materials: The following select list of English Diaries includes all those diaries used in the preparation of this study, together with a selection of others judged to be less notable but worthy of mention. For the sake of convenience I have included in square brackets after the title of each diary the terminal dates covered by its entries.

BARBELLION, W. N. P. (B. F. Cummings). *Journal of a Disappointed Man* [1903–17]. London: Chatto and Windus, 1919.

——. *Last Diary* [1918–19]. London: Chatto and Windus, 1921.

BARRETT, ELIZABETH. *Diary by E.B.B.* [1831–2]. Edited by P. Kelley and R. Hudson. Athens: Ohio University Press, 1969.

BENNETT, ARNOLD. *The Journals of Arnold Bennett* [1896–1928]. Edited by N. Flower. 3 vols. London: Cassell, 1932–3.

——. *The Journals.* Selected and Edited by F. Swinnerton. London: Penguin, 1971. (Includes the 'Florentine Journal' [1910] and the hitherto unpublished Ms. Vol. 6 [1906–7].)

BLUNT, WILFRID SCAWEN. *My Diaries* [1888–1914]. 2 vols. London: Secker, 1920.

BOSWELL, JAMES. *Boswell's London Journal* [1762–3]. Edited by F. A. Pottle. London: Heinemann; New York: McGraw Hill, 1950.

——. *Boswell in Holland* [1763–4]. Edited by F. A. Pottle. London: Heinemann; New York: McGraw Hill, 1952.

——. *Boswell on the Grand Tour: Germany and Switzerland* [1764]. Edited by F. A. Pottle. London: Heinemann; New York: McGraw Hill, 1953.

——. *Boswell on the Grand Tour: Italy, Corsica and France* [1765–6]. Edited by F. Brady and F. A. Pottle. London: Heinemann; New York: McGraw Hill, 1955.

——. *Boswell in Search of a Wife* [1766–9]. Edited by F. Brady and F. A. Pottle. London: Heinemann; New York: McGraw Hill, 1957.

——. *Boswell for the Defence* [1769–74]. Edited by W. K. Wimsatt, Jr., and F. A. Pottle. London: Heinemann; New York: McGraw Hill, 1959.

——. *Journal of a Tour to the Hebrides* [1773]. Edited from the original manuscript by F. A. Pottle and C. H. Bennett. London: Heinemann; New York: McGraw Hill, 1963.

——. *Boswell: The Ominous Years* [1774–6]. Edited by C. Ryskamp and F. A. Pottle. London: Heinemann; New York: McGraw Hill, 1963.

——. *Boswell in Extremes* [1776–8]. Edited by C. M^cC. Weis and F. A. Pottle. London: Heinemann; New York: McGraw Hill, 1970.

BURNEY, FANNY (Mme D'Arblay). *The Early Diary of Frances Burney* [1768–78]. Edited by A. R. Ellis. 2 vols. London: Bell, 1907.

——. *The Diary and Letters of Madame D'Arblay* [1778–1840]. Edited by C. Barrett. 6 vols. London: Macmillan, 1904.

——. *The Journals and Letters of Fanny Burney (Madame D'Arblay)* [1791–1801]. Edited by Joyce Hemlow, with Althea Douglas and Patricia Boutilier. 4 vols. Oxford: Clarendon Press, 1972–3.

——. *Evelina*. Edited by Edward A. Bloom. London: Oxford U.P., 1968.

BURNEY, FANNY ANNE. *A Great-Niece's Journal*. [1830–42]. Edited by M. Rolt. London: Constable, 1926.

BURY, LADY CHARLOTTE. *Diary Illustrative of the Times of George the Fourth* [1810–20]. 4 vols. London, 1838–9 (published anonymously).

——. *The Diary of a Lady-in-Waiting*. Edited by A. F. Steuart. 2 vols. London: Lane, 1908.

BUTLER, LADY ELEANOR. 'Diary' [1785, 1788–90], in G. H. Bell, ed., *The Hamwood Papers of the Ladies of Llangollen and Caroline Hamilton*. London: Macmillan, 1930.

BYRD, WILLIAM. *The London Diary* [1717–21]. Edited by L. B. Wright and M. Tinling. New York: Oxford, 1958.

BYRON, GEORGE GORDON NOEL, LORD. 'Journal' [1813–14] in P. Quennell, ed., *Byron: A Self Portrait*. 2 vols. London: Murray; New York: Scribner, 1950.

CARLYLE, JANE WELSH. Diary Extracts [1855–6] in Letters and Memorials of Jane Welsh Carlyle. Edited by J. A. Froude. 3 vols. London: Longmans, 1883, Vol. II, 257–73.

——. Diary Extracts [1855–6] in *New Letters and Memorials of Jane Welsh Carlyle*. Edited by A. Carlyle. 2 vols. London: Lane, 1903, Vol. II, 87–109.

CAVENDISH, LADY FREDERICK *The Diary of Lady Frederick Cavendish* [1854–80]. Edited by J. Bailey. 2 vols. London: Murray, 1927.

CLIFFORD, LADY ANNE. *The Diary of the Lady Anne Clifford* [1603–18]. Edited by V. Sackville-West. London: Heinemann, 1923.

COLE, WILLIAM. *The Blecheley Diary of the Rev. William Cole* [1765–7]. Edited by F. G. Stokes. London: Constable, 1931.

COWPER, MARY, COUNTESS. *The Diary of Mary, Countess Cowper* [1714–20]. London: Murray, 1864.

DEE, JOHN. *The Private Diary of Dr. John Dee* [1577–1601]. Edited by J. O. Halliwell. Camden Society Publications, XIX, 1842.

DODINGTON, GEORGE BUBB. *The Diary of the late George Bubb Dodington* [1749–61]. Edited by Henry P. Wyndham. London, 1784.

EGMONT, JOHN PERCEVAL, First Earl. *The Diary of Viscount Percival, afterwards First Earl of Egmont* [1728–33]. Edited by R. A. Roberts, 3 vols. London: Historical Manuscripts Commission, 1920–3.

ELIOT, GEORGE. Diary Extracts [1854–80] in Gordon S. Haight, ed., *The George Eliot Letters.* 7 vols. New Haven: Yale U.P.; London: Oxford U.P., 1954–5.

EVELYN, JOHN. *The Diary of John Evelyn* [1640–1706]. Edited by E. S. de Beer. 6 vols. Oxford: Clarendon Press, 1955.

EYRE, ADAM. 'Diary of Adam Eyre' [1646–9] in A. J. Morehouse, ed., *Yorkshire Diaries.* Surtees Society Publications, LXV, 1875.

FARINGTON, JOSEPH. *The Farington Diary* [1793–1821]. Edited by J. Greig. 8 vols. London: Hutchinson, 1922–8.

FIELDING, HENRY. 'Journal of a Voyage to Lisbon' [1754] in Vol. VIII of *The Works of Henry Fielding Esq.* Edited by Leslie Stephen. 10 vols. London: Smith, Elder, 1882.

FIENNES, CELIA. *The Journeys of Celia Fiennes* [1695–7]. Edited by C. Morris. London: Cresset Press. 1949.

FLEMING, MARJORIE. *The Complete Marjorie Fleming: her Journals, Letters and Verses* [1809–11]. Transcribed and Edited by Frank Sidgwick. London: Sidgwick and Jackson, 1934.

FOX, CAROLINE. *Memories of Old Friends* [1835–71]. Edited by H. N. Pym. 3 vols. London: Smith, Elder, 1882.

FROUDE, RICHARD HURRELL. Diary Extracts [1826–7] in *Remains of the Late Reverend Richard Hurrell Froude M.A.* 4 vols. London, 1838–9.

GIBBON, EDWARD. *Gibbon's Journal* [1761–3]. Edited by D. M. Low. London: Chatto and Windus, 1929.

GORDON, CHARLES GEORGE. *General Gordon's Khartoum Journal* [1884]. Edited by Lord Elton. London: Kimber; New York: Vanguard Press, 1961.

GREVILLE, CHARLES CAVENDISH FULKE. *The Greville Memoirs* [1814–60]. Edited by L. Strachey and R. Fulford. 8 vols. London: Macmillan, 1938.

HAYDON, BENJAMIN ROBERT. *The Diary of Benjamin Robert Haydon* [1808–46]. Edited by W. B. Pope. 5 vols. Cambridge, Mass: Harvard U.P., 1960.
——. *The Life of B. R. H. . . . from his Autobiography and Journals.* Edited and compiled by Tom Taylor. 3 vols. London, 1853.

HOBY, MARGARET. *The Diary of Lady Margaret Hoby* [1599–1605]. Edited by D. M. Meads. London: Routledge, 1930.

HOLLAND, ELIZABETH, LADY. *The Journal of Elizabeth, Lady Holland* [1791–1811]. Edited by the Earl of Ilchester. 2 vols. London: Longmans, 1908.

HOOKE, ROBERT. *The Diary of Robert Hooke* [1672–80]. Edited by H. W. Robinson and W. Adams. London: Taylor and Francis, 1935.

HOPKINS, GERARD MANLEY. *The Notebooks and Papers of Gerard Manley Hopkins* [1862–75]. 2nd ed., revised. Edited by Humphry House . . . completed by Graham Storey. 2 vols. London: Oxford U.P., 1959.

JACQUIER, IVY. *The Diary of Ivy Jacquier* [1907–26]. London: Gollancz, 1960.

JAMES, ALICE. *The Diary of Alice James* [1889–92]. Edited by L. Edel. New York: Dodd, Mead; London: Rupert Hart-Davis, 1964.

JAMES, HENRY. *The Notebooks of Henry James* [1878–1911]. Edited by F. O. Matthiessen and K. B. Murdock. London: Oxford, 1947.

JOHNSON, SAMUEL. Diary Fragments [1729–84] in E. L. McAdam, ed., *Diaries, Prayers, and Annals* (Vol. 1 of the Yale Edition of the Works of Samuel Johnson). New Haven: Yale U.P.; London: Oxford U.P., 1958.

JOHNSTON, SIR ARCHIBALD. *The Diary of Sir Archibald Johnston* [1632–60]. Edited by G. M. Paul, D. H. Fleming and J. D. Ogilvie. 3 vols. Publications of the Scottish History Society, ser. 1, LXI, 1911; ser. 2, XVIII, 1919; ser. 3, XXIV, 1940.

JONES, WILLIAM. *The Diary of the Rev'd William Jones* [1777–1821]. Edited by O. F. Christie. London: Brentano, 1929.

JOSSELIN, RALPH. *The Diary of Rev. Ralph Josselin* [1644–81]. Edited by E. Hockliffe. Camden Society Publications, 3rd ser., XV, 1908.

KAY, RICHARD. *The Diary of Richard Kay* [1737–50]. Edited by W. Brockbank and F. Kenworthy. Chetham Society Publications, 3rd ser., XVI, 1968.

KEMBLE, FRANCES ANN. Diary Extracts [1831–2] in her *Records of a Girlhood*. London: Beccles, 1878.

KILVERT, ROBERT FRANCIS. *Kilvert's Diary* [1870–9]. Edited by W. Plomer. 3 vols. London: Cape; New York: Macmillan, 1960.

——. *Collected Verse*. Edited by C. T. O. Prosser. Hereford: Kilvert Society, 1968.

LOWE, ROGER. *The Diary of Roger Lowe* [1663–74]. Edited by W. L. Sachse. London: Longmans; New Haven: Yale U.P., 1938.

MACAULAY, THOMAS BABINGTON. Diary Extracts [1838–59] in G. O. Trevelyan, ed., *The Life and Letters of Lord Macaulay*. 2 vols. London, 1876; *passim*.

MACHIN, HENRY. *The Diary of Henry Machin* [1550–63]. Edited by J. G. Nichols. Camden Society Publications, XLII, 1848.

MACREADY, WILLIAM CHARLES. *The Diaries of William Charles Macready* [1833–51]. Edited by W. Toynbee. 2 vols. London: Chapman and Hall, 1912.

MANNING, HENRY EDWARD, CARDINAL. Diary Extracts [1844–90] in E. S. Purcell, ed., *Life of Cardinal Manning*. 2 vols. London: Macmillan, 1895, *passim*.

MANNINGHAM, JOHN. *The Diary of John Manningham* [1602–3]. Edited by J. Bruce. Camden Society Publications, XCIX, 1868.

MANSFIELD, KATHERINE. *The Journal of Katherine Mansfield* [1904–22]. Definitive Edition. Edited by J. M. Murry. London: Constable, 1954.

MAUGHAM, SOMERSET. *A Writer's Notebook* [1892–1949]. London: Heinemann; New York: Doubleday, 1949.

MONKSWELL, MARY, LADY. *A Victorian Diarist* [1873–1909]. Edited by E. C. F. Collier. 2 vols. London: Murray, 1944, 1946.

MOORE, THOMAS. 'Diary' [1818–49], in Lord John Russell, ed., *Memoirs, Journal and Correspondence of Thomas Moore*. 8 vols. London, 1853.

MUNBY, ARTHUR J. *Munby, Man of Two Worlds: The Life and Diaries of Arthur J. Munby 1828–1910* [1859–98]. Edited by Derek Hudson. London: Murray; New York: Gambit, 1972.

NEVILLE, SYLAS. *The Diary of Sylas Neville* [1767–88]. Edited by B. Cozens-Hardy. London, Oxford U.P., 1950.

NEWCOME, HENRY. *The Diary of the Rev. Henry Newcome* [1661–3]. Edited by T. Heywood. Chetham Society Publications, XVIII, 1849.

NICOLSON, HAROLD. *Diaries and Letters* [1930–62]. Edited by N. Nicolson. 3 vols. London: Collins; New York: Atheneum, 1966–8.

NIN, ANAÏS. *The Diary of Anaïs Nin* [1931–47]. Edited by G. Stuhlmann. Vols. I to IV. New York: Harcourt, Brace, Jovanovich (Harvest paperback); London: Peter Owen, 1966–71.

ORWELL, GEORGE. Diary Extracts [1936–42] in S. Orwell and I. Angus, eds., *Collected Essays, Journalism and Letters of George Orwell*. 4 vols. London: Secker and Warburg; New York: Harcourt, Brace, Jovanovich, 1968.

PEPYS, SAMUEL. *The Diary of Samuel Pepys* [1660–9]. Edited by R. Latham and W. Matthews. Vols. I to VII (out of 11). London: Bell; Berkeley: U. of California Press, 1970–3.

——. *The Diary of Samuel Pepys* [1660–9]. Edited by H. B. Wheatley. 8 vols. London: Bell, 1904–5.

PERCY, ELIZABETH, 1st Duchess of Northumberland. *Diaries of a Duchess* [1752–74]. Edited by J. Greig. London: Hodder and Stoughton, 1926.

POTTER, BEATRIX. *The Journal of Beatrix Potter* [1881–97]. Edited by L. Linder. London: Warne, 1966.

RIDPATH, GEORGE. *The Diary of George Ridpath* [1755–61]. Edited by J. Balfour. Scottish Historical Society Publications, 3rd ser., II, 1922.

ROBINSON, HENRY CRABB. *Diary, Reminiscences, and Correspondence of H. C. Robinson* [1811–67]. Edited by T. Sadler. 3 vols. London, 1869.

ROGERS, RICHARD. 'Diary of Richard Rogers' [1586–7], in M. M. Knappen, ed., *Two Elizabethan Puritan Diaries*. Chicago: American Society of Church History; London: S.P.C.K., 1933.

RYDER, DUDLEY. *The Diary of Dudley Ryder* [1715–16]. Edited by W. Matthews. London: Methuen, 1939.

SCOTT, WALTER. *The Journal of Walter Scott* [1825–32]. Edited by J. G. Tait. 3 vols. Edinburgh: Oliver and Boyd, 1939–46.

SHELLEY, FRANCES. *Diary of Frances, Lady Shelley* [1814–17]. Edited by R. Edgecombe. 2 vols. London: Murray, 1912.

SLINGSBY, HENRY. *The Diary of Sir Henry Slingsby* [1638–49]. Edited by D. Parsons. London, 1836.

——. *Original Memoirs, written during the great civil war; being the life of Sir Henry Slingsby, and memoirs of Capt. Hodgson*. Edited by Walter Scott. Edinburgh, 1806.

STERNE, LAURENCE. *A Sentimental Journey* with *Journal to Eliza* and *A Political Romance*. Edited by Ian Jack. London: Oxford U.P., 1968.

STROTHER. *Strother's Journal* [1784–5]. Edited by Caesar Caine. London: Brown, 1912.

STURT, GEORGE. *The Journals of George Sturt* [1890–1927]. Edited by E. D. Mackerness. 2 vols. Cambridge: University Press, 1967.

——. (George Bourne, pseud.). *The Bettesworth Book*. London: Duckworth, 1920.

——. *Memoirs of a Surrey Labourer*. London: Duckworth, 1907.

SWIFT, JONATHAN. *Journal to Stella* [1710–13]. Edited by H. Williams. 2 vols. Oxford: Clarendon Press, 1948.

SYMONDS, JOHN ADDINGTON. Diary Extracts [1860-88], in H. F. Brown, *John Addington Symonds: A Biography*. Rev. ed., London: Smith, Elder, 1903. *passim*.

TEONGE, Henry. *The Diary of Henry Teonge* [1675–9]. Edited by G. E. Manwaring. London: Routledge, 1927.

THOMLINSON, JOHN. *The Diary of the Rev. John Thomlinson* [1715–22]. Edited by J. C. Hodgson. Surtees Society Publications, CXVIII, 1910.

THRALE, HESTER LYNCH. *Thraliana: The Diary of Mrs. H. L. Thrale (later Mrs. Piozzi)* [1776–1809]. Edited by K. C. Balderston. 2 vols. Oxford: Clarendon Press, 1949.

VICTORIA, QUEEN OF ENGLAND. *The Girlhood of Queen Victoria* [1832–40]. Edited by Viscount Esher. 2 vols. London: Murray, 1912.

——. *Leaves from a Journal* [1855]. Edited by R. Mortimer. London: Deutsch; New York: Farrar, Strauss and Cudahy, 1961.

——. *Leaves from the Journal of Our Life in the Highlands* [1848–61] Edited by A. Helps. London: Smith, Elder, 1868.

——. *More Leaves from the Journal of a life in the Highlands* [1862–82]. London: Smith, Elder, 1884.

WARD, SAMUEL. 'Diary of Samuel Ward' [1595–9], in M. M. Knappen, ed., *Two Elizabethan Puritan Diaries*. Chicago: American Society of Church History. London: S.P.C.K., 1933.

WAUGH, EVELYN. 'The Private Diaries of Evelyn Waugh' [1916–65]. Edited by Michael Davie. 8 parts. *Observer Magazine*. London: 25 March to 13 May, 1973.

WEBB, BEATRICE. *Beatrice Webb's Diaries* [1912–32]. Edited by M. I. Cole. 2 vols. London: Longmans, 1952.

WESLEY, JOHN. *The Journal of John Wesley* [1725–91]. Edited by N. Curnock. 8 vols. London: Culley, 1909–16.

WHITEFIELD, GEORGE. Diary Extracts [1736–70] in J. Gillies, ed., *Works of the Rev. George Whitefield*. 6 vols. London, 1771-2.

WINDHAM, WILLIAM. *The Diary of the Right Hon. William Windham* [1784–1810]. Edited by Mrs. H. Baring. London: Longmans, Green, 1866.

WOOD ANTHONY A. *The Life and Times of Anthony Wood* [1657–95]. Collected and edited by Andrew Clark. Oxford Historical Society Publications, XIX, XXI, XXVI, XXX, XL. Oxford: Clarendon Press, 1891–1900.

WOODFORDE, JAMES. *The Diary of a Country Parson* [1758–1802]. Edited by J. Beresford. 5 vols. London: Oxford University Press, 1924–31.

WOOLF, VIRGINIA. *A Writer's Diary* [1918–41]. Edited by L. Woolf. London: Hogarth Press; New York: Harcourt, Brace, 1953.

WORDSWORTH, DOROTHY. *The Journals of Dorothy Wordsworth* [1798–1803]. Edited by Mary Moorman. London: Oxford U.P., 1971.

WYNNE, ELIZABETH. 'Diary' [1789–1820], in A. Freemantle, ed., *The Wynne Diaries*. 3 vols. London: Oxford U.P., 1935–40.

WYNNE, EUGENIA. 'Diary' [1789–1811] ibid.

WYNNE, HARRIET. 'Diary' [1803–1806], ibid.

YONGE, WALTER. *The Diary of Walter Yonge Esq.* [1604–28]. Edited by G. Roberts. Camden Society Publications, XLI, 1847.

Secondary Materials: The following list includes the various critical studies, works of reference, etc., used in the preparation of the study.

AITKEN, JAMES, ed. *English Diaries of the XVI, XVII and XVIII Centuries.* Harmondsworth: Penguin, 1941.

——. *English Diaries of the XIX Century, 1800–1850.* Harmondsworth: Penguin, 1944.

BASHKIRTSEFF, MARIE. *The Journal of Marie Bashkirtseff* [1873–84]. Translated by M. Blind. 2 vols. London: Cassell, 1890.

BEADLE, JOHN. *The Journal or Diary of a Thankful Christian.* London, 1656.

DELANY, PAUL. *British Autobiography in the Seventeenth Century.* London: Routledge and Kegan Paul; New York: Columbia U.P., 1969.

EVANS, OLIVER WENDELL. *Anaïs Nin.* Carbondale: Southern Illinois U.P., 1968.

GEORGE, ERIC. *The Life and Death of Benjamin Robert Haydon.* Oxford: Clarendon Press, 1967.

GIRARD, ALAIN. *Le Journal Intime.* Paris: Presses Universitaires de France, 1963.

HOCKE, GUSTAV RÉNÉ. *Das Europäische Tagebuch.* Wiesbaden: Limes Verlag, 1963.

KNIGHT, G. WILSON. *Byron and Shakespeare.* London: Routledge and Kegan Paul; New York: Barnes and Noble, 1966.

——. 'Byron's Dramatic Prose', in his *Poets of Action.* London: Methuen; New York: Barnes and Noble, 1967.

LOCKE, JOHN. *An Essay Concerning Human Understanding.* Edited by J. W. Yolton. 2 vols. London: Dent, 1961.

MATTHEWS, WILLIAM, compiler. *British Diaries: An Annotated Bibliography of British Diaries Written between 1442 and 1942.* Berkeley and Los Angeles: University of California Press, 1950; reprinted Gloucester, Mass.: Peter Smith, 1967; London: Cambridge U.P., 1950.

MORRIS, JOHN N. *Versions of the Self: Studies in English Autobiography from Bunyan to J. S. Mill.* New York and London: Basic Books, 1966.

NIN, ANAÏS. *The Novel of the Future.* New York: Collier-Macmillan, 1968; London: Peter Owen, 1969.

O'BRIEN, KATE. *English Diaries and Journals.* 'Britain in Pictures' Series. London: Collins, 1942.

PASCAL, ROY. *Design and Truth in Autobiography*. Cambridge, Mass.: Harvard U.P.; London: Routledge and Kegan Paul, 1960.

PONSONBY, ARTHUR. *English Diaries*. London: Methuen, 1923.

——. *More English Diaries*. London: Methuen, 1927.

——. *Scottish and Irish Diaries*. London: Methuen, 1927.

——. *Samuel Pepys*. London: Macmillan, 1928.

——. *British Diarists*. London: Benn, 1930.

SPALDING, P. A. *Self Harvest: A Study of Diaries and the Diarist*. London: Independent Press, 1949.

STAUFFER, DONALD A. *The Art of Biography in Eighteenth Century England*. Princeton: University Press, 1941.

——. *English Biography Before 1700*. Cambridge: Harvard U.P., 1930.

TRILLING, LIONEL. *Sincerity and Authenticity*. Cambridge: Harvard U.P.; London: Oxford U.P., 1972.

WILLY, MARGARET. *English Diarists: Evelyn and Pepys*. British Council Series 'Writers and their Work', No. 162, London: Longmans, 1963.

——. *Three Women Diarists*. British Council Series 'Writers and their Work', No. 173, London: Longmans, 1964.

Index

✛✛

(Figures in italics indicate the place where the diarist is discussed most fully.)